MODERN BLACK NOVELISTS

A COLLECTION OF CRITICAL ESSAYS

Edited by

M. G. Cooke, comp.

Prentice-Hall, Inc. *Englewood Cliffs, N.J.*

A SPECTRUM BOOK

Acknowledgment is gratefully made to the following:

To Michael Anthony and Andre Deutsch Limited for quotations from
The Year at San Fernando, by Michael Anthony

To George Lamming for quotations from his
In the Castle of My Skin

To Alfred A. Knopf, Inc., and Laurence Pollinger Ltd. for quotations from
New Day, by V. S. Reid

To Andre Deutsch Limited for quotations from
The Middle Passage, by V. S. Naipaul

To Harold R. Kent, Agent for Mrs. J. Mittleholzer, and The Hogarth Press
Ltd. for quotations from
A Morning at the Office, by Edgar Mittleholzer

To The American Folklore Society, Inc., for quotations from
"Andrew and His Sisters," in *Jamaica Anansi Stories,* ed. Martha W. Beckwith,
Memoirs of the American Folklore Society, Vol. 17 (New York, 1924)

To Harper & Row, Publishers, for quotations from
Home to Harlem (© 1928 Harper & Row, Publishers; renewed 1956 by Hope
McKay Virtue),
Banana Bottom (© 1933 Harper & Row, Publishers; renewed 1961 by Hope
McKay Virtue),
Banjo (© 1929 Harper & Row, Publishers; renewed 1957 by Hope McKay
Virtue), by Claude McKay

Prentice-Hall International, Inc. (*London*)
Prentice-Hall of Australia Pty. Ltd. (*Sydney*)
Prentice-Hall of Canada Ltd. (*Toronto*)
Prentice-Hall of India Private Limited (*New Delhi*)
Prentice-Hall of Japan, Inc. (*Tokyo*)

Contents

III. Africa

IV. West Indies

Introduction

by M. G. Cooke

I

The very thing that makes it imperative to come to a clear understanding of the condition of black people in America and abroad also makes it hard even to get a clear image. For that condition is markedly changing. Changing, first, from an enforced and confused uniformity to a complex identity *in* as well as *with* the group. Thus Addison Gayle, Jr., can write about the *"black situation"* but properly confesses that he speaks infallibly only for himself and insists that no one else speaks reliably for him.[1] Changing also from a tight subjection (the back of the bus or the hand) to a surging, searching kinesis ("right on!") or a defiant and self-inspiring slogan ("black is beautiful"). Changing, again, in that the black person is less and less imposed upon by "scientific" evaluations and religious or sociological "laws" that supposedly govern his behavior and experience, on the grounds that these lack the moving spirit of human understanding, or "soul." Of course, the importance of "soul" lies partly in its resistance to an unnatural separation of our sympathetic life from the powers of analysis and in its putting the living community of man above the temptations of ego and institutional power.

Finally, the condition of black people is changing, most importantly —though perhaps least obviously—in the way it now, after looking for so long like a strange and singular visitation, is coming more and more to seem central and prophetic. The scapegoat has turned into the bellwether, or, if that seems too idyllic all of a sudden, into the weathercock that tells which way the wind is blowing. "The Negro," as Richard Wright observed, "is America's metaphor."

The elimination of the principle of the scapegoat, because this principle gives an easy psychic expiation and enrichment as well as material gain through the removal of a curse and the restoration of a bounty, is not simply or swiftly achieved, and remains incomplete. It is, in terms of politics, psychology, and social history, too complex a phenomenon to go into here, yet some of its features can be discerned in the literature on which this collection of critical essays centers. The

---

[1] Addison Gayle, Jr., *The Black Situation* (New York: Horizon Press, 1970).

1

ways in which Ralph Ellison's *Invisible Man* "speaks for" all of us
who are honest, good-natured, fairly intelligent, eager to get along, and
credulous of democratic hopes and dreams are etched in the slightly
demented merrymaking, the divisive suspicion, and the explosive frustration of hardhat and hippie, white and black and red and yellow
and brown. Camara Laye's *The Radiance of the King*, as pregnant and
as problematical in its symbolic values as Saul Bellow's *Henderson
the Rain King*, gives further testimony to the model role of the erst-
while "savage, slave and outcast."

Such novels, perhaps, form part of the literature of protest but they
seem strikingly independent of mere programs and propaganda. They
fluently express a human and aesthetic command about which earlier
writers seemed more diffident. In depth, complexity, and sheer power
of presentation they take a positive step beyond even so compelling a
figure as W. E. B. Du Bois, in *The Gift of Black Folk* and *The Souls
of Black Folk*, and the Wright of *Native Son*. It is this Wright on
whom Baldwin mounts an attack—broadside in "Everybody's Protest
Novel" (1949) and implicit in *Go Tell It on the Mountain* (1952). The
outline of "progress" does not, of course, follow a simple curve. James
Baldwin might seem to have become more fashionably strident and
political in the sixties, but the prevailing tendency really emerges with
Ellison's *Invisible Man* (1952) and Wright's *The Outsider* (1953), two
major novels that, though not purged of doctrine, transcend merely
racial terms. These two novels hold a pivotal place in the passage of
black writers from patently sociological work, throbbing with a felt
alienation, to a profoundly imaginative engagement that takes at once
an empirical view of the liabilities of color and a Cartesian view of
color as less than the quintessence of living or being. This change, coming so long after the mechanical emancipation of the body, betokens
the emancipation of the mind from "aerial chains" through an exorcis-
ing of what Robert Hayden calls "monsters of abstractions [that] police
and threaten us."

It is important to note the way white writers recognize and reflect
what is taking place within the black individual and the general scene.
Leaving aside the obscure and unlikely precedent to be found in
Faulkner, with his Joe Christmas, one may cite Bellow here. Though
his treatment of the black man reverts to a frigid and grossly neurotic
stereotype in *Mr. Sammler's Planet*, in *Henderson the Rain King* he
makes Dahfu in effect his fictive hero's hero. By his ability to come
to terms with himself, both as finite mortal and as absolute monarch,
an individual unto himself and a responsible part of a formal, even
artificial system, Dahfu embodies Henderson's only hope of stability
and purpose in a world where the vacuum of heroism has caused a hol-
lowing out of norms, thus leading to Henderson's incoherent and
grotesque posturings. As this novel and *Invisible Man* remind us, the

hero who has disappeared from the field of action in modern literature abides in the heart of hope.

For all the charges of opportunism and obtuseness that it has triggered, William Styron's *The Confessions of Nat Turner* also illustrates the centripetal movement of the black mythos in the area of white consciousness. Certainly the novel shows that the desperate concentration on survival that once produced the humility of Uncle Tom, the heart-crushing labor of John Henry, and the entertaining antics of Stepin Fetchit is being left behind in a bold quest for significant life that breathes the spirit of independence and self-reverence. Styron's Hark shows this, as does Nat Turner himself in the highest degree, and the point is confirmed in the images of elevation and soaring that Styron calls into use in the culminating episodes of the book. The suggestion that Nat Turner's failure to escape from slavery is analogous to Styron's failure to escape from a Southern mentality would seem unduly pragmatic, and fails to make enough of the *quality* of either attempt. Even if flawed in execution, each shows a breakthrough in conception and a decisive advance in the realm of the spirit, where freedom essentially begins.

Less celebrated works give further evidence of this trend: Jesse Hill Ford's *The Liberation of Lord Byron Jones,* for example, and a handful of recent plays, including *The Great White Hope, The Universal Nigger, The Trial of A. Lincoln,* and *Big Time Buck White.* If we note also the increasing use of the epithet "Uncle Tom" to pinpoint exaggerated meekness regardless of race, the universalization of jazz, and the evidence in popular music that white-favored ballads, with their emphasis on sentiment and melody, have yielded ground to black-inspired rhythm and blues, with their emphasis on dramatization and ritualistic participation, the revision of norms seems graphic indeed. The old canard that the Anglo-Saxon will no more readily admit to taking culture from the black man than a country from the Indian can have no force in a situation where the black person has become a crucial and representative figure.

II

On the other hand, it would be mischievous, and radically misleading, to underplay the symbiotic connection between black literature and Anglo-Saxon culture. The latter, in general, provides a sustaining presence and, more particularly for work in Western tongues, provides the black writer an efficient instrument and vital arena for proving himself. Thus complaints about violence and bleakness in Wright or Ellison may properly be arbitrated by reference to Faulkner or Dreiser or, for a more venerable precedent, Melville. This is not to invoke the axiom that "violence is as American as apple pie," or the excuse that "others are just as much to blame." In effect, blame has nothing to do with the case, which involves far more than the presence, say rather the omnipresence, of violence (Greek literature, ancient and modern, and Russian literature put American varieties of violence in the shade.) The necessary thing is to break the fascination of the collective category "violence" and identify the particular contexts and patterns in which violence occurs, the sense of human character or social behavior that seems to give it form, and the use to which it is put in the structure and action of a given work or body of works.

The notion that violence is cathartic, in that it results in a state of exhausted quiet in body and spirit, does not in this light proffer a sufficient answer. Look in particular at *Invisible Man* or *Native Son* or Wilson Harris's *The Palace of the Peacock* or Samuel Selvon's *Turn Again Tiger* or Chinua Achebe's *A Man of the People,* and the glaring differences in sheer frequency of violent action, to say nothing of relative importance in the aesthetic scheme of each novel, admonish us to look beyond this handy label. Of these five novels, violence has amplest play in *Invisible Man,* which in a sense proceeds in terms of violence or the threat of it or, as with Sybil near the end, the demand for it. Virtually no important development of the action takes place without it. Even the two points of quiescence, in the factory hospital and in the speaker's "residence underground" (his "hibernation"), brood the violence they do not overtly express; and it is consonant with the novel's terms that the samaritan Mary represents an impossible haven for the hero. As a modern picaresque narrative, Ellison's work may justly be said to generate its forward energy by continual physical explosions. All this is true; yet plainly more can and must be said.

For one thing, *Invisible Man* belongs as much to the pilgrimage as to the picaresque tradition. Though it takes the nameless speaker long enough to apprehend this, he has no concrete or positive destination, no city of London and no heavenly city. He is, like the protagonists of Amos Tutuola's *Simbi and the Satyr of the Dark Jungle* and Camara Laye's *The Radiance of the King* in their different ways, involved in the peculiarly romantic and postromantic *pilgrimage to the self.* The system of disruptions that unfolds before and around him helps define a volatile and problematical universe and thereby serves to project the difficulties of being oneself wherein one must strive, within and without, to become oneself. The speaker's namelessness, while making it possible for him to be anyone, today's Everyman, also reemphasizes the precariousness of his "identity" and of "identity" in general. This is evident early, in the factory episode, and later when, to his peril instead of good, he gets mistaken for Rinehart, who is himself a multiple and contradictory personality. Beyond the level of action, then, violence proves to be an instrument of the protagonist's education and self-knowledge, and he knows this, in retrospect, in the midst of the final grotesque upheaval: "I looked . . . and recognized the absurdity

. . . of the simple yet confoundingly complex arrangement of hope and desire, fear and hate, that had brought me here still running, and knowing now who I was and where I was. . . ." It is typical of the novel's basic rhythm of redefinition that he must undergo one more dislocation and surprise before he is "whole" though, typically again, "hurt to the point of invisibility." Thus, the episodes of violence contribute to a rapid gathering of little epiphanies that illuminate at once the speaker's identity and his situation in society. Violence is educative, critical, a complex lens rather than a simple object of attention. It is almost incidental that the hero is seen first in college, a place for formal education, and it is natural that he does not stay there long, but is thrust into the maelstrom of experience for his deepest education.

The violence one meets in Wilson Harris's *The Palace of the Peacock* is akin to that of *Invisible Man* to the extent that the reliability of knowledge and experience and the problem of identity arise as central issues. But Harris makes the reader share in the narrator's quandary, whereas Ellison affords him, till the very last word, a sense of detachment, if not assurance. Moreover, with his exploration of metamorphoses, of reincarnations and interpenetrations of individuals, events, and eras, of the evanescence and reconstitution of natures and substances, Harris carries the reader far from the investigation of the terms and forms of principled conduct that Ellison develops, right into the domain of myth and fantasy. Ellison makes selective use of the pointedly arbitrary dimension of dreams; Harris occupies and manipulates it. If Ellison's pilgrimage is to the self that is possible Harris's pilgrimage, in *Tumatumari* as well as in *The Palace of the Peacock,* is to the self that, having been, must ever be; the flight *from* is the flight *to* death, the greed for life is the path to death (so that, after all, the myth may carry a hint of fatalism, a veiled evaluation of the world of conduct).

In the matter of violence, *Native Son, A Man of the People,* and *Turn Again Tiger,* to deal briefly with the other novels cited, differ markedly both from the works of Harris and Ellison and from one another. The interplay of raw chance and desperate purpose in Wright's novel suggests nothing so much as a deranged or inverted passivity—a characteristic problem of American naturalism, as Dreiser's *An American Tragedy* would seem to show. Bigger Thomas is invested with few of the metaphysical, as opposed to sociological, resonances that enable criminal action in Dostoevski (or even Camus or Norman Mailer) to reach hidden recesses of modern sensitivity. His is an external career, and his tragedy is less powerful in itself than for the quantity of lives it represents.

Achebe, in *A Man of the People,* makes violence an isolated and predictable incident rather than an intrinsic element in experience; it can be brought to bear by a schoolmaster or a politician or a woman in fidelity and grief, but it does not develop anything resembling the independent rhythm it shows in Ellison, Harris, and Wright. In the same way, Okonkwo's violence in Achebe's *Things Fall Apart* is the expression of his peculiar weaknesses and psychic compulsions and not something built into the diurnal patterns of experience.

Selvon, finally, makes relatively slight and yet distinctive and deep use of violence. Matching his stick against his rival's cutlass at the end of *Turn Again Tiger,* Otto develops a poignant rather than a formidable threat of violence. Even so it is more something witnessed than something done; understanding takes place simultaneously with action. Selvon builds the scene into a convincing revelation of *hombría* in a much-mocked and uxorious man who has to fight for his woman and his place in the sun. Violence here is moderated by a sense of humor, humanity, and community and is modified enough to lose its curse but not its credibility. It threatens the community and disrupts the vital activity of reaping, which draws even More Lazy and the dispirited Soylo into its sphere. Indeed violence results in an economic loss, but this is willingly written off in a new spirit of community sympathy, security, and health. For Selvon is motivated to use violence not so much to provide action as to appraise the capacity to act or to pursue the foreseeable effects of action. If in Otto's particular case there seems to be no alternative to violence, Selvon's treatment makes of that violence a rectifying tool that is applied to a given use, then put away: Otto's stick is transformed into "splints" for his rival's broken hand. It is, notwithstanding the passion that runs through the episode, as rational, humane, and social an example of violence as is likely to be found.

Further and more faithful distinctions are no doubt waiting to be made, but distinguishing among styles of violence in even a handful of the novels quickly suggests that this theme, besides being multifaceted in itself, shares unexpected surfaces with other topics: the possibility of individualism and the mechanisms of community or the grotesque (e.g., the finale of *Invisible Man*) or the impact of chance as opposed to organization and reason or the relative value of pastoralism and contemplation (as in Selvon or Abruquah or Camara Laye) or the sources and dimensions of education (already suggested in relation to *Invisible Man*).

III

This question of education, whether defined as the inculcating of a degree of skill and command *vis-à-vis* a practical metier or as the training of the spirit or personality in self-knowledge and self-possession, stands out sufficiently in modern black fiction to warrant dwelling upon. The education of Ellison's hero is exceptional in its ad-lib, traumatic quality and in the psychological and philosophical stripping down to which it leads. (Some readers will find it in this way reminiscent of Conrad's *Heart of Darkness*.) Perhaps the stripping down is the proper result of violence as an anomalous form of education, but as a preparation for a fresh beginning it does convey a positive norm. This appears again in Conrad and, to consider more recent works of nonfiction, Eldridge Cleaver's *Soul on Ice* and *The Autobiography of Malcolm X*, two works that portray, after destructive violence, very strong growth toward personal equilibrium and resolution.

The point is that education takes no typical, established form in these works. While the college novel, as Evelyn Waugh, John O'Hara, Kingsley Amis, and Bernard Malamud serve to remind us, is far from dying, it has no viability for Ellison. *Invisible Man* seems briefly to belong to this type, but its radically eruptive course almost constitutes a criticism of the type. What modern black fiction presents under the rubric of education is in the main a communal rather than a cocooned institutional activity, even if it involves the practical business of going to school. It is (and note again how germane a model *Invisible Man* remains) a cultural system or scheme of life that must be learned and transmitted. Camara Laye's *The African Child* and Joseph Abruquah's *The Catechist* provide important and distinctive examples.

The Catechist reads like the compulsive, self-opinionated, self-vindicating creed of a pathetic old man, his failure blazoned in his ever more bleak and meager succession of posts (again, the symbolic voyage), in the decade of discipline and decency in his household, and in the choice by his sons of ways other than his own. His formal education ends rather early, but the act of teaching, whether his subject be the catechism or his store of autobiographical vignettes, is the very stuff of his existence. His dwindling impact and increasing failures seem to be made up for by nothing more substantial than a self-image of overproof confidence that is scarcely diluted by a suspicion of the world's ingratitude and enmity. To all appearances the Catechist succeeds neither in teaching nor in learning.

But such a reading does not finally stand up. The command of English alone makes it probable that the story is not even told by the old man but in his person by his cultivated son. In this light the story becomes a major act of re-creation and identification, a testimony to the triumph of the Catechist's personality. As a narrative medium, the son both magnifies the old man's presence by effacing himself and, as soon as his own presence is discerned in the narration, tempers the sense of the old man's mere egotism. Instead of the old man's blindness, or rather with his blindness, we see his dedication and resiliency and determination to reclaim an area of order and grace from the ocean of indifference. He has the Faustian temperament without the Faustian talent, and his story embodies the pathos and the ludicrousness but also the struggling heroism of this state. Subtly the father's story turns into the story of the son, who, despite his separation from his father's ways, performs a complete act of piety. The son's overt education as a modern, analytical child of the city is but his second, shallower education. A more spontaneous and pervasive education has established itself in the fibers of his being; in him the catechist has handed himself down whole. Clearly, education in and to the family does not lead to outward imitation of its ways. Just as clearly, there is a natural continuity in the peculiar terms of the narration, and because of this, in part, the implied conflict between the imaginative reconstitution and the partial rejection of the old man's life goes undeveloped.

This conflict comes to the fore in *The African Child,* where both the family experience and the external situation have greater substance and appeal. Ironically, and despite the mother's conservative impulses, it is out of the family's admiration and concern that the boy's advancement (and hence separation) springs. In the home, freedom, deep affection, magic (repeatedly, as with the snake), prestige, and prowess (variously, in the father's metalwork and the uncle's farming) nourish the boy's mind and spirit. Discipline, the overcoming of adversity, logic, and proficiency are the qualities encouraged at school, but they promote intellectual growth at the cost of spiritual starvation. The boy lives to go home, too young to realize there is no way to "go home again." The novel, for all its remarkably candid style, boasts an even more remarkable silence, as the failure of the boy's nostalgic expectations is left unrecorded. He is heading home, all eagerness, at the end of chapter 9, and at the beginning of chapter 10 is again, all business, at school. Much later he laments the gifts and the inertia that carry him so far from home, but not now; it is too much to speak about. The reasons for reticence can be guessed: bafflement at the turn of events, love that would shield his family in their own bafflement and unwonted clumsiness, angry resignation. . . . But this silence speaks for grief that is inexpressible and dumb, and it strikes deep into our sympathies for the spiritually dispossessed who gain their worldly way. One must go to Wordsworth and the *Ode: Intimations of Immortality* for as piercing a recognition of the way a coalition of family and friends and an eager youth can, in fostering a part of his nature, damage that nature as a whole.

Nor is the thought of Wordsworth wildly out of line. One of the things Laye catches in limning the impasse of conflicting educations is a semimystical acuteness in perception and sensation of phenomena, a turning to nature in its details and atmosphere that suggests an apprehension of its essence and which seems liveliest in the child before his "education." Laye conveys more sense of a genuinely Edenlike state than Wordsworth (his snake is a benefactor, a bearer of good knowledge), but shares with him, or with Lawrence, a symbolic sense of landscape and of a contamination that increases with the influence of cities and which is unmistakable in the boy's epochal journey on the train. Some sort of mystical (or at least hyperaesthetic) recognition of landscape appears repeatedly in modern black fiction and may be closer to the center of its interests than any discriminating between Africa and America or other such quasipolitical position.

The idea of the community, of brotherhood—perhaps an extension of the oral tradition of which so much has been made—is also significant. The sense of talking *to someone* is a hallmark of modern black fiction. It reinforces, on the technical and tonal levels, two elements of subject matter: an eye for the momentum of sociopolitical events, which takes the form of an alertness to the vital and complex interplay of individuals and society; and a preoccupation with public activity or public character, as opposed to the filigreed introspection of so much post-Joycean fiction. A striking feature of the communal emphasis is its susceptibility to random developments, with the corollary premium it puts on chance (Ellison's Rinehart and V. S. Naipaul's Mystic Masseur come at once to mind). But one should not say this without noting an undercurrent of fatalism in the novels, which reaches a terrifying force in Orlando Patterson's *Children of Sisyphus*. This fatalism, though not frequently seen, acquires a special interest in that the problem of conduct or the possibility of action is a distinctive *leitmotif* in modern black fiction; understanding is celebrated in the highest degree in *Invisible Man*, but even there as an implied prelude to action.

IV

The foregoing exploration of themes in fiction by modern black authors is selective and, it should not need saying, tentative. Points of contact with nonblack literature as well as within black literature have been suggested, but without intending to prove either dependency or pioneering. The fact is that dependency and pioneering consort together, because this black writing operates as part of a defensive culture, at once delightedly discovering and professing itself and uneasily protecting itself in a problematical environment. Put another way, it is a commodity culture in a consumer society. But the commodity aspect, passive though it would seem, becomes a vehicle for the more animated, creative substance of the culture, and the exponents of that culture have the opportunity and the onus of taking it from there. As Mphahlele says: "how excruciating and exciting it is to be the meeting point of two streams of consciousness. . . ." Ellison, Wright, Baldwin, Achebe, Laye, and Naipaul have already received a fair measure of recognition; others, such as Selvon and Harris, are worthy of no less and may be found to be advancing not just the terms of modern black fiction, but those of modern fiction itself, as Cleaver and Malcolm X have advanced the form of autobiography. At such a point, singularity and centrality in the tradition intersect and interfuse in a new, if speculative, line of development.

It is also true that modern black fiction has evolved new problems for criticism. The essays collected here are diverse in range, temper, and command, without pretending to record samples from all possible layers of the critical field. The very modernity of the material, added to its wide magnetism, has produced a stream of short and so-to-speak promissory critical pieces, where assorted interests are brought to the surface but not to a resolution. This is especially noticeable in the treatment of African literature. At the same time, the need to cope not just with an assortment of single items but with the eager growth of black fiction as a whole has led to adoption of a somewhat stylized critical framework. Thus at times groups of works get treated in the light of questions prompted more by history or sociology than by the literary form itself. Moore and Mphahlele, who both illustrate this phenomenon, may be cited for coming as close as possible to escaping its disadvantages.

By disadvantages I mean that, while the desire—or even the need— to talk about topics like slavery or exile as a critical key to black literature can be all but overpowering, there is no getting away from the fact that only a relative handful of works center upon these subjects, and that the rest lend themselves awkwardly to discussion in these terms. Perhaps "Négritude is in essence the invention of the exile," but it does not follow that exile is the movement theme. In fact, the sociohistorical uses of the recent works that deal forthrightly with slavery and exile turn out to be rather troublesome. As C. W. E. Bigsby has pointed out, Arna Bontemps' *Black Thunder,* impressive as fiction, may be no less vulnerable to cavil than the besieged *Confessions of Nat Turner,* by the nonblack William Styron. Then, on the other hand, L. Edward Brathwaite in his poetic trilogy, *Rights of Passage, Masks,* and *Islands,* offers anything but a conventional image of slavery and exile. The portrayal of Uncle Tom, for example, must be seen as a singular achievement in its fusion of imaginative sympathy, original thinking, and finesse in structuring words.

In this context, the several emphases and suggestive interplay of the articles I have collected here warrant a brief word. The opening section—"Manifesto"—deals with the basic question of what gives modern black fiction its identity. It does so not solely in terms of what this body of writing has manifested and done, but also in terms of what it can and should do. The common engagement of these essays with the problem of *essence* leads to one striking effect: a more or less central concern with the need to win a place independent of both the possessive authority of older literary canons and merely current shibboleths. Brathwaite, again, puts the issue in sharp relief in calling for "a creole culture" in the West Indies:

> There is an argument . . . that holds that our experience is in fact the world's; by which, I think, is meant West Europe's, certainly Britain and North America's. I do not dispute this; although I would seriously qualify it. But I would also add that those people who delight to see our experience, as "international," as "cosmopolitan," tend to see it *only* as these things. When pressed, they are able to provide little basis for their wide horizons. It is my contention that *before it is too late,* we must try to find the high ground from which we ourselves will see the world, and towards which the world will look to find us.

Otherwise, the essays differ significantly in method and viewpoint. Mphahlele and Irele do not see eye to eye on *négritude,* for example; the latter occupies himself with the sorts of discourse *négritude* would seem to imply, the former with the very question of how it works in discourse at all. Again, with Ralph Ellison's "cosmopolitan" stand in mind—one may refresh one's memory with the article by Robert Bone—Wilson Harris's insistence on a West Indian identity that is at once geographical, political, and spiritual gains an extra dimension. And the ironic relation of theory to practice in Ellison and Harris must not go unnoticed: Ellison's is the work that seems steeped in the phenomena of black existence in a white-webbed world, while Harris uses the phenomena of Carribbean experience as a primer for dream-sounding myth.

The section on Africa also involves disagreement within a common frame of reference (see articles by Macaulay and Jahn). In the long run, the diversity may have profounder value, as it ranges from treatment of a single work (Jahn) to investigation of a continental vision as registered in national fictions (July). Other essays, in this and other sections, help to establish a sense of radiant possibilities. Robert Bone not only concerns himself with the issues raised in "Manifesto," but extends one view into the area of biography. Kingsley Widmer is philosophical where Michel Fabre is biographical and psychological in canvassing given themes in, respectively, Wright and Baldwin. Anne Tibble, Kenneth Ramchand, and John Hearne all confront the development of a writer's work, but Ramchand gives greatest play to social issues, Hearne to theme, and Tibble to literary effects. And finally, even if theme appears to be the common preoccupation of Jonathan Baumbach, Gerald Moore, and Gordon Rohlehr, there is no avoiding the differences in amplitude and in formal interest that emerge in their work.

These are connections and discriminations that each reader will, properly, wish to develop for himself. Another sort of connection may lie somewhat out of the way, and so a word on Claude McKay, the novelist to whom the concluding essay of the volume is devoted.

McKay, Jamaican by birth, lived and wrote chiefly in the United States, and this fact did have a material bearing on his work. It is correct to classify him as a West Indian, but proper also to acknowledge his American nurture (not all of it, perhaps, to his palate). Along with a figure like Marcus Garvey, he helps to highlight a vital connection between what would seem to be distinct sociogeographical areas; it is well to recall, as in the case of the impetus given *négritude* by French West Indian writers, that this connection has had a continual and actually widening literary effect. The evolving interrelationship of Africa, the United States, and the West Indies presents itself as an important development of the recent literary situation.

In designating this a recent development, it is necessary to make one qualification. Chronologically the year 1954, which saw the Supreme Court decision outlawing segregation in schools, would seem both crucial to and all of a piece with the literary quickening in the United States, just as, in another key, the beginning of the *uhuru* movement (1953) and of the movement toward federation and independence (1954) obviously counted for much in the writing of, respectively, Africa and the West Indies. But a degree of continuity also exists with the earlier Harlem constellation, in which McKay holds a prominent position. If not the germ, the spirit of the present is manifest in that unprophesied constellation of writers who went on their own, among their own, to open a new field of literary concern and discourse. It is strange but vital to see how close to that time is Richard Wright, who stands so close to us.

The essays in this volume afford as a group a concentrated view of modern black fiction. Other issues and subjects of investigation— an extensive view—may be pursued with the aid of the bibliography. So may the fiction itself, since a substantial list of novels, the counterpart and object of the criticism, receives its due prominence in the bibliography. For whatever reasons, some authors and some works are yet to rise to full stature; about others, the critics have yet to take a stand. One may venture to hope that a volume such as this will help both to further our understanding of well-canvassed reputations and to foster understanding of incipient ones.

Négritude: Literature and Ideology

by *Abiola Irele*

1. Society, History, and Culture

The subordinate role of the Negro in western society had been justified mainly by the allegation that Africa had made no contribution to world history, had no achievements to offer. The logical conclusion drawn from this idea was put by Alioune Diop in this way:

> Nothing in their past is of any value. Neither customs nor culture. Like living matter, these natives are asked to take on the customs, the logic, the language of the coloniser, from whom they even have to borrow their ancestors.

The western thesis that the African had no history implied for the black man that he had no future of his own to look forward to. A good deal of the propaganda effort of French-speaking intellectuals was as a consequence devoted to a refutation of this unacceptable proposition. Cheikh-Anta Diop's writings stand out in this respect. His book, *Nations nègres et culture*, for example, is an impassioned, heavily documented attempt to show that ancient Egyptian civilisation was in fact a Negro-African achievement, and thus to prove that the west owed its enlightenment to Africa. The conclusion to the principal section of his thesis is worth quoting in full, as it illustrates the tenor of the whole book:

> The Egyptian origin of civilisation, and the Greeks' heavy borrowing from it are historical evidence. One wonders therefore why, in the face of these facts, the emphasis is laid on the role played by Greece, while that of Egypt is more and more passed over in silence. The foundation for this attitude can only be understood by recalling the heart of the question.
>
> Egypt being a Negro country, and the civilisation which developed there being the product of black people, any thesis to the contrary would have been of no avail; the protagonists of these ideas are certainly by no means unaware of this fact. Consequently, it is wiser and surer purely

"Négritude: Literature and Ideology" by Abiola Irele. From the *Journal of Modern African Studies*, 3, No. 4 (1965), 513–26. Reprinted by permission of Cambridge University Press.

and simply to strip Egypt of all her achievements for the benefit of a
people of genuine white origin.

This false attribution of the values of an Egypt conveniently labelled
white to a Greece equally white reveals a profound contradiction, which
is not negligible as a proof of the Negro origin of Egyptian civilisation.

As can be seen, the black man, far from being incapable of developing a technical civilisation, is in fact the one who developed it first, in
the person of the Negro, at a time when all the white races, wallowing
in barbarism, were only just fit for civilisation.

In saying that it was the ancestors of Negroes, who today inhabit
principally Black Africa, who first invented mathematics, astronomy, the
calendar, science in general, the arts, religion, social organisation, medicine, writing, engineering, architecture . . . in saying all this, one is
simply stating the modest and strict truth, which nobody at the present
moment can refute with arguments worthy of the name.[1]

The whole thesis is based on an implied correlation between history
and culture which determines the nature of society, and of the individual: and its intention was to prove that the African was essentially
a technical man—*homo faber.* However, by summarily ascribing all
civilisation to the black man in this way, Diop proceeds in the field
of scholarship in the same fashion as Léon Damas in the poem already
cited—by reversing the hierarchy established by the coloniser, without
contesting the basis on which it was founded. It is, in a way, a total
acceptance of the western measure of evaluation, namely technical
achievement.

Négritude may be distinguished from other efforts to rehabilitate
Africa by what can be termed its "ethnological" aspect, which attempted to redefine its terms, and to re-evaluate Africa within a non-
western framework. Here the concept of cultural relativity was to help
in sustaining a campaign whose purpose was to establish the validity of
African cultural forms *in their own right.*

This explains the preoccupation of the French-speaking Negro intellectuals with anthropology, a preoccupation which reveals itself in
the series of special numbers published by *Présence africaine,* especially
the two remarkable volumes *Le Monde noir* (1951) and *L'Art nègre*
(1952). The former, edited by Theodore Monod, brought together a
number of articles by eminent scholars, both European and African,
on various aspects of African cultural expression as well as their
ramifications in the New World, in such a way as to suggest not only
their originality but their world-wide permanence.

The accent was almost invariably placed on the non-material aspects,
on those intangible elements which could distinguish the African's
approach to the world from the western, and which might seem to
underlie his conscious existence as well as his material productions.

[1] Cheikh-Anta Diop, *Nations nègres et culture* (Paris, 1954), p. 253.

Thus African traditional beliefs and, in particular, the native forms of religion received strong emphasis. African "animism" tended in general to be placed on an equal footing with Christianity, though curiously enough by an effort of reconciliation in most cases. The most noteworthy example of this kind of procedure is perhaps a paper by Paul Hazoumé, in which the Dahomean conception of God is likened to that of John the Evangelist.[2]

The anthropological interests of *négritude* came to the fore at the First Congress of Negro Writers and Artists, whose express purpose was to make a total inventory of the Negro's cultural heritage, in an effort to define a Pan-Negro cultural universe. This was at best a very delicate, if not an impossible, undertaking, as the discomfort and reserve of the American participants at the conference was to make clear. It would be tedious to go into the details, but two main lines of thought emerged from the deliberations of this conference. Foremost in the minds of the organisers was the will to demonstrate the specific character of traditional African institutions and beliefs as well as of African survivals in America, in a way that refuted the western thesis of inferiority. The purpose of this was made clear by the Haitian, Emmanuel Paul:

> It was from this [African] past that colonial authors undertook to make the black man inferior. . . . But what we look for from these studies is precisely the awakening of a historical consciousness embracing the millennial past of the race. These black people scattered all over the world who, even under the pressure of the west, still hesitate to deny themselves, have need of this source of pride, this reason for clinging to life.[3]

Secondly, and as a consequence, the concern with the past implied a process of self-appraisal and self-definition, as a solid basis. The Malagasy writer, Jacques Rabemananjara, declared:

> The deliberations [of this Congress] have no other purpose than to assemble and to select material for the dialogue. First among ourselves, with the aim of knowing ourselves more, of grasping, through our diverse mentalities, customs, and countries of origin, the essential human note, the ineffable human warmth that unites us.[4]

These efforts cannot be said to have produced a common cultural denominator, but their significance lay rather in the attitude that inspired them. In direct response to the intolerance that characterised the

---

[2] P. Hazoumé, 'L'âme du Dahoméen, animiste révélée par sa religion', in *Contributions au 1er congrès des écrivains et artistes noirs*, pp. 233–51. See also the collected volume, *Des Prêtres noirs s'interrogent* (Paris, 1957), for a similar approach to African religious beliefs.

[3] E. Paul, 'L'Ethnologie et les cultures noires', in *Contributions au 1er congrès des écrivains et artistes noirs*, p. 152.

[4] J. Rabemananjara, 'L'Europe et nous', ibid. p. 28.

cultural policy of the coloniser, *négritude* developed into a vindication
and an exaltation of cultural institutions which were different from
those of the west; it was thus a conscious attitude of pluralism. The
corollary was a rejection of *assimilation* and a claim to cultural
autonomy and initiative. Alioune Diop expressed this aspect of the
movement in the following terms:

> Unable to assimilate to the English, the Belgian, the French, the Portu-
> guese—to allow the elimination of certain original dimensions of our
> genius for the benefit of a bloated mission of the west—we shall en-
> deavour to forge for this genius those means of expression best suited
> to its vocation in the twentieth century.[5]

2. *Politics and Race*

These efforts to rehabilitate African history and to re-evaluate
African culture were a conscious reaction to the ideology that sustained colonial rule. But the central pole of the colonial situation was
political domination rather than cultural supremacy. The next step
after a demand for cultural autonomy was logically a corresponding
demand for political independence. The arguments for an explicit
political stand came mainly from the Marxist elements in the movement, especially at the second congress in Rome. Frantz Fanon's ad-
dress to this meeting contained an unequivocal summary of their
point of view:

> In the colonial situation, culture, denied the twin support of nation
> and state, withers away in a slow death. The condition for the existence
> of culture is therefore national liberation, the rebirth of the state.[6]

However, if a certain political awareness was an implicit part of the
cultural offensive of the French-speaking black intellectual, which
placed *négritude* in close relationship with African nationalism and
Pan-Africanism, it is none the less quite clear that *négritude* remained
essentially a cultural and intellectual movement, albeit with political
implications. The French-speaking Negro élite tended more towards
an elaboration of ideas concerning the black man's place in the world
than towards the actual mobilisation of the masses for an immediate
and definite political goal.[7] *Négritude* was thus at the most an ideological movement with remote political purposes.

---

[5] Alioune Diop, *Deuxième congrès des écrivains et artistes noirs*, p. 41.

[6] F. Fanon, 'Fondements réciproques de la culture nationale et des luttes de
libération', ibid. p. 87.

[7] G. Balandier observes that, in the development of African political myth, 'the
accent was placed more on . . . cultural liberation . . . than on political liberation'. 'Les Mythes politiques de colonisation et de décolonisation en Afrique', in
Cahiers Internationaux de Sociologie (Paris), XXXIII, 1962, p. 93.

Its link with nationalism is all the same certain in that a special *rationale* was developed along with it; it furnished the most important *mystique* of African nationalism.

In so far then as it is an answer to a certain combination of circumstances, the product of a historical situation, *négritude* is another cultural and political myth: the expression of a justified self-assertion swelling into an exaggerated self-consciousness.[8] *Négritude* has also meant to a considerable extent an assiduous cultivation of the black race.

That Negro nationalism on both sides of the Atlantic should have been based on a vehement racial consciousness can be imputed to the racialism that grew out of and which often came to underlie white domination: black nationalism can in the final analysis be reduced to a challenge to white supremacy. *Négritude*, by confronting white domination with its own racial protest and zealous partisanship of the Negro race, did more than draw together the sentiments and attitudes that went with black reaction and embody them in a heightened form: it moved in fact very distinctly towards a racial ideology.

Even here, most of the ideas expressed by French Negro intellectuals are limited to a refutation of the racial ideology of colonialism. For if, in the literary works, the exaltation of the black race rises to dizzy heights, it has not been reproduced in the non-literary writings with anything like the same abandon. In the single case of Sénghor, this aspect of *négritude* acquires a certain intellectual dimension. So preeminently do his ideas emerge on this question that his conception of *négritude* demands separate consideration.[9]

3. Sénghor and the Theory of Négritude

Sénghor's *négritude* starts out as, and essentially remains, a defence of African cultural expression.[10] It presents itself first as an elaborate apology before it becomes an exposition and a personal view of Africa: it is a passion that is later rationalised. None the less, his ideas over

[8] The following observation by Louis Wirth about minorities' reaction to their situation should be kept in mind when considering *négritude*: 'One cannot long discriminate against a people without generating in them a sense of isolation and of persecution, and without giving them a conception of themselves as more different from others than in fact they are'. R. Linton (ed.), *The Science of Man in the World Crisis*, p. 348.

[9] No other member of the movement has elaborated *négritude* so fully as Sénghor. As a matter of fact, Césaire himself prefers to regard *négritude* as a historical stand, as an attitude, rather than as a comprehensive system (private interview with the author).

[10] The title of one of his early articles is significant: 'Défense de l'Afrique noire', in *Esprit* (Paris), 1945.

the last quarter-century present a coherent and even a consistent pattern.

On several occasions, Sénghor has defined *négritude* as "the sum total of African cultural values," something perhaps more than the simple relation of the African's personality to his social and cultural background. For although Sénghor never speaks of an "essence," he speaks of a "Negro soul," of a special spiritual endowment of the African which is, in some respects, shared by the Negro in the New World, and is therefore a racial mark.[11]

Sénghor describes and defines the African's distinctive qualities mainly by opposition to the western, often by setting a positive value on what the west derided in the African, sometimes proceeding by grounding his own thinking in modern currents of western thought, which he then turns against the west for the benefit of his arguments. He has written, for example:

> Discursive reason merely stops at the surface of things, it does not penetrate their hidden resorts, which escape the lucid consciousness. Intuitive reason is alone capable of an understanding that goes beyond appearances, of taking in total reality.[12]

It is this line of thought that forms the basis for his justification of the African's non-rational approach to the world. He has boldly annexed Lévy-Bruhl's studies on "primitive mentality" to argue the validity of the African's ways of thinking. He seizes in particular upon the French anthropologists' "law of participation";[13] and he uses this in his own formulation of the African's mode of experience, which he presents as essentially one of feeling—of a mystical sympathy with the universe: "The African cannot imagine an object as different from him in its essence. He endows it with a sensibility, a will, a human soul."[14]

For Sénghor, this African mode of apprehending reality through the senses rather than through the intellect is at the root of his direct experience of the world, of his spontaneity. The African's psychology helps to determine a different form of mental operation from the western, a different kind of logic:

> The life-surge of the African, his self-abandonment to the other, is thus actuated by reason. But here, reason is not the eye-reason of the European, it is the *reason-by-embrace* which shares more the nature of the *logos* than *ratio*.

[11] Cf. 'Ce que l'homme noir apporte', in *Liberté*, I: *négritude et humanisme* (Paris, 1964), pp. 22–39.
[12] Sénghor, Preface to Birago Diop, *Les Nouveaux Contes d'Amadou Khoumba*, in *Liberté*, I, p. 246.
[13] Cf. Lucien Lévy-Bruhl, *Morceaux Choisis* (Paris, 1936), pp. 23–27. Although Lévy-Bruhl's ideas have been demolished, and he himself renounced them later in his life, this does not seem to have affected Sénghor's own ideas.
[14] Sénghor, 'Ce que l'homme noir apporte', in *Liberté*, I, p. 24.

He goes on to say, "Classical European reason is analytical and makes use of the object. African reason is intuitive and participates in the object." [15] Sénghor has made this distinction a constant theme in his writings.

The "law of participation" governs the African's sensibility, which to Sénghor is basically emotive. He has pushed this conception of the African mind to a point where emotion has become its cardinal principle. "Emotion is African, as Reason is Hellenic," he has exclaimed, and though this statement has been given careful nuances by him (for the benefit of his critics) he still leaves no doubt about this aspect of his theory of *négritude*: "It is this gift of emotion which explains *négritude*. . . . For it is their *emotive attitude* towards the world which explains the cultural values of Africans." [16]

Sénghor points to creative works to demonstrate the presence of a unique African sensibility which animates them, and insists above all on the privileged position of rhythm in African artistic expression—rhythm is for him the expression of the essential vitality of the African:

> [Rhythm] is the architecture of being, the internal dynamism which shapes it, the system of waves which it sends out towards others, the pure expression of vital force . . . For the Negro-African, it is in the same measure that rhythm is embodied in the senses that it illuminates the Spirit.[17]

In his exposition of the African mind, Sénghor lays emphasis on its intensely religious disposition, on the African's "sense of the divine," on "his faculty of perceiving the supernatural in the natural." [18] The African's mystical conception of the world is for Sénghor his principal gift, and derives from his close links with the natural world. Because the African "identifies *being* with life, or rather with the *life-force*," the world represents for him the manifestation in diverse forms of the same vital principle: "For the universe is a closed system of forces, individual and distinct; it is true, yet also interdependent." [19] Lévy-Bruhl's law of participation is here allied to Fr. Temple's "Bantu Philosophy" to produce a conception of the African world-view as a system of participating forces, a kind of great chain of vital responses in which Man, the personification of the "life-force," occupies a central position: "From God through man, down to the grain of sand, it is a seamless whole. Man, in his role as person, is the centre of this universe." [20]

[15] Sénghor, 'Psychologie du Négro-African', in *Diogène*, 37, 1962; translated by John Reed and Clive Wake, in *Sénghor: Prose and Poetry* (London, 1965), p. 33.
[16] Ibid.
[17] 'L'Esthétique négro-africaine', in *Liberté*, I, p. 212–13.
[18] 'Ce que l'homme noir apporte', in *Liberté*, I, p. 27.
[19] Translations by John Reed and Clive Wake, op. cit., p. 37.
[20] Ibid. p. 43.

For Sénghor, this is not an abstract system but an existential philosophy, a practical view of life; *négritude* is for him not only a way of being, but also a way of living. He therefore extends his theory of the African personality to explain African social organisation. Sénghor believes that the African society is an extension of the clan, which is a kind of mystical family, "the sum of all persons, living and dead, who acknowledge a common ancestor." [21] Thus African society has a religious character—it is not so much a community of persons as "a communion of souls." Where, therefore, western culture insists on the individual, African culture lays emphasis on the group, though without the loss of a sense of the person.[22]

Sénghor's theory of *négritude* is not really a factual and scientific demonstration of African personality and social organisation, but rather a personal interpretation. An element of speculation enters into his ideas, which lays them wide open to criticism. His more subtle formulations often have a specious character; besides, the most sympathetic reader of his theories cannot fail to be disturbed by his frequent confusion of race and culture, especially in his early writings.

On the other hand, these weaknesses are due to the circumstances in which his ideas developed. In assessing the objective differences that cut off the African from western man, his concern is to make a positive re-evaluation of realities which the west considered negative.

Furthermore, Sénghor's political career has given his theory of *négritude* a practical significance—from polemics, it has evolved into an ideology. His social and political thought are set within the general framework of his cultural philosophy. It is in the name of the innate spiritual sense of the African that he rejects the atheistic materialism of Marxism as unfitted for and irrelevant to the African situation.[23]

In a certain sense, therefore, Sénghor may be justified in designating his theory of *négritude* as a cultural and not as a racial philosophy. At any rate, it is not an exclusive racism. Sénghor's views on the African, and even on the whole Negro race, open out towards the larger perspectives of a broader humanism. Here he has been influenced by Teilhard de Chardin's philosophy of the convergence of all forms of life and experience towards the evolution of a superior human consciousness, which has given Sénghor a pole around which he has developed his idea of "a civilisation of the Universal." [24] His defence of cultural and racial mingling is founded on this key concept, which is summed up in the following passage:

[21] Ibid.

[22] Cf. *Nation et voie africaine du socialisme* (Paris, 1961), pp. 71 and 123–24.

[23] Cf. Sénghor, *Nation et voie africaine du socialisme*, pp. 41–66, *and Pierre Teilhard de Chardin et la politique africaine* (Paris, 1962), pp. 17–31. Sénghor does not reject so much the philosophy of Marx as his social ideology.

[24] Ibid., pp. 33 ff.

The only "pan-ism" which can meet the demands of the 20th century is —let us proclaim it boldly—pan-humanism, I mean a humanism which embraces all men at the double level of their contrbiutions and their comprehension.[25]

4. The African Presence and the Black Millennium

An ideology, when it becomes explicit, is a kind of thinking aloud on the part of a society or of a group within it. It is a direct response to the actual conditions of life, and has a social function, either as a defensive system of beliefs and ideas which support and justify an established social structure, or as a rational project for the creation of a new order. The latter type of ideology, even when it includes a certain degree of idealism, also implies a reasoned programme of collective action; it becomes the intellectual channel of social life.

The literature and ideology of *négritude* were by their nature revolutionary, or at the very least radical. Because they spring from a need to reverse an intolerable situation, they are moved in the first instance by a negative principle. They are a challenge to the common lot which western expansion had imposed on non-western man, especially the Negro, whose experience—dispersal, subjugation, humiliation—illustrates the worst aspects of contact with the white man. For black people had in common an experience which, in the words of James Baldwin, placed in the same context their widely dissimilar experience. He continues:

> What they held in common was their precarious, their unutterably painful reaction to the white world. What they held in common was the necessity to remake the world in their own image, to impose this image on the world, and no longer be controlled by the vision of the world, and of themselves, held by other people. What in sum black men held in common was their ache to come into the world as men.[26]

In the circumstances, it is not surprising that this "ache" should have developed sometimes into an intense collective neurosis, which has reached a paroxysm in movements like those of the Black Muslims in the U.S., and the Ras Tafarians in Jamaica. The dilemma in which history placed the black man, and from which the intellectual movements could not escape, was that Negro nationalism of any kind was bound to be even more irrational than any other, for it was to a considerable degree a gesture of despair.

This negative aspect of black reaction to white rule has left a mark on *négritude,* even in its development of positive perspectives. A contradiction, purely emotional in origin, bedevils the movement, which, in

[25] *Nation et voie africaine du socialisme,* p. 108.
[26] James Baldwin, *Nobody Knows My Name* (New York, 1961), p. 29.

its crusade for the total emancipation of black people, has sought to comprise within a single cultural vision the different historical experiences of Negro societies and nations.

It would be a mistake, however, to dismiss the movement as a futile and sectarian obsession with self—a kind of black narcissism. In the larger context of Negro experience, it represents the ultimate and most stable point of self-awareness. For, although its expression has sometimes been exaggerated, it has always had an intellectual content. In the African political context, its role as the ideological spear-point of African nationalism has been sufficiently emphasised. Its profound significance in the cultural and social evolution of Africa has been perhaps less appreciated.

Négritude represents both an African *crise de conscience,* and its most significant modern expression; it is the watershed that marks the emergence of a modern African consciousness. African "messianism" and *négritude* represent the ritualistic and the intellectual facet of the reaction to the same historical, social, and cultural stimulus. Their forms have varied. In African messianism, tradition remains the basis of social behaviour, despite borrowings from western religion, which are absorbed only so far as they will fit in. The reverse is true of *négritude*: despite its championship of a non-rational tradition, it remains rigorously rational. Sénghor's *négritude,* for example, is an anti-intellectualism mediated by the intellect, and the whole movement is expressed through a western mould which absorbs African realities. In short, *négritude* is a break with tradition: although African in content, it is western in its formal expression.

The movement thus marks a transition in the nature of collective expression in Africa—from the myth of the millennium and from the religious undercurrent upon which traditional Africa had relied for human accomplishment, to the lay, intellectually-centred approach to the world which is a legacy of the European Renaissance. It marks a "desacralisation" of African collective life, an attitude which is spontaneous and no longer imposed, and out of which have begun to flow new currents of ideas for tackling present-day African problems.

This is what Balandier has observed as "the progression from myth to ideology" in Africa.[27] Although this progression has been continuous and although, as L.-V. Thomas has remarked, "the originality of modern solutions is inspired by the specific character of former times," [28] none the less the transition is real. African messianism was an archaic reaction to a new situation; *négritude* was a far more appropriate response, adapted to the modern age.

[27] Balandier, op. cit., p. 93.
[28] L.-V. Thomas, *Les Idéologies négro-africaines d'aujourd'hui* (Dakar, 1965), p. 19. Cf. also B. Ogot, 'From Chief to President', in *Transition* (Kampala), 10, 1963, for a study of the same progression in African political organisation and attitudes.

It thus forms an essential and significant part of an African revolution which is marked not only by the emotions it has liberated and the ideas it has thrown up, but also by the forms it has assimilated. The profound character of the transition can best be appreciated by comparing the respective visions of the Absolute in African messianism and in *négritude*. The former was supernatural and apocalyptic—essentially an eschatology. The idealism of *négritude* from the beginning tended towards an earthly utopia:

> We Africans need to know the meaning of an ideal, to be able to choose it and believe in it freely, but out of a sense of personal necessity, to relate it to the life of the world. We should occupy ourselves with present questions of world importance, and, in common with others, ponder upon them, in order that we might one day find ourselves among the creators of a new order.[29]

In their search for identity, the adherents of *négritude* have had to accept and explore to the full their particular situation. But, although preoccupied with a sectional and limited interest, they were inspired by a universal human need for fulfilment. In this, they have never strayed from the central, enduring problem of the human condition.

[29] A. Diop, 'Niam n'goura ou les raisons d'être de présence africaine', in *Présence africaine* 1, 1947 (translated by R. Wright).

Roots

by Ezekiel Mphahlele

At the conference of the American Society of African Culture held at Philadelphia I hit upon a vague desire among some Negroes, to dislodge themselves culturally and seek a reorientation in African values. Mr. Samuel Allen, the Negro poet who writes under the name of Paul Vesey, presented a paper analysing *négritude* as seen and felt by Aimé Césaire, Leopold Sédar Sénghor, and interpreted by Sartre. Briefly, here are Mr. Allen's signposts: Mr. Alioune Diop, secretary of the Paris-born Society of African Culture, gives as the *raison d'être* of *négritude* the fact that the world has been taught there is no culture other than the West's, no universal values which are not hers. The effort to determine the common elements of Negro African culture is but one phase of an historic renaissance which has only begun to reshape the image of man upon the earth. *Négritude,* then, is the complete ensemble of values of African culture, and the vindication of the dignity of persons of African descent.

Jacques Rabemananjara, the Malagasy poet, says the unity of Negro culture is an act of faith. Aimé Césaire is said to be reflecting the essence of *négritude* when he says in a poem:

Hail the royal Kailcedrat!
Hail those who have invented nothing!
Who have explored nothing!
But they abandon themselves, possessed, to the essence of all things,
Heedless of taming, but playing the game of the world. . . .

Sénghor finds the African's heightened sensibility and his strong emotional quality as his chief psychic traits. Two sources, he says, explain the origin of the psychic profile of the Negro African: the millenniums of his tropical experience and the agricultural nature of his existence; the heat and humidity of tropical regions and a pastoral closeness to the earth and the rhythms of its seasons. Emotion, he finds, is at the heart of *négritude*: "emotion is Negro."

Ranged against these opinions, Mr. Allen records, are those of
the late Richard Wright (on American Negro poetry): its common
characteristics, its rebelliousness, its intensity, its despair, can be attributed to the common social factor of oppression. Sénghor, on
the other hand, finds in a poem by Wright an intensity which he
considers as peculiarly African. George Lamming (Barbadian writer):
politics is the only ground for a universal Negro sympathy. Peter
Abrahams (South African born and now living in Jamaica): any sin-
gularities in the Negro's creative art can be attributed to the social fact
of his rejection by the West.

Although Mr. Allen objectively reports these views, he himself
asserts that Africa is looked to by many for a "new humanism, for
new psychic ways, for a vital force." Earlier, in a paper included in
a publication of AMSAC, *The American Negro Writer and His Roots,*
Mr. Allen had said: "Let us consider briefly the possible relevance of
this concept (*négritude*) to the work of the American Negro writer or,
to put it differently, its validity for a writer in our cultural situation.
I think it has a role. This is not necessarily so for all of us, the writer
not being a soldier marching to command. He writes, when he writes
most creatively, pursuant to his own individual and most deeply felt
need. The racial accident of his birth may have little influence or only
indirect influence on the purpose of his writing. . . .

"It is probably true also that it was not by chance that this concept, negritude, originated among the poets rather than among those
working in prose. Except for certain highly imaginative works,
the novelist writes within a framework of what we term reality. He
must in part concern himself with Plato's shadows—with plot and
setting. His characters must grow up. He is constrained to a certain
degree of reasonableness. The poet has probably a greater chance to
penetrate, at once without apology and without a setting of the worldly
stage, to the deepest levels of his creative concern. And so, perhaps
what we are saying may have greater applicability to poetry than to
prose."

Mr. Allen had also observed that for Sénghor the *négritude* of a
poem was *less the theme than the style* (my italics); "its characteristic
manner, the intensity of its passion, its rhythmic flow or the quality of
its imagery, whether he writes of a ritual dance in Dahomey, of the
Brittany sea coast, or of the nature of God and Man."

Look at this poem by Aimé Césaire, of which Mr. Allen renders a
translation in order to demonstrate how Césaire emphasizes the
"dynamic quality" of *négritude*:

My négritude is not a rock, its deafness hurled against the clamour of
   the day
My négritude is not a film of dead water on the dead eye of the earth

My négritude is neither a tower nor a cathedral
It plunges into the red flesh of the earth
It plunges into the burning flesh of the sky
It pierces the opaque prostration by its upright patience.

The theme is, of course, clearly *négritude*. Because the poem is a passionate outcry, a self-vindication, it has an intensity of style, of imagery:
"its deafness hurled against the clamour of the day"; "the burning
flesh of the sky"; "upright patience." Abstract ideas are given a concrete meaning. What have we proved? An intensely conceived subject
begets—or calls for—intensity of style; so that it becoems irrelevant to
talk about theme and style separately. What is so distinctively
négritude about that? One could find in Baudelaire an intensity to
match this. The difference would be that Baudelaire wouldn't talk
négritude, but Césaire does, because he *is* Negro. So we go back to
the theme, the subject of all this talk.

The main reason why *négritude* has enchanted a few American
Negro writers consists in their resistance against the tendency on the
part of the outside world and their fellow-Americans to regard their
work as a tributary to some major American stream, or against the
desire among other writers to join the mainstream of American culture, "a desire for obliteration and passive absorption by the majority."

The American Negro has the right to seek his roots in Africa if he
wishes to, for all the good it might do his art. We must realize that
he is living through a series of crises. Mr. Arthur Davis, another Negro
writer, lays bare the predicament of his people most ably in his essay
in the AMSAC publication referred to above. He says now that the
lynching days are all but over, the enemy that gave Negro writers a
common purpose is capitulating, and integration is taking place, the
most fruitful literary tradition of Negro writing has been shattered:
the protest element is being destroyed; the spiritual climate for integration exists, he says, and "it becomes almost a tragic experience
because it means (especially for the writer in his middle years) giving
up a tradition in which he has done his apprentice and journeyman
work, giving it up when he is prepared to make use of that tradition
as a master craftsman." Some writers have tried to shift the emphasis
from the protest aspect to the problems and conflicts within their
Negro group itself, while retaining the Negro character and background. Some even write about whites. Frank Yerby, for instance, with
ten or more best-selling novels in succession, has never used a Negro
background or Negro principal characters. Mr. Davis says that he
hopes from the integration crisis his people "will move permanently
into full participation in American life—social, economic, political,
and literary. . . ." He (the Negro artist) will discover what we all
know in our objective moments, that there are many facets of Negro

living—humorous, pathetic and tragic—which are not directly touched by the outside world.

It seems to me, an outsider, that the Negro's commitment is so huge in his country that he will probably find it more profitable to concern himself with producing good art inside his social climate, as a "native son." If he finds the American civilization frustrating, he should realize that it is not a parochial malady. Everywhere, especially in Africa, we are up against this invasion by the white world upon our sense of values. It was a healthy thing to discover that the Negro's image of the African was changing to the good. Until President Nkrumah, Dr. Nnamdi Azikiwe, Tom Mboya, Julius Nyerere, Dr. Hastings Banda went to the United States, the Negro thought of the African as a primitive man whose jungle existence had largely outlived the processes of education. The Americans saw these men on TV and heard especially Nyerere and Mboya brilliantly weather the storm of pressmen's questions and often make them look silly. Both middle-class and working-class Negroes told us how revealing these pictures were. I still cannot explain the ignorance of some of the literate Negroes, when United States publishers tell us the book market is glutted with books on Africa, many of them quite good. Negro porters, taxi-drivers, spontaneously revealed their pride in Africa. One old man stopped three of us visiting Africans in Harlem to ask who we were. Then he told us, quite emotionally, how stunned he was by the articulateness of the African leaders he saw on television. On the other hand, we were told, French-speaking Africans who were coming to the United States on and off despised what they regarded as the Negro's lack of fight in response to so much discrimination aimed at them. It reminded me that our French-speaking brothers need a heavy course on African affairs. They just don't seem to know the social forces at work in African countries south of the Equator. They are too often apt to bring a philosophical mind to political and cultural questions in a changing continent.

How similar the American Negro's cultural predicament is to ours in South Africa and in other multi-racial communities. The needle that registers your response as a writer swings between protest and romantic writing, and then, when you are spiritually emancipated, the needle quivers around the central point—the meeting point between rejection and acceptance. Then you know both how excruciating and exciting it is to be the meeting point of two streams of consciousness and the paradoxes they pose. That is what makes our art. If there is any *négritude* in the black man's art in South Africa, it is because we *are* African. If a writer's tone is healthy, he is bound to express the African in him. Stripped of Sénghor's philosophic musings, the African traits he speaks of can be taken for granted: they are social anthropology. We who grew up and were educated in Africa do not find anything new in them. Simply because we respond intensely to situations is no reason why we should think non-Africans are incapable of doing so, or that we are the only section of the human race who are full of passionate intensity. These traits are not anything we need make slogans about, in terms of art. Or are we supposed to dig up the bones of Victorian aesthetes and start beating our drums with them? In my struggle to overcome the artistic difficulty that arises when one is angry most of the time and when one's sense of values is continually being challenged by the ruling class, I have never thought of calling my *négritude* to my aid, except when writing protest material. But is not this elementary—shall I call it "under doggery"?—that Sénghor is talking about? Even he must know, however, that his philosophy will contain his art only up to a point: it won't chain his art for long. He must know that his *négritude* can at best be an attitude, a pose, where his art is concerned, just as it was a pose in my protest writing. Excessive protest poisons one's system, and thank goodness I'm emancipated from that. The anger is there, but I can harness it.

For the rest, I must expose myself to cultural impacts around me, trusting in the truth expressed by Professor J. Newton Hill of Lincoln University at the opening of his paper, "The Idiom in African Art," read at the AMSAC conference:

> It is probably well for us to admit at the very beginning of this study that an artist may express, and frequently with remarkable ability, the sentiments of the race to which he belongs. This is not subscribing to any philosophy regarding environmental influences on the artist, nor is this an admission that the artist is inescapably controlled by ethnological factors. What we mean is rather, that an artist by the simple relationship which he bears to the persons and things all about him, can seldom speak absolutely for himself—as if a being in isolation.

It seems that the two societies of African culture would be more profitably employed if while they preserved traditional works of art in Africa, they sponsored the great amount of talent that is to be found in Africa, artistic talent that has so long been bottled up in countries like South Africa, East and Central Africa. There is plenty of literary art waiting to be published and it needs to be encouraged. In effect, these societies must concern themselves with the artist in his present dilemma. Then, of course, the American Society can continue keeping watch over Negro attitudes towards Africa. I cannot ask much more than this of the Americans, because they are not, like the French-speaking Negro, committed to come back to Africa and lead a movement.

What about identification from the African side? The South African non-white is always looking for symbols of freedom and advancement, as one of his responses to white domination. The magazines *Ebony* (now banned because it highlights Negro achievement and is therefore apt to "mislead" non-whites), *Sepia* and *Bandstand* have done much to project an admirable image of the American Negro in South Africa. Hollywood has done the most in its portrayal of the Negro. The image was automatically transferred in our minds to the West Indian. He too became a symbol. The early American films merely caricatured the Negro in such idiot-looking, clumsy figures as Stepin Fetchit, in the frightened male servant and fat mammy, in the silent, non-committal taxi-driver, the large and menacing black man, the jazz artiste who was always brought in edgeways. But it was enough, to our immature minds, that the Negro was hitting the screen, which we could never hope to do except in shots advertising tea and Vim scouring powder.

Tradition and the West Indian Novel

by Wilson Harris

I would like first of all to point out that the conventional approach to the "West Indian" which sees him in crowds—an under-
privileged crowd, a happy-go-lucky crowd, a political or a cricketing
crowd, a calypso crowd—is one which we have to put aside at this
moment for the purposes of our discussion. The status of the West
Indian—as a person in world society—is of a much more isolated and
problematic character. West Indians in their national context, in their
nation-state, as such, are a minority in the world of the twentieth
century, a very small minority at that. What in my view is remarkable
about the West Indian in depth is a sense of subtle links, the series of
subtle and nebulous links which are latent within him, the latent
ground of old and new personalities. This is a very difficult view to
hold, I grant, because it is not a view which consolidates, which in-
vests in any way in the consolidation of popular character. Rather it
seeks to visualize a *fulfilment* of character. Something which is more
extraordinary than one can easily imagine. And it is this possible
revolution in the novel—*fulfilment* rather than *consolidation*—I would
like first of all to look at in a prospective way because I feel it is profoundly consistent with the native tradition—the depth of inarticulate
feeling and unrealized wells of emotion belonging to the whole West
Indies.

The Potential of the Novel

The consolidation of character is, to a major extent, the preoccupation of most novelists who work in the twentieth century within the
framework of the nineteenth-century novel. Indeed the nineteenth-
century novel has exercised a very powerful influence on reader and
writer alike in the contemporary world. And this is not surprising after
all since the rise of the novel in its conventional and historical mould
coincides in Europe with states of society which were involved in

"Tradition and the West Indian Novel" by Wilson Harris. Text of a lecture
delivered to the London West Indian Students' Union in May 1964. First published
by the Students' Union as a pamphlet; reissued in a collection of essays *Tradition,
the Writer and Society* (London: New Beacon Publishers, 1967), pp. 28–47. Reprinted by permission of the author.

consolidating their class and other vested interests. As a result "character" in the novel rests more or less on the self-sufficient individual —on elements of "persuasion" (a refined or liberal persuasion at best in the spirit of the philosopher Whitehead) rather than "dialogue" or "dialectic" in the profound and unpredictable sense of person which Martin Buber, for example, evokes. The novel of persuasion rests on grounds of apparent common sense: a certain "selection" is made by the writer, the selection of items, manners, uniform conversation, historical situations, etc., all lending themselves to build and present an individual span of life which yields self-conscious and fashionable judgements, self-conscious and fashionable moralities. The tension which emerges is the tension of individuals—great or small—on an accepted plane of society we are persuaded has an inevitable existence. There is an element of freedom in this method nevertheless, an apparent range of choices, but I believe myself that this freedom—in the convention which distinguishes it, however liberal this may appear—is an illusion. It is true of course that certain kinds of realism, impressive realism, and also a kind of fateful honesty distinguished and still distinguishes the novel of individual character especially where an element of great suffering arises and does a kind of spiritual violence to every "given" conception. . . . I would like to break off here for a moment to say that the novel of the West Indies, the novel written by West Indians of the West Indies (or of other places for that matter), belongs—in the main—to the conventional mould. Which is not surprising at this stage since the novel which consolidates situations to depict protest or affirmation is consistent with most kinds of overriding advertisement and persuasion upon the writer for him to make national and political and social simplifications of experience in the world at large today. Therefore the West Indian novel—so-called— in the main—is inclined to suffer in depth (to lose in depth) and may be properly assessed in nearly every case in terms of surface tension and realism—as most novels are assessed today—in the perceptive range of choices which emerges, and above all in the way in which the author *persuades* you to ally yourself with situation and character. I shall return to this point and to a close look at the work of certain West Indian writers. . . . But at the moment I would like to pursue the subtler prospective thread I have raised to your attention. I believe it is becoming possible to see even now at this relatively early time that the ruling and popular convention, as such, is academic and provincial in the light of a genuine—and if I may use a much abused term—*native* tradition of depth.

Native and Phenomenal Environment

The native and phenomenal environment of the West Indies, as I see it, is broken into many stages in the way in which one surveys an existing river in its present bed while plotting at the same time ancient and abandoned, indeterminate courses the river once followed. When I speak of the West Indies I am thinking of overlapping contexts of Central and South America as well. For the mainstream of the West Indies in my estimation possesses an enormous escarpment down which it falls, and I am thinking here of the European discovery of the New World and conquest of the ancient American civilizations which were themselves related by earlier and obscure levels of conquest. This escarpment seen from another angle possesses the features of a watershed, main or subsidiary, depending again on how one looks at it.

The environment of the Caribbean is steeped—as I said before—in such broken conceptions as well as misconceptions of the residue and meaning of conquest. No wonder in the jungles of Guyana and Brazil, for example, material structural witnesses may be obliterated or seem to exist in a terrible void of unreality. Let us look once again at the main distinction which for convenience one may describe as the divide pre-Columbian/post-Columbian. The question is—how can one begin to reconcile the broken parts of such an enormous heritage, especially when those broken parts appear very often like a grotesque series of adventures, volcanic in its precipitate effects as well as human in its vulnerable settlement? This distinction is a large, a very large one which obviously has to be broken down into numerous modern tributaries and other immigrant movements and distinctions so that the smallest area one envisages, island or village, prominent ridge or buried valley, flatland or heartland, is charged immediately with the openness of imagination, and the longest chain of sovereign territories one sees is ultimately no stronger than its weakest and most obscure connecting link.

Vision of Consciousness

It is in this light that one must seek to relate the existing pattern of each community to its variable past, and if I may point to the phenomenal divide again, the question which arises is how one can begin to let these parts act on each other in a manner which fulfils *in the person* the most nebulous instinct for a vocation of being and independent spirit within a massive landscape of apparent lifelessness which yields nevertheless the essential denigration and erosion of historical perspectives. This indeed is a peculiarly West Indian question, strange as it may appear to some, and in fact a question peculiar to every phenomenal society where minorities (frail in historical origin or present purpose) may exist, and where comparatively new immigrant and racial cells sometimes find themselves placed within a dangerous misconception and upon a reactionary treadmill. And it is right here—if one begins to envisage an expanding outward and inward creative significance for the novel—that the monument of consolidation breaks down and becomes the need for a vision of consciousness. And this vision of consciousness is the peculiar reality of language because the concept of language is one which continuously transforms inner and outer formal categories of experience, earlier and representative modes of speech itself, the still life resident in painting and sculpture as such, even music which one ceases to "hear"—the peculiar reality of language provides a medium to *see* in consciousness the "free" motion and to *hear* with consciousness the "silent" flood of sound by a continuous inward revisionary and momentous logic of potent explosive images evoked in the mind. Such a capacity for language is a real and necessary one in a world where the inarticulate person is continuously frozen or legislated for in mass and a genuine experience of his distress, the instinct of distress, sinks into a void. The nightmare proportions of this are already becoming apparent throughout the world.

The point I want to make in regard to the West Indies is that the pursuit of a strange and subtle goal, melting pot, call it what you like, is the mainstream (though unacknowledged) tradition in the Americas. And the significance of this is akin to the European preoccupation with alchemy, with the growth of experimental science, the poetry of science as well as of explosive nature which is informed by a solution of images, agnostic humility and essential beauty, rather than vested interest in a fixed assumption and classification of things.

Let us look at the *individual* African slave. I say *individual* deliberately though this is an obviously absurd label to apply to the persons of slaves in their binding historical context. But since their arrival in the Americas bred a new and painful obscure isolation (which is difficult to penetrate in any other terms but a free conceptual imagination) one may perhaps dream to visualize the suffering and original grassroots of individuality. (In fact I believe this is one of the growing points of both alienation and feeling in modern West Indian literature.) He (the problematic slave) found himself spiritually alone since he worked side by side with others who spoke different dialects. The creative human consolidation—if one dwells upon it meaningfully today—lies in the search for a kind of inward dialogue and space when one is deprived of a ready conversational tongue and hack-neyed comfortable approach.

Irony

I would like to stress again the curious irony involved in this. To assume that the slave was an *individual* is historically absurd since the *individual* possesses certain distinguishing marks, education, status,

background, morality, etc., while a slave—in the American context of
which we are speaking, as in most situations I imagine—was like an
animal put up for sale. (The same qualitative deprivation—though
not in terms of absolute coercion—exists for the illiterate East Indian
peasant, for example, in the twentieth century in the West Indies.)
When therefore one speaks of an inarticulate body of men, confined
on some historical plane, as possessing the grassroots of Western individuality one is creatively rejecting, as if it were an illusion, every
given, total and self-sufficient situation and dwelling within a capacity
for liberation, a capacity for mental and unpredictable pain which
the human person endured *then* or endures now *in* or *for* any time or
place. To develop the point further it is clear that one is rejecting the
sovereign individual as such. For in spite of his emancipation he consolidates every advance by conditioning himself to function solely
within his contemporary situation more or less as the slave appears
bound still upon his historical and archaic plane. It is in this "closed"
sense that freedom becomes a progressive illusion and it is within the
open capacity of the person—as distinct from the persuasive refine-
ments of any social order—within the suffering and enduring mental
capacity of the obscure person (which capacity one shares with both
"collective" slave and "separate" individual in the past and in the
future) that a scale emerges and continues indefinitely to emerge which
makes it possible for *one* (whoever that *one* may be, today or tomorrow)
to measure and abolish each given situation.

Scale

The use of the word "scale" is important, a scale or a ladder, because
bear in mind what we are saying is that the capacity of the person in
terms of words and images is associated with a drama of living consciousness, a drama within which one responds not only to the overpowering and salient features of a plane of existence (which "over-
poweringness," after all, is often a kind of self-indulgent realism) but
to the essence of life, to the instinctive grains of life which continue
striving and working in the imagination for fulfilment, a visionary
character of fulfilment. Such a fulfilment can never be intellectually
imposed on the material; it can only be realized in experiment instinctive to the native life and passion of persons known and unknown
in a structure of time and space.
    Therefore it is clear that the change which is occurring slowly
within the novel and the play and the poem is one which has been
maturing slowly for centuries. Some of the most daring intimations
exist in the works of modern writers, Proust, Joyce, Faulkner, and I
would also venture to say in the peculiar style and energy of Australian
novelists like Patrick White and Hal Porter, a French novelist like

Claude Simon, an English/Canadian novelist like Malcolm Lowry and an African problematic writer like Tutuola. Lowry's novel *Under the Volcano* is set in Mexico where it achieves a tragic reversal of the material climate of our time, assisted by residual images, landscape as well as the melting pot of history, instinctive to the cultural environment of the Central and South Americas.

Let us apply our scale, for example, to the open myth of El Dorado. The religious and economic thirst for exploration was true of the Spanish conquistador, of the Portuguese, French, Dutch and English, of Raleigh, of Fawcett, as it is true of the black modern pork-knocker and the pork-knocker of all races. An instinctive idealism associated with this adventure was overpowered within individual and collective by enormous greed, cruelty and exploitation. In fact it would have been very difficult a century ago to present these exploits as other than a very material and degrading hunger for wealth spiced by a kind of self-righteous spirituality. It is difficult enough today within clouds of prejudice and nihilism; nevertheless the substance of this adventure, involving men of all races, past and present conditions, has begun to acquire a residual pattern of illuminating correspondences. El Dorado, City of Gold, City of God, grotesque, unique coincidence, another window within upon the Universe, another drunken boat, another ocean, another river; in terms of the novel the distribution of a frail moment of illuminating adjustments within a long succession and grotesque series of adventures, past and present, capable *now* of discovering themselves and continuing to discover themselves so that in one sense one relives and reverses the "given" conditions of the past, freeing oneself from catastrophic idolatry and blindness to one's own historical and philosophical conceptions and misconceptions which may bind one within a statuesque present or a false future. Humility is all, says the poet, humility is endless.

Such moments in a scale of reflection (which affect the medium of the arts, however obscurely) are not, of course, peculiar to our time alone. The work of Dante, I believe, was associated with one such "timeless" moment of reality and fulfilment. And it is interesting to recall Eliot's words: "Dante," Eliot remarks, "more than any other poet, has succeeded in dealing with his philosophy, not as a theory or as his own comment or reflection, but in terms of something *perceived*. When most of our modern poets confine themselves to what they had perceived, they produce for us, usually, only odds and ends of still life and stage properties; but that does not imply so much that the method of Dante is obsolete, as that our vision is perhaps comparatively restricted."

Some may interpret the ground of distinction lying between "most of our modern poets" and Dante as one of personal habit (the character of most of our modern poets) and impersonal vision (the character of

Dante). I cannot help feeling, however, that the distinction actually is one between the historical self-sufficient individual, as such, and a living open tradition which realizes itself in an enduring capacity associated with the obscure human person.

I want now to approach the work of certain West Indian writers bearing in mind the background of tradition we have been quickly exploring.

Tragic Premises

One of the most interesting novelists out of the West Indies is George Lamming. Lamming was—and still is—regarded as a writer of considerable promise. What is the nature of his promise? Let us look at his novel *Of Age and Innocence*. This is a novel which somehow fails, I feel, but its failure tells us a great deal. The novel would have been remarkable if a certain tendency—a genuine tendency—for a tragic feeling of dispossession in reality had been achieved. This tendency is frustrated by a diffusion of energies within the entire work. The book seems to speak with a public voice, the voice of a peculiar orator, and the compulsions which inform the work appear to spring from a verbal sophistication rather than a visual, plastic and conceptual imagery. Lamming's verbal sophistication is conversational, highly wrought and spirited sometimes: at other times it lapses into merely clever utterance, rhetorical, as when he says of one of his characters: "He had been made Governor of an important colony which was then at peace with England." It takes some effort—not the effort of imaginative concentration which is always worthwhile but an effort to combat the author's self-indulgence. And this would not arise if the work could be kept true to its inherent design. There is no necessary difficulty or complexity in Lamming's novels—the necessary difficulty or complexity belonging to strange symbolisms—and I feel if the author concentrated on the sheer essentials of his experience a tragic disposition of feeling would gain a true ascendancy. This concentration is essential if the work is not to succumb to a uniform tone which gives each individual character the same public-speaking resonance of voice. I would like to stress a certain distinction I made earlier once again. In the epic and revolutionary novel of associations the characters are related within a personal capacity which works in a poetic and serial way so that a strange jigsaw is set in motion like a mysterious unity of animal and other substitutes within the person. Something which is quite different to the over-elaboration of individual character within the conventional novel. And this over-elaboration is one danger which confronts Lamming. For in terms of the ruling framework he accepts, the individuality of character, the distinctions of status and privilege which mark one individual from another, must be maintained. This is the kind of realism, the realism of classes and classifications—however limited it may be in terms of a profound, poetic and scientific scale of values—the novel, in its orthodox mould, demands. Lamming may be restless within this framework (there are signs and shadows of this in his work) but mere extravagance of pattern and an inclination to frequent intellectual raids beyond his territory are not a genuine breakthrough and will only weaken the position of the central character in his work. He must school himself at this stage, I believe, to work for the continuous development of a main individual character in order to free himself somewhat from the restrictive consolidation he brings about which unfortunately, I find, blocks one's view of essential conflict. This becomes a necessity in terms of the very style and tone of his work. He cannot afford to crowd his canvas when the instinctive threat of one-sidedness is likely to overwhelm all his people and in fact when this one-sidedness may be transformed into a source of tremendous strength in a singleness of drive and purpose which cannot then fail to discipline every tangential field and exercise. The glaring case is Shephard, whom you may recall in *Of Age and Innocence*. Here was an opportunity which was not so much lost—as lost sight of—to declare and develop the tragic premises of individual personality by concentrating on the one man (Shephard) in order to bring home a dilemma which lay in his coming to terms with the people around him by acting—even when he was playing the role of the great rebel—in the way everyone else appeared to see him rather than in the way he innocently may have seen himself.

Comedy of Pathos

It is illuminating at this point to compare V. S. Naipaul's *A House for Mr. Biswas* with George Lamming's *Of Age and Innocence*. Naipaul never loses sight of his Mr. Biswas throughout a very long chronicle in the way Lamming disposes of Shephard again and again. Naipaul's style is like Lamming's in one respect: it is basically conversational though without the rhetoric and considerable power Lamming displays and it follows a flat and almost banal everyday tone. On this flat conversational level the novel has been carefully and scrupulously written. The possibility for tragedy which lay in *Of Age and Innocence*, the vein of longing for a lost innocence associated with Shepard's world is nowhere apparent in *A House for Mr. Biswas*. Mr. Biswas is essentially comic—a mixture of comedy and pathos—where Shephard may have been stark and tragic. Naipaul's triumph with Mr. Biswas is one which—in the very nature of the novel—is more easily achieved, I feel, than a triumph with Shephard for Lamming would have been. To achieve the nuclear proportions of tragedy in Shephard, Lamming

needed a remarkable and intense personal centre of depth; this he
never held, overlooking the concrete challenge which stems from
such a presence in his novel whose status is obscure. On the other
hand the sad figure of Mr. Biswas lends itself to a vulgar and comic
principle of classification of things and people which gives the novel
a conventionl centre. In the first place Naipaul's world is one which
is devoid of phenomenal and therefore corrosive sensibility. He builds
his chronicle around a traditional Hindu family in Trinidad and
therefore persuades his readers to identify with an assumption of individual status, of historical context. The inner and outer poverty of
Naipaul's characters—while achieving at times memorable pathos—
never erupts into a revolutionary or alien question of spirit, but serves
ultimately to consolidate one's preconception of humanity, the comedy
of pathos and the pathos of comedy. It is this "common picture of
humanity" so-called on which Naipaul's work rests. The novel for him,
as for many contemporary readers and writers, restricts the open and
original ground of choice, the vision and stress of transplantation in
the person out of one world into another, the necessity for epic beyond
its present framework, or tragedy within its present framework, since
the assumption remains to the end a contemporary and limited one of
burial and classification, a persuasion of singular and pathetic enlightenment rather than a tragic centrality or a capacity for plural
forms of profound identity.

Moral Distinctions

It is interesting to look at John Hearne in the light of the problems
we have been discussing—the problem of centrality which appears to
be an essential goal for Lamming and the historical status of individual
character as it emerges in Naipaul.

Hearne's solution of this problem I find to be unsatisfactory. He is
a writer of much talent, capable of acute organization and story-telling,
whose aim, it seems to me, is to achieve a certain moral distinction.
This distinction, however, unfortunately, reveals a poverty of creative
perception which springs, to a large extent, from the pure logic of
the conventional novel. Hearne is not instinctively a tragic writer
nor is he comic and therefore since he is a serious novelist *all* his
characters have to be taken seriously in depth within a moral context.
The tragic writer achieves a certain rejection of the "given" historical
situation, the comic writer thrives on the poverty of historical situations once he can maintain the illusion of a common rather than
uncommon humanity, but the moral writer has to be truer than anyone else to a proportionate even classical ground of responsibility. In
order to achieve this classical ground Hearne *imposes* a moral directive

on his situations and this is a considerable creative shortcoming, especially in a context such as the Caribbean and the Americas where the life of situation and person has an inarticulacy one must genuinely suffer with and experience if one is to acquire the capacity for a new relationship and understanding.

Hearne's methods can be seen in a nutshell in his short story *At the Stelling*, which appears in "West Indian Stories" edited by Andrew Salkey. The story, as such, is told with a certain brilliance and economy but once we examine the way in which the moral directive is imposed we are disappointed. What is this moral directive? It has to do with the relationship between master and servant, the officer-in-command and the men he commands, the necessity for proportion and responsibility. John, of Carib descent, shoots his leader Cockburn who is a mulatto, as well as seven or eight men in a survey party. Cockburn has allowed his private sentiment and jealousy of John's prowess in certain matters to obtrude into his public duties. In the end Cockburn is seen as an unfortunate whose training in the traditions of leadership is still lacking at this particular time. The lesson is driven home by the arrival of the previous surveyor and party leader, Mr. Hamilton, an Englishman, and Shirley, also an Englishman, the superintendent of police. Their arrival sets a different tone to the whole affair which would never have happened if Cockburn, who has been shot dead, had been equipped to lead the survey party in the way Hamilton was and still is.

What Hearne is doing here is to arrive at a plausible moral ground by investing heavily in two characters, whose historical status (they are both educated Europeans) allows him to achieve his classical proportion. He has in so doing turned away from the real moral depth and challenge in his material. Let us imagine that the shooting had occurred and Cockburn, the half-baked new leader, had been an Englishman with the given status of Hamilton or Shirley. Then the situation would have opened up and become no longer a matter of relative training and lack of training but of relevant conception and misconception. The full peril of the situation would have invaded all the characters—whose image of themselves would have begun to suffer in a new and unpredictable way—and the obscure status of the Carib descendant as well as the transforming imperative to endure (which is the highest moral principle) would have begun to grow into a creative scale and capacity for self-judgment within the person of each and everyone. It is in this respect I recall Lukacs, the Mexican critic, who points out that a simple affirmation of classical tradition is not enough. And he says a renewal of the classical form can only come by repudiating much in the historical apparatus of the novel or as he puts it in Hegel's words "in the form of a negation of a negation."

Model of Realism

It is at this point that we can see the paradoxical place C. L. R. James occupies in relation to West Indian literature. *The Black Jacobins* is not a novel but it has a curious bearing on the problems we have been discussing. I am not concerned here with James's economic theories of history, which in regard to slavery, in particular, may have exercised some influence since they appear to bob up again in that distinguished book *Capitalism and Slavery* by Eric Williams.

The Black Jacobins first appeared in 1938. The central historical character is Toussaint L'Ouverture. And James seeks to discover him within a dimension of suffering—the stark world of the slaves—and a dimension of revolution—the world of ideological France. The fact that James seeks to implicate both worlds—the world of the slave and the ambivalent world of the free—is consistent with the mainstream tradition and melting pot of the Caribbean. Some may feel the emphasis is too harsh at times, even repulsive and abnormal, but this harshness belongs to a school of extreme realism and to the very nature of many an emotional close-up of historical perspective. James's study therefore is one of the models which may have influenced the realism of certain West Indian novelists who thought they saw an opportunity for commercial investment in historical sensationalism. It is now possible to see how dubious these Mittelholzerian enterprises were and in fact the rise of the comic novel in the West Indies, Selvon and Naipaul, came as a necessary corrective. The dust, however, is now beginning to settle and it is also possible to discover *The Black Jacobins* in relation to the genuine and native capacity of the West Indian. It is a severe and imaginative reconstruction of the historical figure of Toussaint L'Ouverture—Africa, the Caribbean, Europe. The very harshness of line is a repudiation of melodrama and a repudiation of permanent fixtures of value—fascist ornament or liberal self-deception. Toussaint—and this is the curious almost unwitting irony of the work—emerges not because he fits in where James wants him to stand, but because he escapes the author's self-determination in the end. James seeks to smooth over a number of cracks in building his portrait but each significant flaw he wrestles with begins to make its own independent impact.

Toussaint's friendship with and expulsion of Sonthonax, the Frenchman, whom he genuinely appeared to like and admire is one such recalcitrant split or bulge. It seems much more reasonable, in my view, to accept Toussaint's explanation of his action in regard to Sonthonax as one inspired by a reluctance to entertain the counsel of Sonthonax to declare Haiti a sovereign and independent state. In fact this uncertainty of design in Toussaint's mind seems to be borne out by his otherwise inexplicable dealings with his black generals, his equivocation, his secrecy and his alienation from many who were waiting on him to give the final and decisive word. Toussaint was a man of genius, and genius in such phenomenally difficult circumstances must entail, I feel, a strange involvement with both the salvation of grass-roots and the harvest of achievement and labour. The question was— how to reconcile the depth of sacrifice the freed slave must now voluntarily make, with an abstract freedom? Such a vision of reconciliation—slavery with freedom—was essential to retain a continuity of growth and survival in the world at large, the world of Europe, of France, Spain and Britain with whom Toussaint had had diplomatic and strategic dealings—and the world of America, North and South. It was a tragic problem which was to be taken out of his hands with fearful chaotic consequences for Haiti. Furthermore it would appear that this was inevitable. For Toussaint may well have been an agnostic as far as contemporary political faiths are concerned. He may well have had peculiar doubts about the assumption of sovereign status and power. And this was profound heresy even then, much more so now. Where would he have found a real nucleus and following? It is a significant attempt James has made which reflects dedication, self-sacrifice and clarity of intention. Nevertheless in my view—as I said before— the weight of evidence he brings forward refuses ultimately to bow to his fixed purpose. The obscurities and cracks in Toussaint's armour are not amenable to his interpretation of them as a misfortune of secretive temperament. Rather they appear to indicate, when one takes each consistent inconsistency into account, a groping towards an alternative to conventional statehood, a conception of wider possibilities and relationships which still remains unfulfilled today in the Caribbean.

The failure to contain Toussaint sheds a certain paradoxical light beyond the historical framework James set up, upon the seeds of tragedy which are native to a cultural environment whose promise of fulfillment lies in a profound and difficult vision of the person—a profound and difficult vision of essential unity within the most bitter forms of latent and active historical diversity.

Literature and Society

This talk may have been somewhat different, perhaps, to the line I may have been expected to take. But it seems to me vital—in a time when it is easy to succumb to fashionable tyrannies or optimisms—to break away from the conception so many people entertain that literature is an extension of a social order or a political platform. In fact it is one of the ironic things with West Indians of my generation that they may conceive of themselves in the most radical political light but their approach to art and literature is one which consolidates the most conventional and documentary techniques in the novel. In fact many of the great Victorians—Ruskin, Gerard Manley Hopkins, Dickens in *Bleak House* for example, where a strange kinship emerges with the symbolism of both Poe and Kafka—are revolutionaries who make the protestations of many a contemporary radical look like a sham and a pose. The fact is—even when sincerely held, political radicalism is merely a fashionable attitude unless it is accompanied by profound insights into the experimental nature of the arts and the sciences. There are critics who claim that the literary revolution of the first half of the twentieth century may well stem from the work of Pound and Eliot, Joyce and Wyndham Lewis. I am not prepared to go into this claim now but the point is—how is it that figures such as these, described in some quarters as conservative, remain "explosive" while many a fashionable rebel grows to be superficial and opportunistic?

Literature has a bearing on society, yes, a profound and imaginative bearing wherein the life of tradition in all its complexity gives a unique value to the life of vocation in society, whether that vocation happens to be in science, in education, in the study of law or in the dedicated craft of one's true nature and life. For if tradition were dogma it would be entirely dormant and passive but since it is inherently active at all times, whether secretly or openly, it participates in the ground of living necessity by questioning and evaluating all assumptions of character and conceptions of place or destiny. A scale of distinctions emerges, distinctions which give the imagination room to perceive the shifting border line between original substance and vicarious hollow, the much advertised rich and the hackneyed caricature of the poor, the overfed body of illusion and the underfed stomach of reality—room to perceive also overlapping areas of invention and creation, the hair-spring experiment of crucial illumination which divides the original spiritual germ of an idea from its musing plastic development and mature body of expression. It is this kind of scale which is vital to the life of the growing person in society. And this scale exists in a capacity for imagination. A scale which no one can impose since to do so is to falsify the depth of creative experience, the growth and feeling for creative experience.

It is a scale which at certain moments realizes itself in a range and capacity which are phenomenal—the peaks of tragedy, of epic, of myth have been such moments in the dialogue of culture and civilization—while at other times we must be grateful if we are allowed to work at the humility of our task with all of our creative suffering instincts, leaving ourselves open, as it were, to vision.

And this is the germ of the thing the writer feels when he says in everyday talk that "a work begins to write itself," to live its own life, to make its author *see* developments he had not intellectually ordered or arranged.

One last word. As you may have observed I have said nothing about V. S. Reid whose novel *The Leopard* I admire for certain reasons which I leave you to judge after all I have been saying. Nevertheless I feel it is necessary to wait and see what his third novel will be. After all, many West Indian writers—whose novels have been, or are being now written to be published—are relatively young men. And this, of course, is a tremendously hopeful thing. And in this connection I recall Roger Mais, whose work may be naïve in some respects, and unfulfilled in others, but whose life is a symbolic reminder of the brutal philistinism of the middle classes and the upper ruling classes in the West Indies which have thwarted, on many occasions, the rise of the liberal imagination.

Ralph Ellison and the Uses of Imagination

by Robert Bone

*We live only in one place at one time, but far from being
bound by it, only through it do we realize our freedom. We
do not have to abandon our familiar and known to achieve
distinction; rather in that place, if only we make ourselves
sufficiently aware of it, do we join with others in other places.*

—William Carlos Williams

Some twelve years ago an unknown writer, no longer young,
published a first novel and, to no one's astonishment more than his
own, won the National Fiction Award for 1952. There, suddenly, was
the novel, and it spoke eloquently enough, but who was the author of
Invisible Man? We knew only that the curve of his life was a parabola,
moving from Oklahoma City to New York by way of Alabama. In the
intervening years we have had some fleeting glimpses of the man and
his ideas: the acceptance speech itself, an occasional interview, a fragment of his work in progress. We might have noticed his music criticism
in *The Saturday Review,* or the recent exchange with Irving Howe in
The New Leader. But basically the man behind the mask remained invisible.

Now, with the publication of *Shadow and Act,* New York, Random
House, 1964, this remarkable man emerges, at least in silhouette, to
the public eye. The book contains most of Ellison's essays, from the
beginning of his literary career to the present. There are seven apprentice pieces, written in the forties, which reflect the author's social
and political concerns, and seven essays on jazz and the blues, which
appeared principally in the late fifties. There are three interviews of
the *Paris Review* genre, and three first-rate essays on literary topics.
Along the way, we learn a good deal about the author and the forces
that have shaped his sense of life.

The formative years in Oklahoma City are sketched in some detail.
Ellison was born in 1914, just seven years after Oklahoma was admitted

"Ralph Ellison and the Uses of Imagination" by Robert Bone. From *Tri-Quarterly*
6 (Spring 1966), 39–54. Reprinted by permission of the author. All rights reserved.

to the Union. In the early days, his adopted grandfather had led a group of settlers from Tennessee to the Oklahoma Territory. Containing such elements, the Negro community of Oklahoma City developed more a western than a southern tone. Race relations, like all social relations, were more fluid than in established communities. Frontier attitudes persisted well into the present century, and Ellison was raised in a tradition of aggressiveness and love of freedom. He is proud of his frontier heritage, and to it may be traced his fierce individualism and his sense of possibility.

Oklahoma City was a boomtown in the postwar years—a swirling vortex of social styles and human types. There were many masks which an imaginative adolescent might try on, and perhaps one day become:

> Gamblers and scholars, jazz musicians and scientists, Negro cowboys and soldiers from the Spanish-American and First World Wars, movie stars and stunt men, figures from the Italian Renaissance and literature, both classical and popular, were combined with the special virtues of some local bootlegger, the eloquence of some Negro preacher, the strength and grace of some local athlete, the ruthlessness of some businessman-physician, the elegance in dress and manners of some head-waiter or hotel doorman (xv–xvi).[1]

If there was no local writer for a model, there was access to a rich oral literature in the churches, schoolyards, barbershops, and cotton-picking camps. And there was a curious double exposure to the exacting habits of artistic discipline. Through one of the ironies of segregation, the Negro school system placed particular stress on training in classical music. Ellison took up the trumpet at the age of eight and studied four years of harmony in high school. Meanwhile he was exposed to the driving beat of southwestern jazz, of which Kansas City, Dallas, and Oklahoma City were acknowledged centers. From his boyhood onward, he was caught up in that creative tension between the folk and classical traditions which has remained the richest resource of his art.

In 1933 Ellison enrolled at Tuskegee Institute to study composition under William Dawson, the Negro conductor and composer. In his sophomore year, however, he came upon a copy of "The Waste Land," and the long transition from trumpet to typewriter had begun. He read widely in American fiction, and initially scorning the moderns developed a lifelong devotion to the nineteenth-century masters. On coming to New York in 1936 he met Richard Wright, who introduced him on the one hand to the prefaces of Conrad and the letters of Dostoevsky, and on the other to the orbit of the Communist party. One evening he accompanied Wright to a fund-raising affair for the

[1] All references are to Ralph Ellison's *Shadow and Act* (New York: Random House, Inc., 1964).

Spanish Loyalists, where he met Malraux and Leadbelly in person for the first time. It was a notable occasion, symbolic of the times, and of the cross-pressures exerted from the first upon his art.

From these cross-pressures Ellison derived his most enduring themes. How could he interpret and extend, define and yet elaborate upon, the folk culture of the American Negro, and at the same time assimilate the most advanced techniques of modern literature? How could he affirm his dedication to the cause of Negro freedom without succumbing to the stridencies of protest fiction, without relinquishing his complex sense of life? In *Shadow and Act,* Ellison returns again and again to these tangled themes: the relationship of Negro folk culture to American culture as a whole, and the responsibility of the Negro artist to his ethnic group.

As instrumentalist and composer, Ellison had faced these issues for the better part of two decades. When he began to write, it was natural for him to draw upon his musical experience for guidelines and perspectives. Not that his approach to writing is merely an extension of an earlier approach to jazz and the blues; they tend, in fact, to reinforce each other. But his experience with jazz was formative; it left a permanent mark upon his style. His controlling metaphors are musical, and if we are to grasp his thought, we must trace his language to its source. There, in the world of Louis Armstrong and Charlie Parker, Bessie Smith and Jimmy Rushing, we may discover the foundations of Ellison's aesthetic.

Music

The essence of jazz is group improvisation. Its most impressive effects are achieved, according to Ellison, when a delicate balance is maintained between the individual performer and the group. The form itself, consisting of a series of solo "breaks" within a framework of standard chord progressions, encourages this balance. "Each true jazz moment," Ellison explains, "springs from a contest in which each artist challenges all the rest; each solo flight, or improvisation, represents (like the successive canvases of a painter) a definition of his identity: as individual, as member of the collectivity, and as a link in the chain of tradition." "True jazz," he concludes, "is an art of individual assertion within and against the group" (234).

Here is a working model for the Negro writer. By balancing conflicting claims upon his art, he can solve his deepest problems of divided loyalty. As an artist with a special function to perform within the Negro group, the writer must be careful to preserve his individuality. He must learn to operate "within and against the group," allowing neither claim to cancel out the other. Similarly on the cultural plane, where the Negro's group identity is at stake. Here the writer can affirm whatever is uniquely Negro in his background while insisting precisely on the American quality of his experience. "The point of our struggle," writes Ellison, "is to be both Negro and American and to bring about that condition in American society in which this would be possible" (271).

Closely related to the question of individual and group identity is that of personal and traditional styles. Every jazz musician must strike a balance between tradition and experimentation, for "jazz finds its very life in an endless improvisation upon traditional materials" (234). It follows that no jazzman is free to repudiate the past. The jam session, where he must display a knowledge of traditional techniques, will see to that. He must master "the intonations, the mute work, manipulation of timbre, the body of traditional styles" (208), before he can presume to speak in his own voice. The path, in short, to self-expression lies through what is given, what has gone before.

As an American Negro writer, Ellison inherits a double obligation to the past. He must become familiar with a folk tradition which is his alone, and with a wider literary culture which he shares. Moreover, he must strive in both dimensions for a proper blend of past and present, given and improvised. In describing his response to his folk tradition, Ellison draws a parallel to the work of Picasso: "Why, he's the greatest wrestler with forms and techniques of them all. Just the same, he's never abandoned the old symbolic forms of Spanish art: the guitar, the bull, daggers, women, shawls, veils, mirrors" (171). Similarly, Ellison appropriates folkloristic elements from Negro culture, embroiders on them, adapts them to his literary aims and lifts them to the level of a conscious art.

In the wider context of American literature, the same principles apply. Consider Ellison's experimental idiom. Not since Jean Toomer has a Negro novelists been so inventive of new forms, new language, new technical devices. And yet none has been so deeply immersed in the American literary past. As Ellison struggles toward the realization of a personal style, he is *improvising* on the achievement of our nineteenth-century masters. It is this body of writing, he insists, "to which I was most attached and through which . . . I would find my own voice, and to which I was challenged, by way of achieving myself, to make some small contribution and to whose composite picture of reality I was obligated to offer some necessary modifications" (xix).

Still a third balance must be struck between constraint and spontaneity, discipline and freedom. For the jazzman owes his freedom to the confident possession of technique. From his own struggles with the trumpet, Ellison learned how much the wild ecstatic moment depends on patient hours of practice and rehearsal. Freedom, he perceived, is never absolute, but rooted in its opposite. The game is not to cast off all restraint but to achieve, within the arbitrary limits of a musical tradition, a transcendent freedom. Jazz taught Ellison a respect for limits, even as it revealed the possibility of overcoming limits through technique. It was the blues, however, that taught him to discern in this paradox an emblem of the human condition.

The blues begin with personal disaster. They speak of flooded farmlands and reality that gives them birth bespeaks the limits and restrictions, the barriers and thwartings, which the universe opposes to the human will. But the tough response that is the blues bespeaks a moral courage, a spiritual freedom, a sense of human possibility, which more than balances the scales. In Ellison's words, "The blues is an art of ambiguity, an assertion of the irrepressibly human over all circumstance whether created by others or by one's own human failings. They are the only consistent art in the United States which constantly reminds us of our limitations while encouraging us to see how far we can actually go" (246).

The blues begin with personal disaster. They speak of flooded farmlands and blighted crops, of love betrayed and lovers parted, of the black man's poverty and the white man's justice. But what matters is the human response to these events. For the blues are a poetic confrontation of reality. They are a form of spiritual discipline, a means of transcending the painful conditions with which they deal. The crucial feature of the blues response is the margin of freedom it proclaims. To call them an art of ambiguity is to assert that no man is entirely the victim of circumstance. Within limits, there is always choice and will. Thinking of this inner freedom, Ellison speaks of "the secular existentialism of the blues" (218).

This sense of possibility lies at the center of Ellison's art. It explains his devotion to his craft, for what is technique but another name for possibility? It explains his attitude toward protest fiction, for the propaganda novel, in portraying the Negro primarily as victim, gives more weight to circumstance than possibility. Ellison's is a more plastic sensibility. His heroes are not victims but adventurers. They journey toward the possible in all ignorance of accepted limits. In the course of their travels, they shed their illusions and come to terms with reality. They are, in short, picaresque heroes, full of "rash efforts, quixotic gestures, hopeful testings of the complexity of the known and the given" (xv).

If circumstance often enough elicits tears, possibility may release a saving laughter. This blend of emotion, mixed in some ancient cauldron of the human spirit, is characteristic of the blues. It is a lyricism better sampled than described. Note in Ellison's example how the painful humiliation of the bird is controlled, or absorbed, or even converted into triumph by a kind of grudging laughter:

Oh they picked poor robin clean
They picked poor robin clean
They tied poor robin to a stump
Lord, they picked all the feathers
Round from robin's rump
Oh they picked poor robin clean (231).

The blues have nothing to do with the consolations of philosophy.
They are a means of neutralizing one emotion with another, in the
same way that alkalies can neutralize an acid stomach. For the American Negro, they are a means of prophylaxis, a specific for the preven-
tion of spiritual ulcers. It is not a question of laughing away one's
troubles in any superficial sense, but of gazing steadily at pain while
perceiving its comic aspect. Ellison regards this tragicomic sensibility
as the most precious feature of his Negro heritage. From it stems his
lyrical intensity, and the complex interplay of tragic and comic elements which is the distinguishing mark of his fiction.

If the blues are primarily an expression of personal emotion, they
also serve a group need. Perhaps the point can best be made through
a comparison with gospel singing. When Mahalia Jackson sings in
church, she performs a ritual function. Her music serves "to prepare
the congregation for the minister's message, to make it receptive to
the spirit and, with effects of voice and rhythm, to evoke a shared
community of experience" (219). Similarly in the secular context of
the blues. When Jimmy Rushing presided over a Saturday night dance
in Oklahoma City, he was acting as the leader of a public rite: "It was
when Jimmy's voice began to soar with the spirit of the blues that the
dancers—and the musicians—achieved that feeling of communion
which was the true meaning of the public jazz dance" (244).

We are dealing here with substitute rituals. During an epoch which
has witnessed the widespread breakdown of traditional religious forms,
Ellison finds in jazz and the blues, as Hemingway in the bullfight, a
code of conduct and a ceremonial framework for his art. "True novels,"
he insists, "arise out of an impulse to celebrate human life and therefore are ritualistic and ceremonial at their core" (114). Ellison perceives, in short, the priestly office of the modern artist and assumes the
role of celebrant in his own work. Like the blues singer, he is motivated
by an impulse to restore to others a sense of the wholeness of their
lives.

Finally, specific features of Ellison's literary style may be traced to
his musical background. His fondness for paradox and ambiguity, for
example, derives from the blues: "There is a mystery in the whiteness
of blackness, the innocence of evil and the evil of innocence, though
being initiates Negroes express the joke of it in the blues" (53). The
changing styles of *Invisible Man* (from naturalism to expressionism

to surrealism, as Ellison describes the sequence) are based on the principle of modulation. Chord progressions in jazz are called "changes"; they correspond in speed and abruptness to Ellison's sense of American reality, the swift flow of sound and sudden changes of key suggesting the fluidity and discontinuity of American life.

Literature

Let us now turn from Ellison's musical to his literary heritage. We must begin with the picaresque novel and attempt to explain why this form, which first appeared in Renaissance Spain, should be revived by a contemporary Negro novelist. We must then consider Ellison's affinity for the American transcendentalists, in light of his commitment to the picaresque. Finally, we must examine in some detail two devices that are central to his art.

The picaresque novel emerged toward the end of the feudal and the beginning of the bourgeois epoch. Its characteristic hero, part rogue and part outlaw, transcended all established norms of conduct and violated all ideas of social hierarchy. For with the breakdown of static social relations, a testing of personal limits, a bold confrontation with the new and untried, became necessary. Hence the picaresque journey, no longer a religious quest or pilgrimage, but a journey toward experience, adventure, personal freedom. It was the journey of the bourgeois soul toward possibility, toward a freedom possessed by neither serf nor lord under the old regime.

It can hardly be an accident that *Invisible Man* and *The Adventures of Augie March* should win the National Fiction Award within two years of one another. Nor that Ellison and Bellow should each acknowledge a major debt to Twain. For *Huckleberry Finn* is the last great picaresque novel to be written by a WASP. The genre has been abandoned to the Negro and the Jew who, two generations from slavery or the *shtetl,* experiences for the first time and in full force what Ellison calls the magical fluidity of American life. A century after Hawthorne wrote *The Scarlet Letter,* our minority groups are reenacting the central drama of that novel: the break with the institutions and authorities of the past and the emergence into an epoch of personal freedom and individual moral responsibility.

Ellison's revival of the picaresque reflects his group's belated access to the basic conditions of bourgeois existence. These consist economically of the freedom to rise and psychologically of "the right and opportunity to dilate, deepen, and enrich sensibility" (82). The Southern Negro who is taught from childhood to "know his place" is denied these basic freedoms. He is deprived of individuality as thoroughly as any serf: "The pre-individualistic black community discourages individuality out of self-defense. . . . Within the ambit of the black family this takes the form of training the child away from curiosity and adventure, against reaching out for those activities lying beyond the borders" (90–1).

The Great Migration of the Negro masses from southern farm to northern city was picaresque in character. In terms of Negro personality, it was like uncorking a bottle of champagne. Traditionally the journey has been made by railroad, and it is no accident that the blues are associated with freight yards, quick getaways, and long journeys in "a side door Pullman car." No accident either that Ellison should emphasize his own wanderings: "To attempt to express that American experience which has carried one back and forth and up and down the land and across, and across again the great river, from freight train to Pullman car, from contact with slavery to contact with the world of advanced scholarship, art and science, is simply to burst such neatly understated forms of the novel asunder" (104).

The bursting forth of Negro personality from the fixed boundaries of southern life is Ellison's essential theme. And it is this, at bottom, that attracts him to the transcendentalists. For what was the central theme of Thoreau, Emerson, and Whitman, if not the journeying forth of the soul? These writers were celebrating their emancipation from the Custom House, from the moral and political authority of old Europe. Their romantic individualism was a response to the new conditions created by the Revolution, conditions calling for *self* government in both the political and moral sphere. Their passion for personal freedom, moreover, was balanced by a sense of personal responsibility for the future of democracy.

Ellison's debt to transcendentalism is manifold, but what is not acknowledged can easily be surmised. He is named, to begin with, for Ralph Waldo Emerson. In this connection he mentions two specific influences: the "Concord Hymn" and "Self Reliance." The poem presumably inspires him with its willingness to die that one's children may be free; the essay, as we shall see, governs his attitude toward Negro culture. He admires Thoreau, plainly enough, for his stand on civil disobedience and his militant defense of John Brown. Whitman is congenial, for such poems as "The Open Road" and "Passage to India" are squarely in the picaresque tradition.

In broader terms, it may be said that Ellison's ontology derives from transcendentalism. One senses in his work an unseen reality behind the surfaces of things. Hence his fascination with guises and disguises, with the con man and the trickster. Hence the felt dichotomy between visible and invisible, public and private, actual and fictive modes of reality. His experience as a Negro no doubt reinforces his ironic awareness of "the joke that always lies between appearance and reality" (53), and turns him toward an inner world that lies beyond the reach of insult or oppression. This world may be approached by means of the imagination; it is revealed during the transcendent moment in jazz or the epiphany in literature. *Transcend* is thus a crucial word in Ellison's aesthetic.

Above all, Ellison admires the transcendentalists for their active democratic faith. They were concerned not only with the slavery question, but with the wider implications of cultural pluralism, with the mystery of the one and the many. To these writers, the national motto, *e pluribus unum,* was a serious philosophical concern. Emerson discerned a cosmic model for American democracy in the relationship of soul to Oversoul. Whitman, however, made the classic formulation:

> One's self I sing, a simple separate person,
> Yet utter the word Democracy, the word En-Masse.

Ellison reveals, in his choice of ancestors, the depth of his commitment to American ideals. When he describes jazz as "that embodiment of a superior democracy in which each individual cultivated his uniqueness and yet did not clash with his neighbors" (300), he is affirming the central values of American civilization.

It remains to place Ellison in his twentieth-century tradition. What is involved is a rejection of the naturalistic novel and the philosophical assumptions on which it rests. From Ellison's allusions to certain of his contemporaries—to Stein and Hemingway, Joyce and Faulkner, Eliot and Yeats—one idea emerges with persistent force. *Man is the creator of his own reality.* If a culture shapes its artists, the converse is equally the case: "The American novel is in this sense a conquest of the frontier; as it describes our experience, it creates it" (183). This turn toward subjectivity, this transcendence of determinism, this insistence on an existential freedom, is crucial to Ellison's conception of the artist. It finds concrete expression in his work through the devices of masking and naming.

Masking has its origin in the psychological circumstances of southern life: "In the South the sensibilities of both blacks and whites are inhibited by the rigidly defined environment. For the Negro there is relative safety as long as the impulse toward individuality is suppressed" (89). As soon, however, as this forbidden impulse seeks expression, an intolerable anxiety is aroused. Threatened by his own unfolding personality as much as by the whites, the Negro learns to camouflage, to dissimulate, to retreat behind a protective mask. There is magic in it: the mask is a means of warding off the vengeance of the gods.

Consider the jazz solo, one of the few means of self-expression permitted to the southern Negro. Precisely because it is a solo, and the musician must go it alone, it represents potential danger. Ellison writes of certain jazz musicians: "While playing in ensemble, they carried themselves like college professors or high church deacons;

when soloing they donned the comic mask" (126). Louis Armstrong, as Ellison reminds us, has raised masking to the level of a fine art. Musical trickster, con man with a cornet, Elizabethan clown, "he takes liberties with kings, queens, and presidents" (52). In a later development, the bearded mask of the bopster appeared, frankly expressive of hostility, rudeness, and contempt. It is a pose which still finds favor among certain Negro writers of the younger generation.

In his own prose, Ellison employs various masking devices, including understatement, irony, double entendre, and calculated ambiguity. There is something deliberately elusive in his style, something secret and taunting, some instinctive avoidance of explicit statement which is close in spirit to the blues. His fascination with masquerade gives us two memorable characters in *Invisible Man*: the narrator's grandfather, whose mask of meekness conceals a stubborn resistance to white supremacy, and Rinehart, whom Ellison describes as "an American virtuoso of identity who thrives on chaos and swift change" (56). A master of disguise, Rinehart survives by manipulating the illusions of society, much in the tradition of Melville's Confidence Man, Twain's Duke and Dauphin, and Mann's Felix Krull.

Masking, which begins as a defensive gesture, becomes in Ellison's hands a means of altering reality. For if reality is a process of becoming, that process can be partially controlled through manipulation of a ritual object, or mask. "Masking," Ellison remarks, "is a play upon possibility" (54), and possibility is precisely the domain of art. To clarify the matter he summons Yeats, a man not ignorant of masks: "If we cannot imagine ourselves as different from what we are and assume the second self, we cannot impose a discipline upon ourselves, though we may accept one from others. Active virtue, as distinct from the passive acceptance of a current code, is the wearing of a mask" (153). Yeats is speaking of morality, of active virtue, but the function of the artist is implicit in his words. Before pursuing the point, however, we must come to terms with a second feature of Ellison's art.

Naming likewise has its origin in negation, in the white man's hypocritical denial of his kinship ties. For the African slaves received from their Christian masters not only European names, but a massive infusion of European blood, under circumstances so brutal and degrading as to have been virtually expunged from the national consciousness. At once guilty and proud, the white man has resorted to a systematic *mis-naming,* in an effort to obscure his crime. Thus the use of the matronymic to conceal the slave's paternity. Thus the insulting epithets which deny not merely kinship but humanity. In some obscene rite of exorcism, the white man says "nigger" when he should say "cousin." And yet the family names persist as symbols of that hidden truth, that broken connection which will have to be restored before the nation, sick from the denial of reality, can regain its mental health.

Having been misnamed by others, the American Negro has attempted from the first to define himself. This persistent effort at self-definition is the animating principle of Negro culture. The earliest appearance of Negro folklore, for example, "announced the Negro's willingness to trust his own experience, his own sensibilities as to the definition of reality, rather than allow his masters to define these crucial matters for him" (172). Similarly with musical expression: the jazzman who rejects classical technique is affirming his right to define himself in sound. Cultural autonomy, to Ellison, is an elementary act of self reliance. We have listened too long, he seems to say, to the courtly Muses of white America. "Our names, being the gift of others, must be made our own" (147).

For personal as well as historical reasons, Ellison is fascinated by the distinction between one's given and achieved identity. Named for a famous poet, it was half a lifetime before he could define, let alone accept, the burden of his given name. Acknowledging in retrospect the prescience of his father, he speaks of "the suggestive power of names and the magic involved in naming" (151). We are dealing here with the ritual use of language, with the pressure which language can exert upon reality. This is the special province of the poet, and broadly speaking Ellison claims it as his own. He regards the novel as an act of ritual naming; the novelist, as a "moralist-designate" who *names* the central moral issues of his time.

"The poet," writes Ralph Waldo Emerson, "is the Namer or Language-maker." As such, he is the custodian of his language and the guarantor of its integrity. In performance of this function, Ellison has discovered that the language of contemporary America is in certain ways corrupt. "With all deliberate speed," for example, does not mean what it seems to mean when uttered by the Supreme Court of the United States. He proposes a rectification of the language, and therefore of the nation's moral vision. For accurate naming is the writer's first responsibility: "In the myth, God gave man the task of naming the objects of the world; thus one of the functions of the poet is to insist upon a correspondence between words and ever-changing reality, between ideals and actualities" (266).

As with naming, so with the image-making function as a whole. The artist, or image-maker, is guardian of the national iconography. And since the power of images for good or evil is immense, he bears an awesome responsibility. If his images are false, if there is no bridge between portrayal and event, no correspondence between the shadow and the act, then the emotional life of the nation is to that extent distorted, and its daily conduct rendered ineffectual or even patholog-

ical. This is the effect of the anti-Negro stereotype, whether in song or
statuary, novel or advertising copy, comic strip or film. Images, being
ritual objects, or masks, may be manipulated by those who have a
stake in the preservation of caste lines. What is required is a rectification of the nation's icons, a squaring of the shadow and the act.

Nor can this be accomplished through the use of counter-stereotypes.
Protest fiction, by portraying sociological types, holds its readers at
a distance from the human person. But the problem is precisely one
of identification. To identify, in the psychological sense, is to become
one with. For this process to occur between white reader and Negro
character, the writer must break through the outer crust of racial
conflict to the inner core of common humanity. He must evoke, by
his imaginative power, an act of "painful identification." To succeed
requires the utmost in emotional maturity, craftsmanship, and skill.
For what the artist undertakes, in the last analysis, is the rectification
of the human heart.

Politics

If Ellison had remained a jazz musician, he might have been spared
a series of political attacks upon his art. No one would have com-
plained, if he had spoken in a jazz idiom, that his riffs were lacking
in protest content. No one would have accused him, as he blew up
there on the bandstand, of abandoning a posture of clenched militancy.
For it is not expected of a Negro jazzman that, like the first trumpet
in the Dodger Fan Club, he should sit in the stands during every civil
rights contest and play at appropriate moments, "Da da da datta da:
Charge!" So long as he refuses to play for segregated audiences, accepts
no gigs from the State Department, and does an occasional benefit
for SNCC, he is allowed to go about the very difficult business of
interpreting Negro experience in sound.

Not so with the Negro novelist, who works in the medium of words.
For words have a variety of uses, political exhortation being one. The
ideologists therefore move in. The question of militancy is raised,
bearing not upon the novelist's conduct as a citizen, or political man,
but precisely on his creative work, his function as an artist. To those
who feel above all else the urgency of the Negro's political struggle,
it is not enough that a writer demonstrate his solidarity; he must
enlist his image-making powers in the service of the cause. Since no
writer who understands the proper uses of imagination can acquiesce
in this perversion of his talent, he must prepare to walk that lonesome
valley during much of his career, and to accept a good deal of abuse
from those who do not recognize the value of his art.

It was predictable enough, given the rising tempo of the civil rights
struggle, that Ellison should be under pressure from the political

activists. The Freedom Movement, like all great movements of social liberation, is lacking neither in demagogues nor Philistines. But that so sophisticated a critic and humane a man as Irving Howe should join the attack is scandalous. In an article called "Black Boys and Native Sons" (*Dissent,* Autumn, 1963), Howe takes Baldwin and Ellison to task for abandoning the "rasping outbursts," "black anger," and "clenched militancy" of Richard Wright. While he sees some signs of hope in Baldwin's recent work, he plainly regards Ellison as unregenerate. Howe's essay prompted a reply from Ellison, and the result was a sharp exchange in *The New Leader* (Dec. 9, 1963 and Feb. 3, 1964).[2]

One's chief impression of this debate is that the antagonists are arguing at cross purposes. They shout at one another, but little or no dialogue occurs. Howe's original piece is a kind of monument to tactlessness, and Ellison is understandably provoked into a sometimes shrill response. It is a bad show all around, and the issues deserve to be aired in a calmer atmosphere. It is not my intent to mediate, however, for in my opinion Howe is overwhelmingly in the wrong. Nor do I wish to repeat Ellison's arguments which—tone aside—make most of the essential points. I should like rather to explore the philosophical foundations of the controversy. If my argument seems elementary, it is best that we proceed with caution, since plainly each of the contestants feels threatened by the other at the center of his being.

Let me begin with a parable. Imagine a Negro writer in the late nineteen-fifties (I choose the period advisedly, for Howe describes it as a conservative decade) attempting to decide on a subject for a novel. He has before him two projects, each based on the life of a Dodger baseball hero. The one—call it the Jackie Robinson story—is alive with racial drama: the first Negro ballplayer to make the big time; the insults from the stands, the spikings by opposing players, the mixed reception from his teammates. The other—call it the Roy Campanella story—concerns an athlete who, at the height of his career, spun his car around a curve one icy morning and spent the rest of his life in a wheelchair. Within a year or two his wife divorced him, she too a victim of her human frailty.

Suppose, for purposes of argument, that our writer chose to tell the second story. Would that choice suggest to Howe that he was running from reality, the reality of the sharpened spikes? Or is it possible that the Campanella story also contains a reality sufficiently sharp? Nor is there a refusal to confront injustice, for the theme of the second story would have to be injustice on a cosmic scale. Perhaps Howe would attempt a political explanation of our writer's

---

[2] Howe's original piece has been reprinted in *A World More Attractive* (New York, Horizon Press, 1963); Ellison's rejoinder appears in *Shadow and Act* under the title "The World and the Jug."

choice. He might propose that during the militant decade of the thirties such a writer would have turned at once to Jackie Robinson, but that out of his "dependence on the postwar *Zeitgeist*" he turned instead to a subject that was safe. But perhaps these political categories are beside the point. Perhaps our writer chose simply because he felt in one story a deeper sense of human life.

Not all human suffering is racial in origin, that is our initial point. Being Negro, unfortunately, does not release one from the common burdens of humanity. It is for this reason that the blues singer so often deals with other than his racial woes. And it is to this dimension of human, as opposed to racial, pain that Howe gives insufficient attention. Ultimately, Ellison and Howe are divided over the *locus* of human suffering. One stresses man's position in society; the other, his position in the universe at large.

At issue is a crucial distinction between remediable and irremediable evil. The first, roughly speaking, is the domain of politics and science; the second, of art and religion. One's sense of tragedy is linked to one's perception of irremediable evil. What we have, therefore, in the Howe-Ellison exchange, is a confrontation between Howe's revolutionary optimism and Ellison's tragic sensibility. Howe, who still believes in Progress, concentrates on the evil that can be changed to the neglect of that which must be borne.

To the white liberal, racial injustice is a remediable evil. The Negro, however, experiences it in both modes simultaneously. In historical time, things are no doubt getting better, but in one's own lifetime, white oppression is a bitter fact to which one must adjust. The Negro, as Ellison points out, must live with and suffer under the present reality even as he works to change it. Entirely apart from the Movement, he must concern himself with the strategies and techniques of personal survival. It is precisely with this necessity of Negro life that Ellison's art is engaged.

Because of Howe's bias toward remediable evil, it is difficult for him to understand redemptive suffering. Speaking of Richard Wright, he remarks, "He examines the life of the Negroes and judges it without charity or idyllic compensation—for he already knows, in his heart and his bones, that to be oppressed means to lose out on human possibilities." This half truth, it seems to me, dehumanizes the Negro by depriving him of his human triumph over pain. For as Ellison insists, Negro life is not only a burden, but a discipline. Is it idyllic to suggest that Campanella's experience as a Negro might have prepared him in some way for coping with his accident? Was it in any way relevant? Was it, in short, an emotional resource?

If one attends primarily to remediable evil, one may be tempted to make larger claims for politics than history can justify. One may end by making politics the touchstone of a man's humanity: "In response to Baldwin and Ellison, Wright would have said . . . that only through struggle could men with black skins, and for that matter, all the oppressed of the world, achieve their humanity." Perhaps the question of humanity is after all more complex. It would be impertinent to remind Howe, who is a close student of the subject, that in recent Russian history many struggled and were brutalized thereby. But the memoirs of Victor Serge suggest to me that even in the midst of revolution the artist has a special function to perform: to remind the revolution of its human ends.

It will be clear, I trust, that I am speaking out of no hostility to the Freedom Movement or to politics as such. I am arguing not for the abandonment of militancy but the autonomy of art. There is no need for literature and politics to be at odds. It is only when the aesthete approaches politics as if it were a poem, or when the political activist approaches the poem as if it were a leaflet, that the trouble starts. Phrases like "only through struggle" urge the subordination of art to politics. We must stifle these imperialistic impulses and foster a climate of mutual respect. Emerson distinguishes between the Doer and the Sayer, and refuses to honor one at the expense of the other. "Homer's words," he observes, "are as costly to Homer as Agamemnon's victories are to Agamemnon."

And I would add that Homer's words are as valuable as Agamemnon's victories *to the Greeks*. For I am arguing throughout for the social value of art. When Howe touches on this aspect of the question, he tries invariably to preempt all social value for his own position. Ellison, he charges, is pursuing the essentially antisocial goal of "personal realization," while Wright is fulfilling his responsibility to the Negro community. It is a false dichotomy. The Negro writer, who is surely not free of social responsibility, must yet discharge it *in his own fashion*, which is not the way of politics but art; not the lecture platform, but the novel and the poem. Without repudiating his sense of obligation to the group, Ellison has tried to express it through services which only the imagination can perform.

What is at issue is the role of the imagination in that complex process which we call civilization. The visionary power, the power of naming, the power of revealing a people to itself, are not to be despised. If those who can command these powers are diverted from their proper task, who will celebrate the values of the group, who create those myths and legends, those communal rites which alone endow the life of any group with meaning? These gifts are no less precious to a people (and if you like, no more) than those of personal charisma, theoretical analysis, and political organization which are the special province of the revolutionary. Let us therefore give the imaginative faculty its due, concede its social value, and respect its unique contribution to the process of becoming man.

Culture

At least as important as Ellison's defense of the imagination is his contribution to a theory of American Negro culture. Previous work in the field, whether by Negro or white intellectuals, has stressed the autonomous character of Negro culture, viewing it as an alien or exotic tributary to the main stream of American life. Ellison proposes a more integrated view. Negro folk culture, to his way of thinking, is an indestructible monument to the national past. Embodying as it does three centuries of American history, it is a bittersweet reminder of what we were and are as a people. Far from being isolated from the main stream, it marks the channel where the river runs deepest to the sea.

Given the complex interplay of culture and personality, race and social class, that shapes the lives of American Negroes, some degree of theoretical clarity, some modicum of sophistication in these matters, is essential. Not only racial strategies, but one's own sanity and peace of mind are at stake. For every American Negro responds, at some level of his being, to two apparently disjunctive cultural traditions. If this can be shown to be an arbitrary division, false to the realities of American history, not only will the personal tensions ease, but the Freedom Movement will be seen in new perspective. Integration will now appear as a mutual attempt, by American whites as well as Negroes, to restore a splintered culture to a state of wholeness.

The problem of dual identity is particularly acute for members of the Negro middle-class. Suspended between two cultural traditions, each with its own claims and loyalties, the educated Negro has been caught on the horns of a dilemma. To identify closely with the life-style of the white middle-class has generally led to a rejection of Negro folk culture. Conversely, to identify closely with the life-style of the Negro masses has implied a disaffection with the dominant values of American civilization. This conflicting pattern of identification and rejection has produced two broad currents of thought and feeling which I have elsewhere called assimilationism and Negro nationalism. Let me describe them briefly, for purposes of contrast with Ellison's point of view.

Assimilationism is a natural response to the experience of upward mobility. As the Negro middle-class becomes differentiated from the masses by virtue of income, education, and social status, it looks back upon its origins with embarrassment and shame. Negro folk culture, this rising middle-class would argue, is the creation of an illiterate peasantry. It is vulgar and often shocking, permeated with the smell of poverty, reminiscent of our degradation and our pain. However well it may attest to what we were, it contains nothing of enduring value for us or for our children. On the contrary, it is a major obstacle to integration. The white middle-class will accept us only to the extent that we become like them. It is therefore necessary to expunge every trace of "Negroness" from our behavior.

To these arguments Ellison would counterpose the richness of his folk tradition. He insists upon the relevance of folk experience to the conditions of modern urban life, and more important still, to the condition of being man. The assimilationist demands that in the name of integration the Negro self be put to death. But Ellison regards this proposal as a projection of self-hatred. To integrate means to make whole, not to lop off or mutilate; to federate as equals, not to merge and disappear. Anything else is a denial not only of one's racial identity, but one's national identity as well. For slavery really happened on American soil, and it has made us both, Negro and white alike, what we are today.

Negro nationalism is a natural response to the experience of rejection. Rebuffed by the whites, the Negro nationalist rebuffs in turn. Rejecting the white man's civilization as thoroughly corrupt, visibly in decay, and hopelessly compromised by its oppression of the blacks, he asks in anger and despair, "Why should we integrate into a burning house?" From this mood of separatism and alienation flows his attitude toward the folk culture. For here is a system of values to oppose to those of the white middle-class. All that is distinctive in Negro life is thus exalted as a matter of racial pride. Traditionally this point of view has been fortified by some sort of African mystique, the current version being the concept of *Négritude*.

Here Ellison would counter with the richness of the dominant tradition. European civilization, of which he is a part, cannot be written off so lightly. Emerson and Einstein, Mozart and Michelangelo, Jefferson and Joyce are part of his tradition and he has paid for them in blood. He is not about to bargain them away in exchange for *Négritude*. The Negro nationalist demands that for the sake of injured pride the Western self be put to death. But if the injury is real, the remedy is disastrous. What is separatism but the sulking of a rejected child? The American Negro, after all, is no stranger to the affairs of this nation. Nor can he stand aside from its appointed destiny. For if the house burns, one thing is certain: the American Negro will not escape the conflagration.

Assimilationism and Negro nationalism both involve a maiming of the self, an unnecessary loss. Why not combine the best of both traditions? Between these opposite and symmetrical errors, Ellison steers a steady course. On the one hand, he wants in: no one, white or colored, will persuade him that he is an outsider. Talk about the main stream! He's been swimming in it since sixteen-nineteen. On the other hand, he is not about to trade in his tested techniques of survival on some

white man's vague promise: "Be like us and we will accept you maybe."
When he comes in, he brings his chittlins with him. If in the process he
transforms America into a nation of chittlin-eaters, so much the better
for our ethnic cooking.

While assimilationism and Negro nationalism make opposite evaluations of Negro folk culture, they both regard it as in some sense
un-American. To all such formulations Ellison objects that they abstract distinctive Negro qualities from the concrete circumstances of
American life. The American Negro *is* different from his white countrymen, but American history and that alone has made him so. Any
serious attempt to understand these differences will therefore lead,
by a thousand devious paths, across the tracks to white America.
Always there is a connection, however hidden; always a link, however
brutally severed. It follows that "any viable theory of Negro American
culture obligates us to fashion a more adequate theory of American
culture as a whole" (253).

To this end, Ellison offers what might be called some Notes toward a re-Definition of American Culture. There is a gross distortion,
he suggests, in America's self-image. It begins with the white man's
artificial attempt to isolate himself from Negro life. But Negro life
is not sealed off hermetically from the historical process. On the
contrary, it is the most authentic expression of that process as it has
actually unfolded on the North American continent. Ellison argues,
in effect, that the life-style of the Negro ghetto is *more* American than
the so-called standard American culture of white suburbia because
the latter, in the very impulse that gave it birth, denies a vital dimension of American experience. There is no possibility, he warns, of
escaping from the past. What is required is that we bring our distorted
image of ourselves into line with the historical reality.

Paradoxically, what is most distinctive in Negro life is often most
American. Jazz, for example, is not simply Negro music, but the
definitive rendering of American experience in sound. Similarly with
folklore: "In spilling out his heart's blood in his contest with the
machine, John Henry was asserting a national value as well as a
Negro value" (270). Where do we turn for the truth about American
slavery: to Negro spirituals or the songs of Stephen Collins Foster?
Why is the current slang of American teen-agers drawn from the
speech of the Negro ghetto? Why the persistent vogue for Negro
dance forms unless we have been growing, from Charleston to Watusi,
steadily less inhibited as a nation?

American culture is still in process of becoming. It is not a finished
form, a house that one day will be rented out to Negroes. On the
contrary, in the process of racial integration the culture will be
radically transformed. This transformation will amount to a correction
of perspective. By degrees, the white man's truncated version of Amer-

ican reality will be enlarged. The American eye will be retrained to see sights hitherto ignored, or if seen, misconstrued for venal ends. Connections formerly obscure will now be plain; the essential oneness of American civilization will merge. Ultimately Americans will develop a new image of themselves as a nation.

"I was taken very early," Ellison remarks, "with a passion to link together all I loved within the Negro community and all those things I felt in the world which lay beyond" (12). This passion is the driving force of his career. It can be felt in his response to jazz as well as his approach to fiction. It accounts, moreover, for his views on politics and art. For the linking together which he has in mind can barely begin in courthouse and in workshop, neighborhood and school. It must be consummated in some inner realm, where all men meet on common ground. Such are the links that Ellison would forge, the new reality he would create, the shattered psyche of the nation that he would make whole.

Nightmare of a Native Son:
Invisible Man, by Ralph Ellison

by Jonathan Baumbach

Who knows but that, on the lower frequencies, I speak for you?
                                                    —*Invisible Man*

I hesitate to call Ralph Ellison's *Invisible Man* (1952) a Negro novel, though of course it is written by a Negro and is centrally concerned with the experiences of a Negro. The appellation is not so much inaccurate as it is misleading. A novelist treating the invisibility and phantasmagoria of the Negro's life in this "democracy" is, if he tells the truth, necessarily writing a very special kind of book. Yet if his novel is interesting only because of its specialness, he has not violated the surface of his subject; he has not, after all, been serious. Despite the differences in their external concerns, Ellison has more in common as a novelist with Joyce, Melville, Camus, Kafka, West, and Faulkner than he does with other serious Negro writers like James Baldwin and Richard Wright. To concentrate on the idiom of a serious novel, no matter how distinctive its peculiarities, is to depreciate it, to minimize the universality of its implications. Though the protagonist of *Invisible Man* is a southern Negro, he is, in Ellison's rendering, profoundly all of us.

Despite its obvious social implications, Ellison's novel is a modern gothic, a Candide-like picaresque set in a dimly familiar nightmare landscape called the United States. Like *The Catcher in the Rye*, *A Member of the Wedding*, and *The Adventures of Augie March*, Ellison's novel chronicles a series of initiatory experiences through which its naïve hero learns, to his disillusion and horror, the way of the world. However, unlike these other novels of passage, *Invisible*

Man takes place, for the most part, in the uncharted spaces between the conscious and the unconscious, in the semilit darkness where nightmare verges on reality and the external world has all the aspects of a disturbing dream. Refracted by satire, at times, cartooned, Ellison's world is at once surreal and real, comic and tragic, grotesque and normal—our world viewed in its essentials rather than its externals.

The Negro's life in our white land and time is, as Ellison knows it, a relentless unreality, unreal in that the Negro as a group is loved, hated, persecuted, feared, and envied, while as an individual he is unfelt, unheard, unseen—to all intents and purposes invisible. The narrator, who is also the novel's central participant, never identifies himself by name. Though he experiences several changes of identity in the course of the novel, Ellison's hero exists to the reader as a man without an identity, an invisible "I." In taking on a succession of identities, the invisible hero undergoes an increasingly intense succession of disillusioning experiences, each one paralleling and anticipating the one following it. The hero's final loss of illusion forces him underground into the coffin (and womb) of the earth to be either finally buried or finally reborn.

The narrator's grandfather, whom he resembles (identity is one of the major concerns of the novel), is the first to define the terms of existence for him. An apparently meek man all his life, on his deathbed the grandfather reveals:

> Son, after I'm gone I want you to keep up the good fight. I never told you, but our life is a war and I have been a traitor all my born days, a spy in the enemy's country ever since I give up my gun back in the Reconstruction. Live with your head in the lion's mouth. I want you to overcome 'em with yesses, undermine 'em with grins, agree 'em to death and destruction, let 'em swoller you till they vomit or bust wide open.[1]

Though at the time he understands his grandfather's ambiguous creed only imperfectly, the hero recognizes that it is somehow his heritage. In a sense, the old man's code of acquiescent resistance is an involved justification of his nonresistance; it is a parody on itself, yet the possibility always remains that it is, in some profound, mysterious way, a meaningful ethic. On a succession of occasions, the hero applies his grandfather's advice, "agreeing 'em to death," in order to understand its import through discovering its efficacy. On each occasion, however, it is he, not " 'em," who is victimized. Consequently, the hero suffers a sense of guilt—not for having compromised himself but for failing somehow to effect his grandfather's ends. Ironically, he also feels guilty for deceiving the white "enemy," though he has "agreed 'em"

---

[1] Ralph Ellison, *Invisible Man* (New York: New American Library, 1953), p. 19. All quotations are from this edition.

not to death or destruction, only to renewed complacency. For example:

> When I was praised for my conduct I felt a guilt that in some way I
> was doing something that was really against the wishes of the white
> folks, that if they had understood they would have desired me to act
> just the opposite, that I should have been sulky and mean, and that
> really would have been what they wanted, even though they were fooled
> and thought they wanted me to act as I did. [p. 20]

The hero's cynical obsequiousness has self-destructive consequences. Having delivered a high school graduation speech advocating humility as the essence of progress, he is invited to deliver his agreeable oration to a meeting of the town's leading white citizens. Before he is allowed to speak, however, he is subjected to a series of brutal degradations, which teach him, in effect, the horror of the humility he advocates. In this episode, the first of his initiatory experiences, the invisible man's role is symbolically prophesied. The hero, along with nine other Negro boys, is put into a prize ring, then is blindfolded and coerced into battling his compatriots. Duped by the whites, the Negro unwittingly fights himself; his potency, which the white man envies and fears, is mocked and turned against him to satisfy the brutal whims of his persecutor. That the bout is preceded by a nude, blond belly dancer whom the boys are forced to watch suggests the prurience underlying the victimizer's treatment of his victim. The degrading prizefight, a demonstration of potency to titillate the impotent, in which the Negro boys blindly flail one another to entertain the sexually aroused stag audience, parallels the riot in Harlem at the end of the novel, which is induced by another institution of white civilization, the Brotherhood (a fictional guise for the Communist party). Once again Negro fights against Negro (Ras the Destroyer against the hero), although this time it is for the sake of "Brotherhood," a euphemism for the same inhumanity. In both cases, the Negro unwittingly performs the obscene demands of his enemy. In magnification, Harlem is the prize ring where the Negroes, blindfolded this time by demagoguery, flail at each other with misdirected violence. The context has changed from South to North, from white citizens to the Brotherhood, from a hired ballroom to all of Harlem, but the implication remains the same: the Negro is victimized by having his potency turned against himself by his impotent persecutor.

After the boxing match, what appears to be gold is placed on a rug in the center of the room and the boys are told to scramble for their rewards. The hero reacts: "I trembled with excitement, forgetting my pain. I would get the gold and the bills, I thought. I would use both hands. I would throw my body against the boys nearest me to block them from the gold." [p. 29]

He is, on the rug as in the boxing ring, degraded by self-interest. Though his reaction is unpleasant, it is, given the provocation, the normal, calculable one. He has been tempted and, unaware of any practicable ethical alternative, has succumbed in innocence. When the temptation recurs in more complex guises later in the novel and Ellison's nameless hero as adult falls victim to his self-interest, he is, despite his larger moral purposes, culpable and must assume responsibility for the terrible consequences of his deeds. In each of the various analogous episodes, the hero is torn between his implicit commitment to his grandfather's position—subversive acquiescence—and his will to identify—the primal instinct of self-assertion. Both commitments dictate pragmatic, as opposed to purely ethical, action, with, inevitably, immoral and impractical consequences. The rug becomes electrified, the gold coins turn out to be brass—a means, like the bout, of mocking the Negro's envied potency. That the fight and electrification follow in sequence the naked belly dancer in the course of an evening of stag entertainment for tired white businessmen indicates the obscene prurience behind the white citizen's hatred of the Negro. By debasing and manipulating the Negro's potency, the white mutes its threat and at the same time experiences it vicariously. It is in all a mordant evocation, satiric in its rendering and frightening in its implications. The white man's fascination with the Negro as a source of power (potency) is another of the thematic threads that holds together what might otherwise be a picaresque succession of disparate episodes. The ballroom humiliation serves as a gloss on the following scene, in which the hero is expelled from the Negro state college for, ironically, the consequence of his obedience to a white trustee.

The president of the Negro college, Dr. Bledsoe (all of Ellison's names characterize their bearers), entrusts the hero, up to then a model student, with the responsibility of chauffeuring a philanthropic white trustee, Mr. Norton, on a tour of the manicured country surrounding the campus. Driving aimlessly—or perhaps with more aim than he knows—the hero suddenly discovers that he has taken the trustee to the backwoods homestead of Jim Trueblood, the area's black sheep, an "unenlightened" Negro whose sharecropper existence (and incestuous, child-producing, accident with his daughter) is a source of continued embarrassment to the "progressive" community of the college. The hero would like to leave, but Norton, curiously fascinated by the fact that Trueblood has committed incest (and survived), insists on talking with the sharecropper. At Norton's prodding, Trueblood tells his story, an extended and graphically detailed account of how he was induced by a dream into having physical relations with his daughter. The story itself is a masterpiece of narrative invention and perhaps the single most brilliant scene in the novel. As Trueblood finishes his story, we discover in a moment of ironic

revelation that the bloodless Norton is a kind of euphemistic alter ego
—a secret sharer—of the atavistic Trueblood. Earlier, while being
driven deeper into the backwoods country—the reality behind the ivy
league facade of the college—Norton had rhapsodized to the narrator
about the unearthly charms of his own daughter, for whose death he
feels unaccountably guilty:

> Her beauty was a well-spring of purest water-of-life, and to look upon
> her was to drink and drink and drink again. . . . She was rare, a perfect
> creation, a work of purest art. . . . I found it difficult to believe her my
> own. . . . I have never forgiven myself. Everything I've done since her
> passing has been a monument to her memory. [pp. 43–44]

Trueblood, then, has committed the very sin that Norton has, in the
dark places of his spirit, impotently coveted. Upon hearing Trueblood's
story, Norton participates vicariously in his experience, has his own
quiescent desires fulfilled while exempted, since Trueblood has acted
for him, from the stigma of the act. Underlying Norton's recurrent
platitude that "the Negro is my fate" (he means that they are his
potency) is the same prurience that motivates the sadism of the white
citizens in the preceding scene. However, in an ironic way, Trueblood
is Norton's fate. When Trueblood finishes his story, Norton feels compelled to pay him, as the white citizens reward the Negro boxers, in
exchange for, in a double sense, having performed for him. When
Norton (who exists here really as idea rather than character) leaves
Trueblood's farm, he is exhausted and colorless, as if he had in fact
just committed incest with his own daughter.

Having exposed Norton to the horror of his own philanthropic
motives, after a further misadventure among inmates of a Negro insane asylum, the hero is expelled from school by Bledsoe because
"any act that endangered the continuity of the dream is an act of
treason." The boy, sensing his innocence, feels haunted by his grandfather's curse. Through Ellison's surrealistic rendering, we sense the
nightmare reality of the hero's experience (as we do not with Norton's
comparable nightmare):

> How had I come to this? I had kept unswervingly to the path before me,
> had tried to be exactly what I was expected to be, had done exactly
> what I was expected to do—yet, instead of winning the expected reward,
> here I was stumbling along, holding on desperately to one of my eyes
> in order to keep from bursting out my brain against some familiar ob-
> ject swerved into my path by my distorted vision. And now to drive me
> wild I felt suddenly that my grandfather was hovering over me, grinning
> triumphantly out of the dark. [p. 131]

Accepting responsibility for the sins of his innocence, the hero goes to
New York, armed with several letters of "identification" which Bledsoe
has addressed to various trustees for the ostensible purpose of finding

him a job. When the hero discovers that the letters have been written "to hope him to death, and keep him running," that the renowned Negro educator Bledsoe has betrayed him treacherously, has in effect ordered him killed as an almost gratuitous display of power, he experiences a moment of terrible disillusion. At the same time he senses that this betrayal is in some way a reenactment of the past: "Twenty-five years seemed to have lapsed between his handing me the letter and my grasping its message. I could not believe it, yet I had a feeling that it all had happened before. I rubbed my eyes, and they felt sandy as though all the fluids had suddenly dried." [p. 168]

In a way, it *has* happened before; for Bledsoe's act of victimization (the beating of Negro by Negro) is analogous to the punishment the hero received in the prize ring at the hands of the largest of the other Negro boys. Bledsoe's deceit, like its analog, is motivated by the desire to ingratiate himself with the white society which dispenses rewards —which provides, or so he believes, the source of his power.

As one episode parallels another, each vignette in itself has allegorical extensions. Employed by Liberty Paints, a factory "the size of a small city," the narrator is ordered to put ten drops of "black dope" into buckets of optic white paint in order, he is told, to make it whiter. The mixing of the black into the white is, of course, symbolic: the ten drops are analogous to the ten boys in the prize ring, and in each case the white becomes whiter by absorbing the Negro's virility, by using the black to increase the strength of the white. Yet the name "optic white" suggests it is all some kind of visual illusion. When the black dope runs out, the hero as apprentice paint mixer is ordered by his boss, "the terrible Mr. Kimbro," to replace it, without being told which of seven possible vats has the right substance. Left to his own discretion, the hero chooses the wrong black liquid, concentrated paint remover, which makes the white paint transparent and grayish; this act symbolizes the implicit threat of Negro potency left to its own devices. The paint-mixing scene is paralleled by the violence of the insane Negro veterans at the bar (the Golden Day) in which they beat their white attendant Supercargo into grayness and terrorize the already depleted Norton. It anticipates the antiwhite violence of Ras the exhorter-turned-destroyer, the only alternative to invisibility the white man has left the Negro.

Yet there is the illusion of another alternative: when the narrator adds the black drops to the paint which already contains the black remover, though the mixture appears gray to him, it passes for white in Kimbro's eyes. This is, in symbol, the role of subterfuge and infiltration—his grandfather's legacy and curse:

> I looked at the painted slab. It appeared the same: a gray tinge glowed through the whiteness, and Kimbro had failed to detect it. I stared for a minute, wondering if I were seeing things, inspected another and an-

other. All were the same, a brilliant white diffused with gray. I closed
my eyes for a moment and looked again and still no change. Well, I
thought as long as he's satisfied. . . . [p. 180]

Kimbro permits the gray-tinged paint to be shipped out and the hero
wonders whether, after all, he has been the deceiver or the deceived.
He suspects, when Kimbro dismisses him, that he somehow has been
the dupe. That the paint passes for white in Kimbro's eyes suggests
that the black with which it was mixed was, like the hero's existence,
to all intents and purposes, invisible.

Essentially invisible, the narrator undergoes a succession of superficial changes of identity—in a sense, changes of mask—each entailing
a symbolic, though illusory, death and rebirth. Knocked unconscious
by the explosion of a machine which makes the base of a white paint,
a machine that he was unable to control, the hero is placed in another
machine, a coffin-like electrified box, in order to be "started again."
The shock treatments surrealistically rendered recall the electrification
from the rug, however magnified in intensity. Like most of the episodes
in the novel, it is on the surface a comic scene, though in its implications (lobotomy and castration) it is a singularly unpleasant nightmare.
The hero's first awareness upon awakening is that he is enclosed in a
glass box with an electric cap attached to his head, a combination
coffin-womb and electrocutor. When he is blasted with a charge of
electricity, he instinctively screams in agonized protest, only to be
told in response as if he were indeed a piece of equipment, " 'Hush
goddamit. . . . We're trying to get you started again. Now shut up!' "
[p. 203] After a while he is unable to remember who he is or whether
he has in fact existed before his present moment of consciousness: "My
mind was blank, as though I'd just begun to live." Like the charged
rug, though considerably more cruel, the shock treatments are intended
to neutralize him, in effect to castrate him. In his moments of confused consciousness he hears two voices arguing over the proper method
to treat his case. One is in favor of surgery, the other in favor of the
machine:

> "The machine will produce the results of a prefrontal lobotomy without
> the negative effect of the knife," the voice said. "You see, instead of sever-
> ing the prefrontal lobe, a single lobe, that is, we apply pressure in the
> proper degrees to the major centers of nerve control—our concept is
> Gestalt—and the result is as complete a change of personality as you'll
> find in your famous fairy-tale cases of criminals transformed into amia-
> ble fellows after all that bloody business of a brain operation. And
> what's more," the voice went on triumphantly, "the patient is both
> physically and neurally whole."
> "But what of his psychology?"
> "Absolutely of no importance!" the voice said. "The patient will live
> as he has to live, with absolute integrity. Who could ask more? He'll ex-

perience no major conflict of motives, and what is even better, society will suffer no traumata on his account."

There was a pause. A pen scratched upon paper. Then, "Why not castration, doctor?" a voice asked waggishly, causing me to start, a pain tearing through me.

"There goes your love of blood again," the first voice laughed. "What's that definition of a surgeon, 'A butcher with a bad conscience'?"

They laughed. [pp. 206–207]

I quote this passage at length to suggest the high-voltage charge of Ellison's satire, capable at once of being mordantly comic and profoundly terrifying. The clinical attitude of the psychologist ("society will suffer no traumata on his account") suggests the northern white position toward the Negro, as opposed to the butcher-surgeon who represents the more overtly violent southern position. The ends of both, however, are approximately the same—emasculation; the difference is essentially one of means.

The narrator is, in this scene, almost visibly invisible, discussed impersonally in his presence as if he were not there. When he is unable to recall his name, his mother's name, any form of his identity, any form of his past, the doctors seem pleased and deliver him from the machine, the only mother he knows:

I felt a tug at my belly and looked down to see one of the physicians pull the cord which was attached to the stomach node, jerking me forward. . . .

"Get the shears," he said. "Let's not waste time."

"Sure," the other said. "Let's not waste time."

I recoiled inwardly as though the cord were part of me. Then they had it free and the nurse clipped through the belly band and removed the heavy node. [p. 213]

In describing the birth from the machine, Ellison suggests through evocation that it is also a kind of castration. Insofar as it leaves the hero without the potency of self, it is, in implication, just that.

Aside from the Prologue and parts of the Epilogue, which have an enlightened madness all their own, the experience of the machine birth is the least realistic, the most surrealistic, in the novel. And this brings us to what I think is the novel's crucial flaw, its inconsistency of method, its often violent transformations from a kind of detailed surface realism in which probability is limited to the context of ordinary, everyday experiences to an allegorical world of almost endless imaginative possibilities. Often the shift is dramatically effective, as when the hero and Norton enter the insane world of the Golden Day (here the truth is illuminated by a nominal madman who has the insane virtue of pure sight) and Norton is forced into a frightening moment of self-recognition. On other occasions, the visional shifts jar us away from the novel's amazing world into an awareness of the

ingenuity of its creator. Since Ellison is at once prodigiously talented
and prodigiously reckless, *Invisible Man* is astonishingly good at its
best. By the same token the book is uneven; on occasion it is very
bad as only very good novels can be. Given the nature of his vision,
Ellison's world seems real—or alive—when it is surrealistically distorted, and for the most part made-up or abstract—when it imitates
the real world. Largely recounted in the manner of traditional realism,
the hero's adventures in the Brotherhood up until the Harlem riot
constitute the least interesting section of the novel.

In joining the Brotherhood, the narrator gives up his past to assume
a new identity or rather new nonidentity, Brother———. Because of
his remarkable speech-making abilities, as well as his conscious ambition to be some kind of savior, he becomes one of the leading figures
of the Harlem Brotherhood. Finally, his controversial activities make
it necessary for him to disguise himself in order to get through Harlem
safely. Brother ———'s disguise—dark glasses and a wide-brimmed hat
—which he has hoped would make him inconspicuous in Harlem,
creates for him still another identity, which is, in effect, just a new
aspect of nonidentity. Wearing the hat and glasses, Brother ——— is
unrecognized as his Brotherhood self, but is mistaken for a man
named Rinehart, a charlatan of incredible diversification. Rinehart,
whose identities include numbers runner, police briber, lover, pimp,
and Reverend, is, the hero discovers, a kind of alter ego to his invisibility. If you are no one, you are at the same time potentially
everyone. The hero has disguised himself in order to avoid the consequences of his acts and instead finds himself held responsible for
Rinehart's inordinate sins—for all sins—which are, in the Dostoevskian
sense, his own. When the Brotherhood's theoretician Hambro informs
the hero that, with the alteration of the larger plan, his role has
changed from exhorter to pacifier, he senses his likeness to his dazzling
alter ego:

> "Besides I'd feel like Rinehart. . . ." It slipped out and he looked at me.
> "Like who?"
> "Like a charlatan," I said.
> Hambro laughed. "I thought you learned about that, Brother."
> I looked at him quickly. "Learned what?"
> "That it's impossible *not* to take advantage of the people."
> "That's Rinehartism—cynicism. . . ." [p. 436]

In following the dictates of the Brotherhood, the hero has hurt,
he discovers to his pain, the very people he has intended to help. Without benefit of glasses and hat, he has been a Rinehart in disguise all
the time. He has been, paradoxically, an unwitting cynic. Duped by
his self-conscious, romantic ambitions to be another Booker T. Wash-
ington, the hero has let the Brotherhood use him for their cynical

"historic" purposes. As a Brotherhood agent, he demagogically incites the Harlem Negroes to potential action only to leave them prey to the misdirected violence of Ras, their violence ultimately turned, like that of the boys in the prize ring, against themselves. With awareness comes responsibility, and the hero recognizes that he alone must bear the guilt for the Brotherhood's betrayal of the Negro. The ramifications of his awful responsibility are manifested generally in the hellish Harlem riot at the end of the novel and particularly in the disillusion and death of the most admirable of the Brotherhood, Tod Clifton (the name suggests a kind of Promethean entrapment), whose career prophesies and parallels that of the hero.

Earlier in the novel, Ras, after sparing Tod's life, has exhorted his adversary to leave the Brotherhood and join his racist movement (a fictionalized version of the Black Muslims). Their confrontation, an objectification of the hero's interior struggle, anticipates Tod's defection from the Brotherhood:

> "Come with us, mahn. We build a glorious movement of black people. *Black people!* What do they do, give you money? who wahnt the damn stuff? Their money bleed black blood, mahn. It's unclean! Taking their money is shit, mahn. Money without dignity—that's *bahd* shit!"
>
> Clifton lunged toward him. I held him, shaking my head. "Come on, the man's crazy," I said, pulling on his arm.
>
> Ras struck his thighs with his fists. "Me crazy, mahn? You call me crazy? Look at you two and look at me—is this sanity? Standing here in three shades of blackness! Three black men fighting in the street because of the white enslaver? Is that sanity? Is that consciousness, scientific understanding? Is that the modern black mahn of the twentieth century? Hell, mahn! Is it self-respect—black against black? What they give you to betray—their women? You fall for that?"
>
> "Let's go," I repeated. He stood there, looking.
>
> "Sure, you go," Ras said, "but not him. You contahminated but he the real black mahn. In Africa this mahn be a chief, a black king!" [pp. 322–23]

In this eloquent scene, Clifton finally rejects Ras, but he is undeniably moved by his enemy's crude exhortation. Ras—the name suggests an amalgam of race and rash—is a fanatic, but given his basic premise, that the white man is the Negro's natural enemy, his arguments are not easily refutable. Unable to answer Ras, Clifton, out of a sense of shame or guilt, knocks the Exhorter down, committing an act of Rasian violence. The punch is an acknowledgment, a communion, an act of love. As they leave, the hero discovers that Clifton has tears in his eyes. Clifton says, referring to Ras, " 'That poor misguided son of a bitch.' 'He thinks a lot of you, too,' I said." [p. 326]

Clifton is sympathetic to Ras's motives, but he is nevertheless too civilized to accept his methods. The Brotherhood, then, with its cant of "historic necessity," represents to Clifton the enlightened alternative to racist violence through which the Negro can effect his protest. Entrapped by the Brotherhood through the commitment imposed by his integrity, Clifton becomes, even more than the narrator, a victim of the Brotherhood's betrayal. Like the implicit suicide of Conrad's Lord Jim, Clifton's death (he provokes a policeman into shooting him) is a sacrifice to a culpability too egregious to be redeemed in any other way, and, at the same time, a final if gratuitous act of heroism. In giving himself up to be murdered, Clifton takes on the whole responsibility for the Brotherhood's betrayal of the Negro. If by his sacrifice he does not redeem the hero from his own culpability, he at least through his example sets up the possibility of Brother ———'s redemption. If the various characters with whom the "invisible" hero is confronted represent possible states of being, Clifton symbolizes the nearest thing to an idea.

Clifton's death, because it permits the hero to organize the Negroes around a common cause (the narrator's funeral oration is a magnificent parody of Antony's), is potentially an agent of good, for Clifton can be considered in a meaningful sense a sacrifice. However, even that is denied him. At the last minute the Brotherhood withdraws its support from the hero, and, left to their own devices and the exhortation of Ras, the aroused Negroes perform arbitrary acts of plunder and violence. That Clifton's death initiates the Harlem riots, which serve the Brotherhood's new purpose of pacifying the Negro by exhausting his hate-charged energies in meaningless self-conflict, is a last terrible mockery of his decent intentions.

In hawking the chauvinistic "Sambo dolls" which dance at the tug of an invisible string, Clifton was not so much mocking the Brotherhood's attitude toward the Negro as he was parodying himself. His own comment about Ras suggests in a way the impulse of his nihilistic act:

> "I don't know," he said. "I suppose sometimes a man *has* to plunge outside history. . . ."
> "What?"
> "Plunge outside, turn his back. . . . Otherwise, he might kill somebody, go nuts." [p. 328]

Deceived by the bogus historians of the Brotherhood, Clifton has "plunged outside history," though in punching the white policeman he demonstrated that he had not quite "turned his back." As an alternative to violent reprisal—Clifton was an essentially gentle man racked by rage—he became a heckler of the Brotherhood, of the Negro, of the white man's treatment of the Negro, of himself, of the universe. Though he is one of the few noble characters in Ellison's world, his destruction is less than tragic. A man of tragic stature, Clifton is a captive participant in an absurd world which derogates him and mocks the significance of his death as it did his life. Clifton's sacrificial act, its intention perverted, is mostly invisible. The others of the Brotherhood—Wrestrum (rest room), Tobitt (two bit), Jack (money, masturbation)—who in their commitment to "science" have become as dehumanized and corrupt as those they oppose, survive the shift in tactical policy.

When the hero discovers that it is through him that the Brotherhood has betrayed Clifton, he feels responsible for his friend's death. Earlier, in outrage he spat at one of Clifton's dancing puppets, knocking it "lifeless," performing symbolically what the policeman does actually —the murder of Clifton. When the hero knocks over the doll, an outsider laughs at what he thinks is the likeness between the spitter and the spat-on doll. Just as Clifton in selling the obscene doll has been mocking himself, the hero in spitting at the doll has been attacking himself as well as Clifton, though without benefit of awareness. Only after his showdown with the Brotherhood, and even then incompletely, does the hero become aware that he has been performing all along as if he were, in life size, the dancing puppet doll.

At his moment of greatest self-awareness, the hero suffers his most intense sense of guilt. Watching two nuns in the subway (one black, one white), he remembers a ritual verse he had once heard:

> Bread and wine,
> Bread and wine,
> Your cross ain't nearly so
> Heavy as mine. . . . [p. 382]

The rhyme comes to him as an automatic response, its singsong at first overriding its sense. Momentarily, almost without awareness, as the pain of wound travels from flesh to brain, he comes to assume its implications. As he watches some Negroes maltreat a white shopkeeper, he experiences a terrible revelation:

A pressure of guilt came over me. I stood on the edge of the walk watching the crowd threatening to attack the man until a policeman appeared and dispersed them. And although I knew no one could do much about it, I felt responsible. All our work had been very little, no great change had been made. And it was all my fault. I'd been so fascinated by the motion that I'd forgotten to measure what it was bringing forth. I'd been asleep, dreaming. [p. 384]

A sleepwalker in a world never real enough for him to believe in, the hero experiences a succession of awakenings, only to find himself participating in still another level of nightmare. In accepting Clifton's role as martyr-saint, in taking on the responsibility for all of Harlem, all of Brotherhood, in extension, *all,* he succeeds only in setting himself up for a final, self-destroying victimization. Aware of the futility of all his past acts and, in implication, all acts in the absurd context of his world, the hero commits an act of meaningless violence. Entrapped by a situation for which he is at least partly responsible, with his neck quite literally at stake (Ras wants to hang him), he impales the demonic innocent, Ras, through the jaw with his own spear.

That Jack, the leader of the Brotherhood, has one eye (as earlier the euphemistic preacher Barbee is revealed as blind) is symbolic of the distorted perspective of the Brotherhood's "scientifically objective view" of society, in which the human being is a casual puppet in the service of the "historic" strings that manipulate him. Clifton makes only *paper* Negroes dance; it is Jack and Tobitt who treat flesh-and-blood Negroes as if they were puppet Sambo dolls. (By having Clifton charge a "brotherly two bits" for the puppet dolls, Ellison, through suggestion, transfers the onus of traitor to Tobitt and in extension to the Brotherhood itself.) When the hero discovers that the Brotherhood has betrayed him, he consciously resolves to impersonate the puppet doll he has so long mimicked unwittingly—to, as his grandfather advised, "overcome 'em with yesses . . . agree 'em to death and destruction." For all his Rinehartian machinations, he manages, however, only to abet the scheme of the Brotherhood.

Seeking redemption from his compounded guilt, he is sucked into the maelstrom of the Harlem riot for which he suffers a sense of limitless, unreclaimable responsibility. He realizes that "By pretending to agree I had indeed agreed, had made myself responsible for that huddled form lighted by flame and gunfire in the street, and all others whom now the night was making ripe for death." [p. 478] The flaming buildings and streets, the burnt tar stench, the black figures moving shadowlike through the eerily illumined night become an evocation of Hell, a mirror for the hero's raging interior guilt. At the center of the riot—at the very seat of Hell—he experiences the deaths of his various corrupted identities, shedding the false skins to get at the pure invisibility underneath. As Ras approaches, the hero searches for his "Rineharts," his dark glasses, only to "see the crushed lenses fall to the street. 'Rinehart, I thought, Rinehart!'" as if he had just witnessed Rinehart himself—his Rinehart self—collapse in death before him. To propitiate Ras and stop the riots, the hero disavows allegiance to the Brotherhood, killing in effect his Brotherhood self. But as he is invisible, he is unheard, his words as always not communicating his meanings. Struck by the absurdity of the demonic Ras on horseback, of the senseless pillage and murder around him, and, after all, of existence itself, the hero is for the moment willing to relinquish his life if it will make the white man see him and consequently see himself. But the example of Clifton's meaningless sacrifice dissuades him. The hero, faced with death, decides that it is "better to live out one's own absurdity than to die for that of others, whether for Ras's or Jack's." When in self-protection he impales Ras, who is in a sense the deepest of his identities, he experiences the illusion of death and rebirth: "It was as though for a moment I had surrendered my life and begun to live again." [p. 484]

Newly baptized by an exploded water main, like the birth from the machine, a somewhat illusory (and comic) resurrection, the hero seeks to return to Mary, his ex-landlady, who has become a symbolic mother to him. But as he is unable to imitate Christ, he is unable to reach Mary. Instead, chased by two white looters, he falls through an open manhole. Unable to find the exit to his coffinlike cell, he burns various papers of his past (high school diploma, Sambo doll, Brotherhood card) for torches to light his way out, only to discover in a moment of terrible realization that the Jacks and Nortons have left him no exit, that without his paper symbols he has no past and consequently no home, no identity. With this knowledge he relaxes in the carrion comfort of his dank hole, having returned at last to the womb of the earth. It is, as he puts it, a "death alive," from which emergence will be rebirth, his victimization transcended, his guilt perhaps purged, his soul if possible redeemed. A nonparticipant in existence, an invisible man by choice, the hero continues to live in his private cellar, which he has illumined by 1,369 lights (a symbolic attempt at transcending his invisibility—at seeing himself), the electricity supplied gratuitously in spite of themselves by Monopolated Light and Power. As the whites had mocked his potency and used it for their own ends, he is now paying them back in kind. Though he is protected from the pain of disillusion while isolated from the brutal, absurd world he hates and, in spite of himself, loves, the hero plans some day to emerge into the outside world because, a son of God and man, one of us, he is willing to believe that "even the invisible victim is responsible for the fate of all." [p. 487]

Much of the experience in Ellison's novel is externally imposed; that is, each scene, through allusive reference, is made to carry a burden of implication beyond that generated by its particular experience. Consequently the weight of the novel, its profound moral seriousness, resides primarily in conception rather than rendering. Given the problem of transforming large abstractions into evocative experiences, Ellison is nevertheless able more often than not to create occasions resonant enough to accommodate his allegorical purposes. Finally, one senses that the novel, for all its picaresque variety of incident, has a curiously static quality. This is not because the episodes are the same or even similar—on the contrary, one is compelled to admire the range and resourcefulness of Ellison's imaginative constructions—but because they are all extensions of the same externally imposed idea; they all *mean* approximately the same thing.

Like so many of our serious writers, Ellison is not prolific. It took him, by his own testimony, some seven years to write *Invisible Man*, and now eleven years after its publication his second novel is still not completed. If Ellison's reputation had to rest, as it does at the time of this writing, on his one impressive if uneven novel, *Invisible Man* is, I suspect, vital and profound enough to survive its faults—to endure the erosions of time. As a satirist and surrealist, Ellison excels among his contemporaries and can bear comparison with his mentors—Kafka, Joyce, and Faulkner. As a realist, he is less adept: talky, didactic, even at times, if the term is possible for so otherwise exciting a writer, tedious. For all that, Ellison has written a major novel, perhaps one of the three or four most considerable American novels of the past two decades.

An excerpt from his forthcoming novel, "And Hickman Arrives," published in the first issue of *The Noble Savage*, exhibits some of the same evangelical rhetoric that gives *Invisible Man* its terrible impact. Still, it is idle from a fifty-page fragment to prophesy what kind of novel it will make. Moreover, "And Hickman Arrives" has many of the damaging excesses of the first novel. Ellison has a penchant for letting good things go on past their maximum effectiveness. Yet his excesses are also his strength; like Faulkner before him, Ellison is a writer of amazing verbal energy and at his best he creates experiences that touch our deepest selves, that haunt us with the suffocating wisdom of nightmare. American novelists have often had a predilection for large, protracted books, as if great length were a virtue in itself. Ellison is no exception. However, he is one of the few novelists on the scene today who seems capable of producing a large, serious novel, justified by the size of its experience and the depth of its informing intelligence. On the lowest (and highest) frequencies, he speaks for us.

Black Existentialism: Richard Wright

by *Kingsley Widmer*

In Richard Wright's most successful fiction, the novella *The Man Who Lived Underground* (first complete version 1944; collected posthumously in *Eight Men*, 1961), his isolated black man hiding out in the sewers and contemplating crimes thinks to himself, "Maybe *any*thing's right. . . . Yes, if the world as man has made it was right, then anything else was right, any act a man took to satisfy himself. . . ." Yet the man who says it, bitter author as well as desperate underground character, ends tormented with isolation, overpowered by obscure guilts, and urged towards self-destruction.

This is the preoccupying, indeed obsessive, moral drama focusing almost all of Wright's writings. Traditionally, we and Wright recognize it as Ivan Karamazov's brain-fevered perplexity, his just conclusion that in a cruel and purposeless world "Everything is permitted." But father and God and all values dead, only guilty anguish remains, the demon of destruction and self-destruction. Wright repeatedly and overwhelmingly felt that perplexity, not only individually but as a black in white America, though he was one who came to recognize much of that "blackness" as the universal human condition. With the old myths gone, he discovers that black revenge *is* permitted —violation, crime, hatred, killing—but that it results in ultimate revenge against the self. Just as the final obedience the authoritarian parent exacts from the son is self-hatred, and the major work the master exacts from the slave is self-abasement, so American racist injustice exacts guilty black self-destruction. Domination, exploitation, and other human viciousness succeed all too well, and most horribly in the victim's vengeance against himself for being a victim.

The Man Who Lived Underground seems paradigmatic. Fred Daniels, a simple black falsely accused of murdering a white woman, hides out underground but feels terribly guilty of some unnameable crime. In the lonely and foul depths, each black man finds "the secret of his existence, the guilt that he could never get rid of," the

"Black Existentialism: Richard Wright" by Kingsley Widmer. Revised version of "The Existential Darkness: Richard Wright's *The Outsider*" from *Wisconsin Studies in Contemporary Literature*, 1, No. 3 (1960), 13–21. Copyright © 1971 by Kingsley Widmer.

"dreadful offense" of his very being in the world of white contempt
and hatred. Living for days in a cave off the city sewers, the outcast
collects and plays with the "serious toys" of the overground world—
money, jewels, machines, clocks, a meat cleaver. But, in his dreadful
freedom and anxious isolation, those things can have no meaning.
Nor can the lives of that other world. From his subterranean access
to stores and offices, to a church and a movie theatre and a funeral
parlor, he looks in on the phantasmagoric pathos and obscenity and
guilt of the ordinary social order. In his separation, he crouches free
of such mis-reality, so free that his very identity (even his sense of his
own name) begins to dissolve in the lonely and placeless and timeless
depths. So he comes above ground to declare to the police, though he
did not kill the woman: "I'm guilty!" All men are. To be, he must in
this society be guilty of something. But the police have found a different criminal to blame for that particular woman's death. Reluctantly
following the crazedly submissive guilty outcast back toward his secret
sewer cache, the white cops kill him: "You've got to shoot his kind.
They'd wreck things." Though naturalistic in much of its detail, this
fervid guilt fantasy is a nightmare which can only end with the
black man's death in the sewer with a "mouth full of thick, bitter" understanding.

This harshly seminal fable, indebted to Dostoyevsky's *Notes from the
Underground* and providing the basic tropes for Ellison's *Invisible
Man*, is what Wright could best do, and perhaps only do. From the
pathetically fumbling murders and self-hatred of Bigger Thomas in
Chicago in Wright's first, quasi-Marxian determinist novel, *Native Son*
(1940), through the slyer crimes and self-disgusted flight imposed by
the white South on black Fishbelly in his last work of rhetorical
naturalism, *The Long Dream* (1958), Wright mostly played variations
on the black outsider as guilty underground victim. The isolated and
despised black compulsively strikes out for his freedom in violations
which demand self-destruction in a world of whited sepulchers.

The personal dimensions of Wright's existential paradigm may be
followed out in his most poignant book, the autobiographical *Black
Boy* (1945). Raised fatherless in Mississippi by a fanatical puritan
mother, his later isolated heroes usually guiltily punish an uncomprehending "good woman." White Southerners gave Wright every
reason for the sense of degradation, self-disgust and embittered flight
which compels all of his protagonists. And the sensitivity and intelligence of the black boy brutally victimized by white Americans demand Wright's intense commitment to rage, accusation and exacer-
bated black insight.

The intellectual dimensions of this outcast being receive fullest development in his "novel of ideas," *The Outsider* (1953). Though fal-
tering in style and characterization—Wright's rage drove him into

rhetorical abstraction in all of his books—it was his most thoughtful novel. Written with partial detachment provided by some years of deracinated escape from America in exile in Paris, it is often condemned by other black writers and those identifying with them. For though the central figure is a black man in ghettoized America, and ghetto experiences inform most of the scenes and themes, the issues, as Wright pointed out in the novel, are not confined to "racial consciousness" and its "self-loathing." Blackness but provides special emphasis on the more universal outsider state. Similar perplexities of "freedom and dread" apply to all men, all of us guilty. The race issue is the broadly human, not merely ethnic, one. All sensitive men must recognize their "black existence."

The Outsider is an explicitly philosophical novel framed with epigraphs from Kierkegaard and Nietzsche and developed on Sartrean dialectics. One of the few self-consciously American existentialist fables, it is, except for those imposing some parochial thesis about "American Black Culture" on the author, Wright's most interesting novel. Critical charges against it for melodrama, for passages of didactic abstraction and jargon and awkwardness, and for obsessive pessimism, correctly apply to all of Wright's books. Nor, as I have already suggested in discussing his work of a decade earlier, is the existential moral focus an imposition of the author's Paris days. As black boy from Natchez, as naturalist writer from Chicago, and as left-Negro militant from New York, Wright had always practiced the "literature of extreme situations," dramatized the "gratuitous acts" of an "ethical criminal," centered on the isolation of American Raskolnikovs meditating on man's terrible freedom and compulsion, and insisted on revealing "the horrible truth of the uncertain and enigmatic nature of life." Black Wright was a birthright existentialist.

The dramatization in *The Outsider*—the title, says his biographer, was suggested by a reader of the manuscript—employs the melodrama usual to philosophically insistent literature, as in Marlowe, Dostoyevsky and Sartre, to highlight choice. The protagonist, ex-philosophy student Cross Damon, rebels against the humiliations of a resentfully aspiring black middle-class family, the tedium of a postal clerk's job, the sense of failure in sexual complications, the oppressive Protestant ethos of his milieu, and the whole complex of Negro-American "nonidentity." (The allegorical emphasis includes the demonic crucifixion suggested by the name of the hero and the parody of Soren Kierkegaard's use of the postman as archetypal Christian in *Either/Or*, as well as novelistic sub-division into an existential pentad of "stages": Dread, Dream, Descent, Despair and death-Decision.) A fortuitous subway accident, in which a mangled black body with the wrong coat is misidentified as Cross Damon, allows the protagonist to pretend to be dead and flee his past life. Damon attains the moral limbo of totally alienated freedom—a hugely appealing contemporary fantasy. In the following days he kills a "Negro clown" (his Jim Crow antithesis) who could identify him with his past, tricks several kind people whose pathos would impose obligations on his freedom, covers his masqueraded identity by burning the Selective Service office (it was, with appropriate irony, in the basement of a church), and, with moral impartiality, kills a fascistic racist and an exploitative Communist. Soon after, dreadfully free logic drives him to murder another suspicious political functionary. He attempts to achieve a sense of purpose in anguished love for the victimized wife of one of his victims (Eva, the primal sensitive artist), but she, confronted with knowledge of Cross Damon's past and amoral acts, commits suicide, leaving her Damon in ultimate loneliness and despair. Such is the dread of truth in others, and the price of truth for the self. Cross Damon's own death, at the hands of bureaucratic functionaries who must destroy him because they cannot understand him, simply closes the absurd rebellion to get "outside history," social morality, and the meaningless self.

Cross Damon's destructive acts, of course, also reflect psychological compulsions. He finally recognizes that he was partly in rebellion against his puritan mother: "It had been her moral strictures that had made him a criminal. . . ." His "ungovernable compulsions" to murder his enemies also reflect the social oppression and outcastness of those who "live in but not of the normal rounds of ritualized life." But Wright also wants to fuse these circumstances with the existential-outsider crux in which a man can propound gratuitous crimes, i.e., make a "free" selection of assertions by a "petty god" in a "Godless world." Like Raskolnikov, Cross Damon comes to treat people as "insects." A Dostoyevskian psychological policeman (Ely Houston, the crippled "outsider" District Attorney) points out the metaphysical logic of Damon's destructive actions, his reasonable but inhuman responses to a world losing its mythologies of values. The "logic of atheism," of total disbelief in man and men, cannot give sufficient shape to personal desires and promises in a meaningless universe. Recognized truth is not enough for life. Sadly, this outsider must also discover under his arguments the truth revealed by the earlier underground man: "the feeling that had sent him on this long, bloody, twisting road: self-loathing. . . ."

Can Wright sufficiently relate the dialectic about existential awareness and the compulsions of his black American? It remains problematic, perhaps because of inadequate artistry. Wright does show Cross Damon's mistake in letting "contingency" become "destiny" in some scenes. His purposes were insufficient and perverse, though it is not clear what else would have worked in a world dehumanized into Communists versus policemen. Partly because of his personal disillusionment in the forties with Communist manipulation (the detail appears in Wright's contribution to *The God Who Failed*), he dramatizes his Communists, if not his policemen, as too cynical, as men inhumanly pursuing only the "sensuality of power" (the point may come from George Orwell). They all only play in existential "bad faith" with "the far-flung conspiracy pretending that life was tending toward a goal of redemption."

Thus Wright's Cross Damon ends making demonic criss-crosses for the author, cancelling each lie with another lie, each crime with another crime. For a non-political example, early in the novel Damon becomes estranged from his wife, Gladys, the epitome of the black bourgeoise, of the predatory middle-class virtues:

> as he suffered her nagging, he felt increasingly walled off from her; but the more he felt it the more he sought to hide it, and finally there crept into his dealings with her a weird quality of irony. It first manifested itself in an innocent question: How could he help Gladys? And the moment he asked that question he knew he did not love her and perhaps had never loved her. . . . She had become for him an object of compassion. He was now haunted by the idea of finding some way to make her hate him. Her hatred would be a way of squaring their relationship, of curing her of her love for him, of setting her free as well as himself.

In his ornate "psychological attack" upon his wife, and upon himself, Damon draws upon his earlier aberrant behavior, upon a fluke episode, and comes home unexpectedly, walks in like a mute and mad stranger, hits his wife, walks out, and later returns at his usual time as if nothing had happened. This perversely ironic psychological dramatization drives him into the total alienation he demands and makes flight imperative. Thus "contingency" reveals "destiny," though one as destructive, and self-destructive, as the materials from which it is made. Here, perhaps with more irony than Wright intended, we find a naturalistic delineation of Sartre's maxim that "man chooses himself," which must include the idea that man significantly desires to be that which has happened to him.

As in this representative episode, Wright's usual deployment of inverse and doubling emotions (hate as love, destruction as compassion, compulsion as freedom) ends in self-rejection since each insistently reversed self becomes unacceptable. But, we should note, this goes beyond Wright to characterize much of existentialism's analysis of man. Our suspicion that Cross Damon's "weird irony" reflects self-hating compulsion as much as freedom also applies to the gratuitous murder and embracement of death by Camus' Mersault in *L'Etranger*. (*The Outsider* also parallels *The Stranger* several times in the incapacity for remorse, etc.) But the ambiguities between existential freedom and the compulsions to self-destruction appear not only in Wright and Camus but in Sartre, Genet, Bowles, Mailer, and other self-consciously existential fabulists, and become crucially definitive of modern Western man's loss of positive myth and community. We might also note that, in spite of the usual arguments of traditional moralists, art can locate its insights in hatred as well as in love.

In profound ambiguity, Cross Damon serves as the hero and the victim of existential lucidity. While his choices of action and identity appear free, they also reveal "dark compulsions" in the three pathetic women he chooses, in the betrayals, the acts of violence, the self-confessions, the disguises, the flights, and the self-destruction. He insists, like many contemporary political leaders, nihilistic juveniles, and certain other criminals, that "no ideas are necessary to justify his acts." *That idea* is but another version of Raskolnikov's final dream in *Crime and Punishment* of the "new men," the amoralists of the totalitarian and apocalyptic age.

The existential scene in which Wright places his amoralist tends to only one tonality—an *a priori* blackness. His dark-skinned hero-victim moves solely through the dark wintry season, the black ghettos of Chicago and New York, the dark despair of the "literature of the irrational" (his favorite reading, which gives him away to the intellectual policeman), and even a black levity. The blackness, of course, provides practical images to embody the darkness of dread. Where Sartre in *Nausea* has some difficulty in reasonably presenting Roquentin's repulsion to the "viscous" horrors of his own body, Wright's Damon can more readily see, and treat, his black body as "an alien and despised object" because the white society in its Manichean fears does just that. To "stand outside the world" in the moral and social darkness, for Wright's protagonist, depends on an actual as well as metaphysical alienation of the black man from the white rationalizations of ordinary life and social order.

In his effort to find the "relationship of himself to himself," to escape from his "burden of nonidentity," Cross Damon diabolically takes on "the project of deception," which must finally mislead himself as well as others. Some of this anguished dramatization of the theology and self-defeat of living lies seems to draw upon Sartre's analysis of *mauvaise foi* (*L'Etre et le Néant,* Chapter 2). In both, the systematic bad faith used to hide inner emptiness becomes a bitter parody of the daily compromises and resentments of most men, though the lies and other deceptions American whites demand from blacks may be the most debilitating.

The deceptions and ambiguities and inversions so crucial to the existentialist unfolding of human behavior rest in a desperate romantic irony: enlightenment perversely requires a descent into the darkness. Only thus does one get "outside" not only the usual history and ideas but mere control by circumstances. For Wright's figure, however, very little can be found down and out. Damon's repeated existential maxim, "Man is nothing in particular," shows a greater sense of futility than its source, Sartre's "Man is a useless passion." Is embittered blackness the basis of the difference? For Wright's Damon, anyway, there remains after the descent no irreducible value in the human individual. His desperate individualistic assertion of free value ends treating men as "insects," "meaningless obstructions," "nothings," including himself. Wright has carried the existential quest to a dead end.

Perhaps there is a peculiarly American insistence here, and not just in the obvious mockery of our pious idealistic and manipulative optimisms. Where Kierkegaard's "single one" could fall back before the horror of the arbitrary absolute on a humble moral identity (the familial postman in *The Deer Park*), or more atheistic and antibourgeois European existentialists establish themselves in honorific identities (as traditional artistic and political rebels), the American outsider cannot achieve an adequate role for his metaphysical pathos. Wright is aware that when one is being nothing in particular, passion spent, an unsettled society presents "no form or discipline for living." The apparent mobility, the patently fortuitous order, the lack of heroic patterns, the chameleon styles, of American mass society do confuse even negative limits. Though a victimized black, a Cross Damon has apparent access to much; he can borrow money, travel first class, anonymously shift places and take on deceptive roles. He can even make an elliptical confession of his crimes to the inquisitor and go technically free, though to little purpose and satisfaction. The slightness of American community and identity make concrete his apocalyptic existential question: "Could there be a man in whose mind and consciousness all the hopes and inhibitions of the last two thousand years have died?" It receives the Nietzschean answer in the final chapter of *The Outsider*: "The real men, the last men, are coming." The sloughing off of the old consciousness and culture threatens to be soon and complete in America.

The rage of disbelief in anything, heightened by Wright's own angrily heavy sensibility, his whiskeyed and bitter black intellectual hero, and a black-and-white winter urban world, takes unfortunate political focus. It may be, though I doubt it, appropriate to show the rise of "valueless men" in the guise of power-longing and manipulative political figures, Communist functionaries. But the didactic and obsessive debating with them, by Damon-Wright, turns out to be more than a heavy artistic failure since it also contains no political resolution. The nineteen-fifties politics of leftist disillusionment leaves only a total *apolitics.* In his, and the decade's, last years Wright sometimes prophetically yearned to go beyond it by identifying with a Third World Politics of the oppressed. But in *The Outsider* the political rhetoric reveals larger intellectual and moral inadequacies. For instance, the disenchantment with all political ideology and idealism does not acknowledge the need of most men to rely on faiths in order to act. Wright quite obscures the differences in his characters' convictions, allowing no significant conflict of views between Christian and Communist and cop, or anyone else. All come out as pathetic victims "playing god." All those "suspending ethical laws" get mashed together even though criminal, Communist, cop, artist, lover and existentialist do and mean something rather different. Wright, like his protagonist, descends only into negative belief, even though he aims to bitterly expose that failure.

Why did Damon commit his crimes? Intellectually, it was because "I don't *believe* in anything." The lies, the murders, the flight, the self-destruction, are the "ludicrous protest" of an "inverted idealist." He "wanted to be free" to find out "What living meant." And he has broken through to the answer: "Nothing."

But not quite nothing. The insight of *The Man Who Lived Underground* has been in several ways extended in *The Outsider*: "Men hate themselves and it makes them hate others." Like Wright, Cross Damon could shed much of the white middle-class American way imposed, at best, on the black American, but not the hatred and self-hatred. He didn't finally get "outside." Cross Damon's last words, "I'm *innocent.* That's what made the horror . . .", simply completes the "underground man's" plaintive demand, "I'm guilty!" Neither brings justice. Guilt and innocence have lost meaning. Thus the restatement of Nietzsche's prophecy for our Age of Nihilism: "The myth men are going. . . . The real men, the last men, are coming."

In this existential anti-existentialism, Wright can see, but not present, the resolution of the failing outsider quest for meaning: "Alone a man is nothing." Wright reinforces that existential discovery with the rages responsive to the unjust and false American social order and the anxieties responsive to the heroic theology of Protestant atheism. He dramatizes the way attempts to live by isolated moral logic, such as killing men who "deserve" to be killed, ends in nothing. Neither the logics of salvational ideologies nor the rebellions against repressive circumstances can sufficiently create authentic being. Wright's half-hearted asides calling for a humanized scientism and benevolent moral idealism also seem quite inadequate for any community of genuine and humane being.

Even the crucified atheist criminal, the modern form of the saint, cannot sufficiently transcend our destructive compulsions and emerge with trust in the other and with the passion and richness of *unjustified* life. And the very texture of Wright's art cannot present a sufficient positive sense of living, of adequate scenes of tangible life. *The Outsider,* then, considerably fails, though it does achieve some wisdom. Existential awareness, we are reminded by Wright, provides an extreme exploration into truth, but no mythos to live by. Its insights may be considerable but remain alienated from a full sense of life, maintaining themselves only by endless self-purgings and demonic catharsis. To attempt to be outside reveals black truths about those inside but is no sufficient escape from them. A heroic negativity, primarily critical and diagnostic, existential explorations display the limits of rebellion, defiance and perversity. That black awareness, I have argued along with Wright, is true but won't do. It intensifies individual understanding but won't further the mutuality we need.

Such heroic nothingness does provide devastating insights into the covert nihilisms of most contemporary social, scientistic, and religious as well as political ideologies. The black writer like Wright who courageously, however falteringly, refuses to conceive himself writing just for and of blacks, and who purges his black self-hatred, reaches towards our better purposes. Black writing can only be fully serious and pertinent when it goes beyond being black, both ethnically and philosophically. Like us others, it must, even in the Age of Nihilism, come inside and find a "new man" who cannot only transform violently guilty self-hatred but achieve a community of joyous acceptance of self.

Fathers and Sons in James Baldwin's
Go Tell It on the Mountain

by Michel Fabre

Go Tell It on the Mountain deals with the religious conversion of a black adolescent who on his fourteenth birthday accepts his family's faith, in a Harlem storefront church. The protagonist, John Grimes, constantly claims our attention and presents himself as the only hero. However, on closer examination, the reader perceives that fewer than half the novel's three hundred pages are seen from John's point of view, and these pages are placed at the beginning and the end like the side panels of a triptych, the central panel of which ("The Prayers of the Saints") presents the converging histories of John's aunt, his stepfather, and his mother. These characters are so taken up with their pasts that the figure of Gabriel, flanked by Florence and Elizabeth, emerges as something of a Christ figure between two Holy Women. John appears in each section of this novel-as-retable, rather like the donor whose portrait appears in each panel of the painting. Gabriel dominates. The son is dispossessed of his own story by the fatal image of his father. Gabriel stays in the foreground so long that his presence and that of the two reunited women cast an ominous shadow on the space reserved for John in the novel. From the second line, the future of the child is defined in relation to his father: "Everyone had always said that John would be a preacher when he grew up, just like his father."

Like a folktale with its archetypal resonances, this story seems to have no other function than the fulfillment of this prophecy. It ends with an ultimate confrontation:

> He turned to face his father—he found himself smiling, but his father did not smile.

"Fathers and Sons in James Baldwin's *Go Tell It on the Mountain*" by Michel Fabre. From *Études Anglaises* 23, no. 1 (1970), pp. 47–61. Translated by Katherine P. Mack and used by permission of Michel Fabre. Translation © 1971 by Katherine P. Mack.

They looked at each other a moment. His mother stood in the doorway, in the long shadows of the hall. (303)[1]

As it must be, the mother stays in the shadows, withdrawn.

Certain verbal patterns reinforce this structural grouping in the novel. In John's story, the words designating the father are twice as numerous as those designating the mother (three times as numerous in the last section, which presents the spiritual confrontation between father and son). In "Gabriel's Prayer," words referring to the Lord are predominant, as they ought to be in the mouth of a preacher (more than two per page), but the son takes second place. The preacher defines himself less in terms of his three successive women than by the line of saints he must father in order to be sure his name will be inscribed in the Book of Heaven. In the exact center of the novel is placed the crucial sentence which expresses Gabriel's dilemma:

. . . it came to him that this living son, this headlong, living Royal, might be cursed for the sin of his mother, whose sin had never been truly repented; for that the living proof of her sin, he who knelt tonight, a very interloper among the saints, stood between her soul and God. (150)

The interloper—John—stands not only between God and the salvation of his (natural) mother but also between God and the salvation of his stepfather:

But how could there not be a difference between the son of a weak, proud woman and some careless boy, and the son that God had promised him, who would carry down the joyful line his father's name, and who would work until the day of the second coming to bring about His Father's Kingdom? (151)

This is the question which the novel continually exerts itself to answer. For Gabriel, the desire for the return of his prodigal son is matched by the fear that "the son of the bondwoman" will take his place. For the relationship of paternity is self-multiplying; it explodes like a mirror whose fragments reflect all possible combinations, their specious symmetry driving on the plot. The quasi-Faulknerian unveiling of the family situation reveals an unsuspected complexity: nothing in John's account tells us that Gabriel is not his father or justifies the latter's scornful hardness towards the boy. The explanation which first presents itself is that of an irrational preference for Roy, the younger of the boys. It would seem a matter of supersedure, with John finding himself stripped of his rights as the elder son. The

[1] All page references are to Baldwin's *Go Tell It on the Mountain* (New York: Grosset & Dunlap, Universal Library edition, 1952).

mother, however, loves her two sons equally. She favors John for a time (she is the only one not to forget his birthday) to compensate for Gabriel's injustice, but she quickly turns to Roy when he is hurt. John looks into himself in vain for the unknown fault which causes him to be rejected. He finds a partial explanation in his own failings: his Oedipus complex, his desire to leave the ghetto, his intelligence, which sets him apart, his resentment towards his father. This psychological explanation for John's rejection gives way only before the historical one set forth in "Gabriel's Prayer." There is a double secret: Roy is truly the son of Gabriel and Elizabeth, but John is the natural son of Elizabeth and Richard, who died before he was able to marry her. John is ignorant of this but Gabriel cannot forget it. This illegitimacy has a symmetrical counterpart: during a first marriage with Deborah, who was barren, Gabriel himself had a bastard son, Royal, by Esther. Royal has been killed in a fight and Roy is for his father the legitimate replacement. Their names—chosen by Gabriel to mark the line of kings he hopes to father—unite them less than the aggressive and rebellious temperament inherited from their father, and less still than their violent fates: the knife which cut Royal's throat has just disfigured Roy.

Gabriel's fault is not only unknown to John but to Elizabeth, and Gabriel is a pharisee who can look down on her, the former sinner, and scorn her illegitimate fruit because his own sin, though very similar, remains unsuspected. The preacher's sister, Florence, could reveal his fault because she alone has irrefutable proof in the form of a compromising letter. She appears as John's fairy godmother: she has already protected him, as has Elizabeth, from the flames of Gabriel's wrath, and the weapon which she holds could make Gabriel vulnerable. Here the plot closely resembles an archetypal situation in folktale: an unknown person is about to dethrone a tyrant with the help of a woman who gives him a talisman and also, we will see, with the help of a companion of his own age. But this archetypal situation is not exploited because Baldwin himself prefers a symbolism more appropriate to the religious context of the novel, the symbolism of an Old Testament struggle for succession.

The family relationships are further complicated by the inability of fathers and sons (as of husbands and wives) to communicate. Reciprocal love is prevented, it seems, as much by a psychological inevitability—holiness standing opposed to happiness—as by a divine ordonnance—the saint being in reality a sinner. To mortify his flesh, Gabriel marries Deborah, who has been despoiled by being raped by a gang of whites, of her gracious and fertile femininity. This woman, who loves him and whom he does not love, cannot give him a legitimate heir. Esther, the woman whom he desires and who loves him totally, gives him a son even though he does not want to marry her. From this situation proceeds a drama of impossible recognitions: Gabriel cannot legitimize the child whom he loves tenderly and the child can never know that Gabriel is his father. There is an irony of fate or natural justice: when the preacher passes by, Royal makes a classic and obscene joke about his sexual prowess without knowing that he himself is the living proof of that prowess. And the only time that Gabriel can (metaphorically) call Royal his son is the moment when they are united through the danger of castration by white men.

After the deaths of Royal and Deborah, Gabriel welcomes as a sign from the Lord the meeting Florence arranges with Elizabeth and her son. He believes they are sent to him so that he can atone for his own sin by marrying a repentant sinner. The drama then might have ended, had not the preacher's pride and bad faith prevented him from treating John as his own son. In Gabriel's eyes, the child represents the sin of Elizabeth and also a means of projecting and rejecting his own guilt. Ready to love, John encounters hatred which forces him to hate in return in order to survive. He becomes the anti-son ("the Devil's son") and Gabriel becomes the anti-father. Though the birth of Roy finally gives the preacher a legitimate heir, Roy later rejects his heritage. The true son calls his father a bastard, a term which, hypocritically, Gabriel hated to hear Esther call Royal but which he applies willingly enough himself to John. And while Roy, the prodigal son, withdraws from the bosom of the family, the adopted son tries to enter in and only succeeds insofar as he himself resembles the returning prodigal son.

Moreover, while Esther's existence remains under a cloud for Elizabeth, Richard remains in half-shadow for Gabriel. And for John, who is his true son, Richard does not exist at all. He is only defined for the reader as the mythical father endowed with all those qualities which would contrast with Gabriel: he was handsome, intelligent, generous, loved life, wanted to learn and to improve himself. Some of these qualities are inherited by John, as well perhaps as a certain weakness of character, joined to a sense of his own dignity, like that which led Richard to cut his wrists after being put in prison.

The novel plays, then, with a whole constellation of fathers—father unknown and mythical, real and legitimate, putative father, possible father, adulterous husband and father of a bastard—which corresponds to a whole constellation of sons—sons natural, born of adultery, adopted, prodigal, etc. These are the different roles adopted by Richard, Gabriel, John, Roy, and Royal in a tragic game of hide and seek. The novel draws its plot from this tragi-comedy of errors. If the author had wanted to use the *deus ex machina* of classical theater, he would have needed only to reveal the mistake in order to resolve the mystery. Curiously, however, only the reader knows the full truth in *Go Tell It on the Mountain*. John learns nothing: the existence of his real father remains as hidden from him as that of Gabriel's bastard son. Florence, in a final act of cruelty towards the brother she has always hated because he took the first place in their mother's heart, threatens to reveal all:

> "[I'll] make Elizabeth to know," she said, "that she ain't the only sinner . . . in your holy house. And little Johnny, there—he'll know he ain't the only bastard." (293)

The discovery by John that he is a bastard would be in effect a glorious revelation, because the shame of his illegitimacy would fade before the glory of having such a perfect being as Richard for a father, and would disappear entirely if the existence of the first Royal were revealed. But Florence does not speak. This logical and "mechanical" resolution to the drama could only take place in a problematical "fifth act."

If mutual recognition and reconciliation are not brought about by an artificial intervention on Florence's part, it would seem to be because Baldwin wants to bring them about by divine intervention. Just so, at the moment of his conversion, when the saints are praying before the altar, John comes to know his identity and heritage, and these take root in the discovery and acceptance of his own sin. Religion appears as a means of knowing that self which is guilty of sins against purity, charity, racial and human solidarity.

John would like to escape the prophecy: "He would not be like his father, or his father's fathers. He would have another life." (15) An ambiguous and multiple refusal! He refuses to become either a preacher or a "Great Leader of His People." He chooses for a time material success—to the well-fed, well-dressed, go to the movies—what amounts to a rejection of his racial as well as his religious heritage. The trip to midtown Manhattan offers this symbolic significance: from the top of the hill in Central Park, John dominates the city as Rastignac did Paris. He makes watching a movie not an act of social participation but a gesture of defiance against morality and religion because he identifies with the white heroine, a rebel who "thumbs her nose at the world."

In his intelligence John has discovered an almost magic power, a road to salvation which others cannot follow. What does he hope to gain by it? Only love: ". . . perhaps, with this power he might one day win that love which he so longed for." (17) But interior force and the power to make oneself loved are inseparable from the capacity to resist and to hate. The boy cherishes both powers, hugging them close, unable to separate them from the "wickedness" which his father tries to beat out of him. He admits to seeking for hate as much as for love. He lives for the day when he can curse his father on his deathbed. His survival as an individual requires this hate, but it keeps him from being truly converted and makes him resist his father's place in the church hierarchy:

> His father was God's minister, the ambassador of the King of Heaven, and John could not bow before the throne of grace without first kneeling to his father. On his refusal to do this had his life depended, and John's secret heart had flourished in its wickedness until the day his sin first overtook him. (17–18)

The father is protected by his sacred function, and he does not hesitate to use religion as an instrument of power. Religion prohibits the son from being himself unless he can find a way either to remove that prohibition or to turn it into a shield. But, says Baldwin, his sin catches John out every time. This sin is his discovery of his sexuality, which he feels to be a deep abyss. Woman is everywhere present: Ella Mae before the altar, with her breasts and her thighs under her thin robes, standing beside Elisha the handsome youth; the stain on the ceiling which transforms itself into a woman's shape; the couple John saw making love leaning against a wall; the temptations of the street. . . . Woman is also, and first of all, his mother. When John, cleaning the kitchen, thinks, "He who is filthy, let him be filthy still," he looks at his mother at the same time, only he sees her with the face of her youthful photograph, a woman desirable and fit to be taken. The Oedipus complex is everywhere. The son is sexually jealous of his father and of that virile power which fills him with disgust. In the bathroom (the place of sin, where his secret sin and his voyeurism meet), he has, like the son of Noah, beheld "his father's hideous nakedness. It was secret, like sin, and slimy, like the serpent, and heavy, like the rod. Then he hated his father, and longed for the power to cut his father down." (267) The allusion is clear: castrate his father and seize the rod, both as scepter and sexual image. And the symbolic serpent appears again, in bronze and poised to strike, among those so very important family photographs. The voyeurism which makes John "diabolic" is also his revenge, for with it he can reveal his father's sin:

> "I know what you do in the dark, black man, when you think the Devil's son's asleep. I heard you, spitting and groaning and choking—and I *seen* you, riding up and down, and going in and out. . . . I don't care about your long white robe. I seen you under the robe, I seen you!" (269)

His father's puritanism makes John's normal instincts appear to him as proof of his own damnation. Submerged in guilt, John dreams of his punishment, the terror of castration: "His father raised his hand. The knife came down." (270) The knife thus unites Gabriel's three sons as possible victims in an echo of Abraham's sacrifice. But John is only dreaming: he is not a true son of Gabriel and the knife will not really harm him. While in a mystical trance at the foot of the

altar, he projects his fantasies and accepts his guilt. Such is the role
of religion: to aid men to make their terrors objective and thus more
distant. And religion gives the adolescent the means of disqualifying
his father as superior before taking his place: he becomes the son of
God and is able to count on God as an ally. This implies a renaissance,
a literal rebirth:

> . . . sown in dishonor, he would be raised in honor, he would have been
> born again.[2]
>
> Then he would no longer be the son of his father, but the son of his
> Heavenly Father, the King. Then he need no longer fear his father, for
> he could take, as it were, their quarrel over his father's head to Heaven—
> to the father who loved him. . . . Then he and his father would be
> equals. . . . His father could not cast him out, whom God had gathered
> in. (194)

John thus enlists God on his side, apparently to rejoin his father
in a shared affection, but really to supplant him. He dreams of hating
until the end of time this "everlasting father" who must die to be
removed from his path. As the Lord's anointed he can vanquish Gabriel
on the same ground where Gabriel had once supplanted the Fathers
of the Church: as the better preacher, John will be a saint, one of the
elect, sacrosanct.

Moreover, John enlists the aid of an intercessor in order to speak
to God while bypassing the church hierarchy in which his father figures as one of his immediate superiors. This intercessor is Elisha, the
prophet, the older brother, the young priest, but also the temptingly
attractive youth, the too-beautiful guardian angel. When Gabriel
raises his hand against the adolescent who has presumptuously seen
into the depths of his soul, Elisha finds himself literally and physically
interposed between them. Elisha is John's ideal—handsome, robust,
angelic. Like Jacob with the angel, John wrestles with Elisha in the
empty chapel. His strength is almost equal to Elisha's, and they become
locked in an embrace in which tenderness is mixed with homosexuality.
Elisha is a character as ambiguous as love between men always is, and
he reappears in different guises throughout Baldwin's work. In "The
Outing," he becomes a father substitute: John turns to David as to
a big brother after his father has humiliated him in public, and the
scene is surrounded by a nimbus of copper-colored sun, of golden joy,
and a quasi-divine presence. In *Go Tell It on the Mountain*, Elisha
supports John in his ecstasy; like Jesus he commands "Arise, and
walk!"; like the Creator in the frescoes of the Sistine Chapel, he holds
out his hand to man:

---

[2] The references to dishonor and to John's illegitimacy are numerous, even in
his own part of the narrative, but always in ambiguous terms. He does not know
he is illegitimate. If he did his anguish would vanish, for he could then hate his
stepfather and dream of his (true) father.

"Rise up, Johnny," said Elisha, again. "Are you saved, boy?" . . .
Elisha stretched out his hand, and John took the hand, and stood—so
suddenly, and so strangely, and with such wonder!—once more on his
feet. (280)

Elisha attests to John's salvation and invulnerability; he sponsors
his rebirth in a scene that could not be more symbolic:

"He come through," cried Elisha, "didn't he, Deacon Grimes? The Lord
done laid him out, and turned him around and wrote his *new* name
down in glory. Bless our God!"
    And he kissed John on the forehead, a holy kiss. . . . The sun . . .
fell over Elisha like a golden robe, and struck John's forehead, where
Elisha had kissed him, like a seal ineffaceable forever. (302)

Invited by Elisha to recognize that John belongs henceforth to the
elect, Gabriel refuses. He does not reply, he does not smile on Johnny,
he gives no sign of admitting his defeat. However, there *is* a defeat.
The equality of the saints does not imply their mutual recognition,
and John feels superior because he has already potentially replaced
the deacon in his ecclesiastical functions. The young preacher uses
religion to affirm his own identity as the old one had to repudiate his
sin, and thus by religion John murders his father in a manner that
is as effective as it is symbolic. The Church is the holy place where
the adolescent can escape the world, and also the tabernacle where
he can escape his father. It is the battleground, the ring where he can
triumph over him.[3] As one might expect from John's intense resentment, his reunion with Gabriel is false and no relation of equality is
established between them. The conversion takes place for other ends
than the service of the Lord; it becomes a means to escape the ghetto
and his father, what Baldwin calls "a gimmick" in *The Fire Next
Time*. It is therefore not surprising that John's liberation is illusory.
A more efficacious illusion is added to John's childish dreams, those
dreams of grandeur where he was no longer the ugly duckling. Like
the author, we sympathize with the protagonist, but we suffer to see
his inability to free himself confirmed. His identity remains that of a
child. The Father Almighty does not cause a sentimental change of
heart in his father, and, on a psychological as well as on a dramatic
level, the ending is referred to as a "fifth act."

One of the causes of this impossible ending can perhaps be found
in the multiplicity of metaphoric functions which the author gives to

---

[3] Space symbolism occurs throughout the novel: Broadway and the strait gate of
ecstasy; the threshing-floor, the circumscribed space where the wheat is separated
from the chaff; the fall into the abyss and flight on the wings of an eagle. The
closed square, ring, pulpit, threshing-floor are *par excellence* the place of trial and
of triumph. In "Sonny's Blues," the same symbolism occurs as the music-hall represents the holy tabernacle.

John's story. His destiny is presented as a quest for identity and the whole conversion episode as an initiation. The story is reminiscent of the Oedipus myth of the lost father and the death of the king. It incorporates a myriad of Biblical stories, and it is through the mediation of the Bible that it becomes a metaphor for race relations in general in the United States, thus denying for the immediate future a happy outcome in keeping with the title of the novel.

Explicit allusions tie John's condition to that of the black American (in a linking more artificial than organic). But the parallel between Gabriel's behavior and that of white America does not fail to shed light on the good conscience (another name for "bad faith") of a racist, although, as we will see, it is impossible to push this metaphor to its logical limits within the framework of the novel, a fact that constitutes one of its weaknesses.

John's triumph is Gabriel's defeat, and Gabriel sees his fears realized: "Only the son of the bondwoman stood where the rightful heir should stand." (128) John represents the "son of the bondwoman," and the allusion recalls the scene in Genesis where Sarah demands that Abraham banish the son of Hagar the Egyptian. Certain of Baldwin's characters can be compared with the Biblical ones: Gabriel-Abraham, Roy-Isaac, Elizabeth-Hagar, and finally John-Ishmael. Ishmael the turn-coat, the Wandering Jew, the accursed. On other pages, Gabriel evokes an image of king David, with Roy his son an Absalom hung from a tree like a lynched Negro. But, above all, Gabriel is Noah, the father drunk and naked on whom Ham threw, instead of the mantel of modesty, the mocking stare of rebellion. John-Ham-Ishmael thus becomes the black son of a white father. And the author says explicitly: "he . . . looked, as the accursed son of Noah had looked, on his father's hideous nakedness," and, six lines later:

> . . . [was] his deadly sin, having looked on his father's nakedness and mocked and cursed him in his heart? Ah, that son of Noah's had been cursed, down to the present groaning generation: *a servant of servants shall he be unto his brethren.* (267)

And he explains almost laboriously:

> All niggers had been cursed, the ironic voice reminded him, all niggers had come from this most undutiful of Noah's sons. . . . Could a curse come down so many ages? (267–268)

The ironic voice of his critical sense frees John from a curse on him as an individual (deserved because he has seen his father's nakedness) to lay upon him the collective curse of his whole race. But Baldwin at the same time explodes this religious pseudo-justification of slavery by stressing the reality of time: can a fatal curse come down through all the ages? Does John live in time or in a moment of time? in the duration or in an instant? And is the instant not eternal, out of time, like an ecstasy? Thus, at the very moment when the metaphoric equation of Gabriel=white man/John=black man is put, it is challenged in terms of causality and functions only on the level of psychological exploration.

The white man does not appear as a father in the stories of each protagonist. Rather, white men are remote executioners whose blind brutality corners Richard and drives him to suicide; whose domineering sexualism leaves Deborah devastated by the side of the road; whose imposing power makes the misery of the ghetto all the more somber. The white man does not create, but when he procreates, he rejects the fruit of his sin. The relationship of adulterous father-natural son, Gabriel-John, is metaphorically true. Moreover, the story of their relationship (since the days of slavery, days which the novel makes a point of briefly recollecting) turns the black American into the natural son of the white American, a son disowned by his father. This is precisely the point at which Gabriel's behavior works best as a symbol. As the White Man, he cannot squarely face the evil in himself. Secret father of a bastard child, he hides his guilt so as not to tarnish his image as the Lord's chosen propagator of the race of the elect. To preserve his good opinion of himself, he holds his guilt at a distance, repudiating it by attributing it to others. By his bad faith, Gabriel casts a pall over the lives of those close to him: he refuses to pardon Elizabeth's "sin," he offers John in expiation for his own sins, a sacrifice which costs him nothing. As well as the role of victim—the ugly duckling, the Cinderella of the house—the child must play the role of scapegoat (the very lamb who replaced Isaac at the last moment under the knife). But John is not guilty. Though a bastard, he is not Gabriel's natural son and the correspondence does not work point for point. It only holds good in the mind of the reader (interpreting the novel as a parable, a "fable") insofar as it symbolizes the bad faith of the white man who protects himself from the sin which gnaws at his soul by transforming the black man into the "Devil's son," into an incarnation of evil, branded by his color, blighted by the whole symbolism of the Bible.

The contrast of black and white, shadows and light, underlies the entire novel. We immediately think of the immaculate robes of the newly baptized, and Gabriel's sermon on the theme: "I am a man with unclean lips," or John's meditation: "He who is filthy, let him be filthy still." We recall the choice of a name for Grimes, and the Sisyphus figure of the child who works at the everlasting dirt in the carpet. A prisoner of his shame, the black child seeks the causes of his rejection just as John seeks the reasons for his ugliness. Blackness and ugliness become interchangeable in the equation made by white religion, since Scriptural symbolism seems to validate racial prejudice.

Religion, the pretext of the white man, also becomes a "gimmick" for the black, and Robert Bone describes this in a happy phrase: "spiritual bleaching cream." [4] Thus the black American calls on the Father Almighty to surround him with the golden rays of His Glory. He uses religion as a tactic for survival. But if, for a brief moment, the hero's situation may recall that of the torn and tragic mulatto so dear to novels of the nineteenth century, of the bastard who could be redeemed by a single word from his Caucasian father, the existential drama of John's situation expands rapidly into a parable of the history of the black people in the United States: it chronicles the means of survival which the black American drew from Christianity —Judgment Day, the last who will be first, the son of the bond-woman who will stand between God and his father because the legitimate heir of the king has turned against him and because his legitimate spouse has remained barren. The father may not want to recognize his bastard, but God will recognize his own. The belief which sustains John after he accepts his heritage (Gabriel's negative example forbids him any real self-rejection) is born of the same faith which has sustained colored pastors and preachers since the days of slavery. It is the dream of a revenge by holy mandate, of a revenge without that violence condemned by religion. The white man thinks himself the chosen race, but he belongs to the race of the pharaohs, not to the race of the Lord's elect, as the Bible points out to the black man who in turn identifies himself with the Jews of Exodus. The story of Jacob and the mythology of the Black Muslims reflects the same conviction of belonging to the chosen race.

Let us follow the implications of this racial metaphor to a conclusion. Does the black man belong, as he believes, to the chosen people? Yes, says Baldwin, but only to the degree that he does not yield to the temptation to foist onto others those instincts in himself which he fears, to the exact degree that he is not a Gabriel. This part of his humanity, of his blackness and his sin, which John assumes in order to be saved—is it not exactly this "humanity" which the novelist demands that the Afro-American writer accept in his essay, "Everybody's Protest Novel"?

> "Bigger's tragedy," writes Baldwin of the hero of *Native Son*, "is not that he is cold or black or hungry, not even that he is American and black, but that he has accepted a theology that denies him life, that he admits the possibility of his being sub-human and feels constrained, therefore, to battle for his humanity according to those brutal criteria bequeathed him at his birth."

Up to this point, Baldwin seems to suggest that the black man ought to reject the definition imposed on him by the white man as

---

[4] *The Negro Novel in America* (New Haven: Yale University Press, 1962), p. 223.

John refuses that imposed on him by Gabriel. But Baldwin goes further:

> our humanity is our burden, our life, we need not battle for it; we need only do what is infinitely more difficult, that is, accept it.[5]

Such a "humanity" can only arise as the black man's definition of himself, and implies acceptance of his negative aspects. The black takes on himself all those defects which the white man tries to load onto him in making him his scapegoat. He becomes a sort of redeeming Christ in a view which links ritual lynching with holy communion. The black man cannot save himself without also saving the white man, Baldwin repeats in *The Fire Next Time*. However, this is precisely the problem: John cannot save himself without saving Gabriel. Hence, at the end of the novel, he does not really save himself in spite of that beautiful blaze of mysticism which restores his confidence. Either (and I think this to be the case), religion is a "gimmick" and cannot save us spiritually, or it is not a gimmick and the efficacy of its grace redeems the world. As we have no proof of Gabriel's salvation, John's salvation remains problematical. *Go Tell It on the Mountain* appears to me to fail on precisely this point, not only in terms of psychological motivation, but also because the racial metaphor cannot function completely, and especially because the structure of the novel suffers from the very postulate which gives it its "suspense" and interest. John can only take up the burden of Gabriel's sins if he knows about them, and he never learns what the reader knows—the past of his ancestors, his true lineage, his stepfather's secret. The history of his race, implicit in him as protagonist, is never made substantial. The converging rays of the destinies of his father, his mother, and his aunt meld in a flash of brilliance at the ideal meeting point: the child. But the child is the filament which transmits the light and not the eye which beholds it. The transubstantiation does not come about, nor the communion of saints, and John remains prisoner of the definition imposed on him by Gabriel; he does not acquire his own adult identity in a true mystical experience. Thus the racial conflict cannot be resolved metaphorically within the limits of the story. The illumination of the soul is only a spark without a future, a spasm of sensibility in search of love. True knowledge is absent, rebirth impossible.

While psychological explanations are problematical, because they are partial, I would like to try to throw more light on this limitation in the effectiveness of the racial metaphor which becomes, in effect, a limitation of the novel. I mean to consider a type of mental block which I sense hinders the novelist. One cannot hope to explain every-

[5] "Everybody's Protest Novel," *Partisan Review*, 15 (June 1949), 585.

thing, but only to explore a tendency in Baldwin's work apparently deep enough to have stemmed from a youthful psychological trauma. I am convinced that the thin line which separates fiction from autobiography in *Go Tell It on the Mountain* allows us to take this risk.

The novel is a barely fictionalized account of James Baldwin's own life. The childhood is the same: the preacher David Baldwin marries Emma Berdis Jones three years after James is born, but this stepfather prefers the younger boy, Sam, his son by a first marriage, although his affection is not reciprocated. He despises James, on whom falls the responsibility for the care of the children born after him. His mother's right arm, James is also the ugly duckling of the story, "frog-eyes" with the bulging eyes and too-wide mouth which were the sport of his schoolmates. He identifies himself with Topsy, the urchin of *Uncle Tom's Cabin*. He is the model student of P.S. 24 and is given tickets to the 1939 World's Fair by a white substitute teacher there. He is the little boy who dreamed of greatness on top of that hill in Central Park. He is the one who is mortifyingly arrested and searched by the police, and who feels a mixture of hatred for white cops, his stepfather, and his crude schoolmates, and an immense, unsatisfied thirst for tenderness which (just as John becomes a preacher) drives him to write not for recognition but for love.

The account of Baldwin's religious conversion is found in *The Fire Next Time*. At the age of fourteen, he was converted by an evangelist (Margaret in *The Amen Corner*, Praying Mother Elizabeth in the novel) and escaped the wages of sin by joining the Calvary Church. He experienced the heady ecstasy described in "Down at the Cross." He was "saved," at once from his father and from Lenox Avenue, by using religion as his escape hatch. As a "holy roller" preacher he made himself in three years obviously superior to his father. The relationship between John and Gabriel follows closely that between James and David until David's death in 1943.

The writing of *Go Tell It on the Mountain* represents, then, for Baldwin, an attempt to free himself. He threw himself into it in the same way that he left Harlem for Greenwich Village after the death of his stepfather. At the age of eighteen he began "Crying Holy," a first fragmentary effort, but he needed ten more years to assimilate and order his experiences. In 1946, he could read to his friends some chapters of a confession which later became "In My Father's House." At this time he met Richard Wright. He had read Wright's work, three profound, dignified, pitiless works in which the older man had defined his identity in withstanding the white world. All the respect that one can feel for a literary celebrity separated Baldwin from Wright, but the latter held out his hand: he recommended the beginner for a grant, approaching his friend Ed Aswell, administrator of the Rosenwald Foundation. Wright had not singled Baldwin out from his other protégés and saw nothing exceptional in this gesture of solidarity. But for the budding novelist, it took on a religious value—it designated him as a writer. It was the kiss of Elisha, the sign of a merciful father who consecrated him. At once Baldwin, freed from the image of his father David, constructed a new myth, projecting onto Wright an image of the spiritual and fraternal father who would recognize his worth. The novel-in-progress (it would become *Go Tell It on the Mountain*) served primarily as a means of winning Wright's acceptance. But the composition took time and the writer felt guilty:

> I was ashamed—I thought I'd done something terrible to Richard—because he—he counted on me—as I thought, y'know, to do it. And I'd failed.[6]

The son could not be satisfied unless he proved himself worthy before his father, and Baldwin as writer worthy before Wright.

For the moment, he could not progress, and it was not his fault. He found himself cast, by the predominantly white world of American criticism, editors and literary agents, into the role of a militant and combative black writer in the Wright mold. At the time this was not his calling. He wanted only to be loved and accepted. He sought to stir people's emotions, while the Wright spirit pushed him to demand respect and to come to grips with his public. One demanded tenderness, the other dignity. Their courses were different, almost opposite, and Baldwin found that others had placed Wright as a sort of obstacle to his natural bent, somewhat as his father had formerly blocked his development. "Everyone had always said that Baldwin would be a militant novelist when he grew up, just like Richard Wright," we could say, paraphrasing the first sentence of the novel. This appears to be the essential reason why in 1949 Baldwin wrote the essay "Everybody's Protest Novel," to react not only against the view expressed by *Uncle Tom's Cabin* but also against the conception of the militant writer as represented by Wright—in order to claim, in fact, his right *not* to be such a writer. He wanted to conceive of race relations as other than a fierce struggle:

> The failure of the protest novel lies in its rejection of life, the human being, the denial of his beauty, dread, power, in its insistence that it is his categorization alone which is real and which cannot be transcended.[7]

By this general declaration, Baldwin claimed first of all the freedom to write as he felt. However, what went on in his soul would

---

[6] Fern Marja Eckman, *The Furious Passage of James Baldwin* (New York, 1967), pp. 105–6.

[7] "Everybody's Protest Novel," p. 585.

remain incomprehensible to Wright, who did not understand that, to succeed, Baldwin needed his "paternity," and that the critical essays of the confused young man aimed, in effect, to force Wright to extend his friendship. Wright published in *Zero* an essay in which he called down Baldwin and expressed astonishment over his attack. He kept his distance and refused a deeper friendship. In the meantime, apparently freed by this self-definition, Baldwin had reoriented his style, his writing, his art. He was now capable of ending his novel in three months. His friend Lucien Happersberger offered him the family chalet at Loches-les-Bains near Lausanne, and on February 26, 1952, Baldwin literally descended from the mountain to mail off his manuscript of *Go Tell It on the Mountain*.

The later relationship between Wright and Baldwin is minor literary history, but is important to know if we are to understand what is latent in Baldwin's behavior. He was pursuing the destruction of his father-idol and, as one might expect, his final victory brought him only unhappiness. A friendship which might have flourished remained for Baldwin a love deceived, and makes us think, once more, of John:

> Oh, that his father would *die!*—and the road before John be open, as it must be open for others. Yet in the very grave he would hate him; his father would but have changed conditions, he would be John's father still. (195)

It is tempting to see, woven into the fabric of the novel, the thread of this simultaneously ambiguous and unstable relationship which was established between the two writers in 1952, this story of an aborted relationship. Deeply exasperated by this humble and self-effacing quest for his affection, Wright refused the friendship. Baldwin interpreted the refusal as pride or jealousy of his literary success. Soon his articles on the meetings on the Franco-American Fellowship in 1951 and on le Premier Congrès des Ecrivains et Artistes Noirs at the Sorbonne in September, 1956, were presenting Wright as a man who thought himself superior. Because he suffered from not being recognized by Wright while others, like Chester Himes, were Wright's friends in exile, Baldwin went so far as partially to invent the account of a happy evening when Wright, Himes, and he met in a Parisian café, on a footing of equality and without friction. We ought to read here the projection of a dream of reconciliation rather than the description of a harmony which never existed. Then, the feeling turned sour, and Baldwin seems to have devoted himself to maneuvers designed to knock the figure of Wright—grown too large—off the pedestal erected by American criticism. It was not, I think, careerism which compelled Baldwin to seek assignments for Mr. Luce's magazines. It was rather a sort of psychological fatality, comparable to the life struggle he had had with his stepfather, a deep need to supplant the spiritual father whom he had chosen and who had rejected him. A strange situation, because it was Baldwin himself who had, without his consent, established Wright in this role! When the older man died in November, 1960, Baldwin the novelist at last was free to be himself. Yet, as he matured, Baldwin had less need to feel accepted and his writing became more militant, more biting, in a word more like the protest literature which he had criticized in 1950.

Certainly his work never has lost its sentimental overtones, its simultaneously religious and homosexual ambiance (the homosexual is, in another order the priest, such as Elisha represents), but it became more shaped to the spiritual state of the blacks for whom Baldwin spoke during the big civil rights campaigns. In 1960, then, he found no more difficulty in walking in Wright's shoes as a protest writer than he had had walking in his father's shoes as a preacher. His political evolution coincides with his deep psychological evolution, the one throwing light on the other. He became a militant writer for civil rights in the self-chosen role of spiritual father.

One can deplore the initial misunderstanding which separated the two novelists. Baldwin would certainly have been content with a friendship in which he did not play the dominant role. His ambition was less strong than his desire to be accepted by Wright. One can also deplore the pettiness which, in "Alas, Poor Richard" compelled Baldwin to flog a dead horse. But this last reaction should be understood, it seems to me, as a gesture of despair and powerlessness. Wright, now dead, became the father who would never recognize the man who wanted to be his son. Having found it necessary to attack Wright when alive because he stood in the way of the younger writer's development, Baldwin seems to have wanted to attack Wright even after his death to efface the eternal regret for a friendship which might have been.[8] This attitude, recalled in the controversy between Irving Howe and Ralph Ellison about black protest literature,[9] proceeds in Baldwin's case less from a theoretical conviction than from an emotional reaction. It is not the expression of a man who fights for his ideas, but the sentimental response, at times almost pathological, of a wounded soul.

After *Go Tell It on the Mountain,* Baldwin has seemed determined to remain an Ishmael in search of a father, or, at least, of a brother. Such is the central and traumatic reaction which the behavior of the writer betrays and repeats and which crops up in all his work, more as

[8] Baldwin, moreover, admits this candidly in "The Exile," from *Nobody Knows My Name* (New York, 1961).

[9] See Irving Howe, "Black Boys and Native Sons," *Dissent*, 10 (Fall 1963), pp. 353–68, and Ralph Ellison, "The World and the Jug," *Shadow and Act* (New York, 1964).

therapy than as a conscious literary strategy. Without wanting to reduce man to a single relationship, and without trying to use as support a novel which explores all aspects of religion, sexuality, and interracial relations, it does seem to me impossible not to consider the father-son relationship as of prime importance. At this level, *Go Tell It on the Mountain* risks becoming not another literary production but another "gimmick," a tactic of survival just like religion, a system for projecting the fantasies which have haunted the "bastard" son since infancy. From this proceeds its rich autobiographical resonances, and perhaps its limitations. But the greatness of the work and its incontestable literary value proceed perhaps from the fact that this drama of the quest for a father is not limited to a history of Baldwin's personal trauma. It lends itself admirably to a metaphoric expansion because it calls naturally on one of the fundamental archetypes of human history.

The African Personality in the African Novel

by Robert W. July

During the past few years much has been said, both inside and outside Africa, about *négritude* and the African personality. The discussion has been carried on in a variety of ways—by anthropologists and sociologists concerned with the structure of a changing African society, by African statesmen intent on rallying their people behind the new independence movements, by journalists and political commentators, and by artists and writers in Africa seeking new means of expression to match a new social order. Though the artistic and literary world has been increasingly active in pursuing the debate— witness the voluminous proceedings of the two congresses of African artists and writers sponsored by *Présence Africaine* in 1956 and 1959 —very little attention has thus far been given to the evidence of an African personality as presented through literary and artistic works. Yet these offer a great deal, not only in the form of sociological or political reporting, but in the perceptive insights which art can sometimes provide where more analytical methods fail.

To illustrate the richness of this source of information, let us examine four novels which have appeared in Africa within the recent past, and which are concerned with exploring the quality of the contemporary African mind and how it operates.[1] Each work presents a major character and a number of lesser figures whose lives are made by the world they live in, and whom we can see as authentic modern Africans, presenting the rich detail of internal mental stress, external physical action, and environmental force whose tensions balance to form these particular African personalities. Two of these novels come from Nigeria—*Jagua Nana* by Cyprian Ekwensi, and *Blade Among the Boys* by Onuora Nzekwu. The third, more strictly a long short

"The African Personality in the African Novel" by Robert July. From *Introduction to African Literature: An Anthology of Critical Writings from "Black Orpheus"*, ed. Ulli Beier (Evanston, Ill.: Northwestern University Press; London: Longmans, Green & Co., Ltd., 1967), pp. 218–33. Reprinted by permission of the publishers.

[1] *A Walk in the Night,* by Alex La Guma, Ibadan, Mbari, 1962; *Jagua Nana,* by Cyprian Ekwensi, London, Hutchinson, 1961; *Blade Among the Boys,* by Onuora Nzekwu, London, Hutchinson, 1962; *L'Aventure Ambiguë,* by Cheikh Amidou Kane, Paris, Julliard, 1961.

story, is *A Walk in the Night* by the South African writer, Alex La Guma. The fourth, *L'Aventure Ambiguë*, is by the Senegalese writer and public servant, Cheikh Amidou Kane. What kind of person emerges?

A Walk in the Night presents a few hours of one day in an African district of Capetown. A young African, Michael Adonis, has just lost his job because he was "cheeky" to his white foreman. He roams the neighbourhood, meeting acquaintances with whom he bitterly discusses his plight. He soon gets drunk on cheap wine, returns to his lodging where he unpremeditatedly and senselessly kills a neighbour, an old Irishman dying of alcoholism. By chance Adonis escapes detection and all suspicion falls on Willieboy, a footloose young drifter, unemployed and with a record of petty crime. Willieboy is hunted down and killed in the street by the police. Michael at the same moment is to embark on a criminal career by participating in a robbery.

These are the bare bones of a story on which is built a picture of such vividness and verisimilitude that one can almost taste and smell the air, the streets, the buildings against which the characters move in sure and full three-dimensional reality. The world of these Africans is an urban slum—narrow garbage-filled streets, grimy tenements with vestibules smelling of urine, dark stairs leading to narrow corridors and eventually to cheerless rooms where rats and roaches compete with the human inhabitants for possession. They eat their meals in greasy cafés that smell of rancid oil, of sweat, of stale smoke. They seek their recreation gambling in clandestine pool halls which exist only through police corruption, and they find some escape from their sordid meaningless lives in the local pub where cheap wine offers a momentary false courage against the forces which are grinding them down to hopeless dreary extinction. Bit by bit the author adds to the picture. Here a shabby store window containing "rows of guitars, banjoes, mandolins, the displayed gramophone parts, guitar picks, strings, electric irons, plugs, jews'-harps, adaptors, celluloid dolls all the way from Japan, and the pictures of angels and Christ with a crown of thorns and drops of blood like lipstick marks on his pink forehead." Down the street the entrance to a tenement where a row of dustbins "exhaled the smell of rotten fruit, stale food, stagnant water and general decay," while "a cat, the colour of dishwater," tried to paw "the remains of a fishhead from one of the bins." Inside "the staircase was worn and blackened, the old oak banister loose and scarred. Naked bulbs wherever the light sockets were in working order cast a pallid glare over parts of the interior, lighting up the big patches of damp and mildew, and the maps of denuded sections on the walls. . . . From each landing a dim corridor lined with doors tunnelled towards a latrine that stood like a sentry box at its end, the floor in front of it soggy with spilled water," while in the air was the smell of "ancient cooking, urine, damp-rot and stale tobacco."

And what of the people living in this slum? There are the "derelicts, bums, domestic workers, in-town-from-the-country folk, working people, taxi-drivers, and the rest of the mould that accumulated on the fringe of the underworld: loiterers, prostitutes, *fah-fee* numbers runners, petty gangsters, drab and frayed-looking thugs," the gangsters at once identifiable by their "lightweight tropical suits with pegged trousers and gaudy neckties, yellowish, depraved faces and thick hair shiny with brilliantine." Despite the plethora of apparently exotic types, it is the ordinary people who form the majority of this population—"the worn, brutalised, wasted, slum-scratched faces of the poor," hardworking, ignorant, little understanding their losing fight for existence against forces they cannot control. Typical is the stevedore who "worked like hell in the docks" all day only to come home to his dingy, dirty, crowded room occupied by himself, his wife, and their five children:

> He wore a singlet and a pair of old corduroys shiny with wear, and there was coal dust in the grooves where the furry cotton had not been worn away. He had an air of harassment about him, of too hard work and unpaid bills and sour babies. . . . His wife had a few minutes earlier announced that she was once more pregnant and he was trying to decide whether it was good news or bad.

The drabness and hopelessness of such lives drove many to seek romantic fulfilment in criminal unsettled lives which, if they inevitably ended in tragedy and futility, at least gave a momentary illusion of success and a small measure of personal distinction. Thus we have the lookout for a bawdy house, "an old decrepit ghost of a man . . . [who] nursed a sort of pride in his position . . . which raised him a dubious degree out of the morass into which the dependent poor had been trodden."

Thus too, Willieboy, who is perhaps the author's major protagonist:

> Willieboy was young and dark and wore his kinky hair brushed into a point above his forehead. He wore a . . . crucifix around his neck, more as a flamboyant decoration than as an act of religious devotion. He had . . . an air of nonchalance, like the outward visible sign of his distorted pride in the terms he had served in a reformatory and once in prison for assault. . . . He was also aware of his inferiority. All his youthful life he had cherished dreams of becoming a big shot. He had seen others rise to some sort of power in the confined underworld of this district and found himself left behind. . . . He had affected a slouch, wore gaudy shirts and peg-bottomed trousers, brushed his hair into a flamboyant peak. He had been thinking of piercing one ear and decorating it with a gold ring. But even with these things he continued to

remain something less than nondescript, part of the blurred face of the crowd, inconspicuous as a smudge on a grimy wall.

This then is the backdrop and these the people. We can see how their world acted upon them and what their reaction was. But how self-conscious are they, how aware of their predicament? What motivation, if any, stirs them to action? There appears to be very little—a narrow range from total unawareness to adolescent dreams. At one extreme is the unselfconscious amorality of the gangsters, implicit in their actions and, of course, never articulated. The middle ground is occupied by the ordinary citizen—decent, hard working, vaguely aware that his life lacks something but unable to understand what it is and how to go about getting it. The younger people, hopelessly unable as they are to deal with their lives and encumbered with values which only a lunatic might find of service, at least do have some conscious standards and the warped courage to live by them. Michael Adonis, freshly out of a job, full of bitter self-pity, gets drunk, sees himself as the romantic hero of the escapist Westerns which are his constant emotional diet—"Okay, trouble-shooter. You're a mighty tough *hombre*. Fastest man in Tucson"—kills a man. With difficulty he overcomes an urge to confess, to discuss all the details, an urge born not of remorse or a sense of wrong, but from a desire to achieve status. In the end he sinks into a life of crime. Willieboy lives by similar values and if they lead him to a violent end it is not so much because he doubts them as because he is less well equipped to survive. Only one person in the whole cast of characters seems able to see the futility of this way of life. And he is cast in a minor role as Joe, a nondescript homeless beggar, a half-insane boy who yet has some vision of human dignity. Vainly begging Adonis to stay clear of criminal entanglements, his pitiful cry goes unheeded, "Jesus, isn't we all people?"

The scene is Capetown, South Africa, the people African, but where is the African personality? The conditions we see, the actions and motives of the characters could fit with equal authority a city slum in Europe or America: Chicago, St. Louis, New York, London. Willieboy with his hollow bravado is at once reminiscent of young Studs Lonigan, similarly undernourished physically and psychically, moving across the urban squalor and meanness of South Side Chicago with a swagger which never quite makes up for the sense of inadequacy and ultimate failure. East Harlem in New York City today contains blocks which are at once recognisable in La Guma's powerful narrative. The similarity between Harlem and Capetown, however, does not result from the fact that they are both Negro quarters, but that they are both city slums. People living in crowded tenements amidst dirt and disease, lacking the means for a normal family life with its security, its childhood pleasures and adult satisfactions, constantly brushing against the brutalised amorality of criminals, develop characteristics and attitudes of identifiable similarity. These people are authentic Africans without question, but they belong to the new Africa of the industrial city. If none of the ways of tribal Africa shows through, it may be because consciously or otherwise they have left that world far behind. Joe, the strange young drifter, puts it best when he describes how his father deserted his family, forcing his mother to sell her few things and go back to live with his grandmother in the country. "Me, I ran away when I heard they were going . . . I wasn't going to the outside. To the country. Man, that would be the same like running away. . . . My old man, he ran away. I didn't want to run, too."

Jagua Nana provides another view of the new urbanised African. The details are different: Lagos is not Capetown and the Nigerian is not to be confused with the South African, but the essential identity is unmistakable. Both display the African city with its way of life, its physical appearance and its values so different from those of the traditional village. Both tell the story of how these forces have shaped the African city dweller, making him in turn equally different from his country cousin. The plot of this novel need not detain us; it is the characters who interest us as they already exist when we first encounter them: vibrant, bawdy, optimistic, unmoral, opportunistic, living from day to day in the noisy, crowded, yeasty, lusty West African city of Lagos where the heat and the dampness never seem to deprive the Nigerian of his energy and his enthusiasm for living.

Jagua Nana might be called an amateur prostitute, not in the sense of lacking skill or eschewing remuneration, but in the sense of loving her work. Physically impressive, she found as a girl that village life was much too restrictive to one of her talents and enthusiasm and, like many others similarly affected, came to Lagos to live. There she carries on a bewildering succession of affairs, living on the favours of the men she sleeps with, guided by a code of ethics derived from the *Tropicana*, a nightclub which serves as her base of operations and source of spiritual refreshment. This is the world of the fast sports car, the tired business man, the crooked politician, the hoodlum, and packaged sex. The girls wear undersize dresses designed to make men ogle, their faces are masked with powder, pencil, and lipstick, their hair is combed straight and heavily oiled, and their feet are clad in high-heeled sandals through which can be seen the tips of lacquered nails. And Jagua is always the best of the lot. "She lowered the neckline of her sleeveless blouses and raised the heels of her shoes. She did her hair in the Jagua mop, wore ear-rings that really rang bells, as she walked with deliberately swinging hips." This is the standard for the Lagos demimonde and possibly for others as well. When Jagua is about to enter the *Tropicana* on one occasion, she is examined with approval by a woman selling cooked yams near the entrance, who

bursts out, "Heh! . . . One day ah will ride motor car and wear fine
fine cloth."

Others from this boisterous world attract our attention and hold
our interest. There is Uncle Taiwo, the indefatigable politician, who
drives an enormous Pontiac and pursues his career of misleading the
voters and misappropriating his party's funds to his destiny of death
in the streets, a twisted swollen corpse in a muddy gutter. There is
Freddie who combines infatuation for Jagua with a fondness for the
dignified westernised respectability of a British Council lecture, who
studies law in England as a means to wealth, power, and esteem, but
who also falls victim to the corruption and violence of Lagos politics.
There is Dennis, a young hoodlum, and his gang who live their violent lives briefly but with no sense of regret that they might have had
something better. There are others, anonymous but no less sharply
defined:

> The influential men of Lagos. Private business men . . . dabblers in
> party politics . . . men in their early fifties, and what they lost in youth-
> ful virility and attractiveness they made up by lavishing their money on
> women like Jagua Nana. . . . Jagua saw them now as with white collars
> off they struck a different mood from the British Council: the "expatriate"
> bank managers, the oil men and shipping agents, the brewers of beer and
> pumpers out of swamp water, the builders of Maternity Block, the heal-
> ers of the flesh. German, English, Dutch, American, Nigerian, Ghanaian,
> they were all here.

Like Jagua, most of the Africans in Lagos have come from small villages, driven to the city by boredom, ambition, or circumstance. Like
her, they occasionally return home either actually or figuratively. Jagua
may be firmly attached to city ways but she has brought with her a
heritage of beliefs and attitudes which disappear slowly. She is not
above belief in witchcraft and juju, particularly where affairs of the
heart are concerned. Neither, for that matter, is the ostensibly better-
educated Freddie. He broods over his affair with Jagua and wonders
at her powers:

> Could it really be . . . that Jagua was resorting to black magic to torture
> him? Was she a witch with black powers over his soul? Only that morn-
> ing he had been telling the pupils at the College that there was no such
> thing as black magic or witchery, only the imagination. Scientific facts,
> he held, could be demonstrated; but these extra-sensory qualities de-
> pended too much on vague circumstances and conditions.

But ultimately these are city people wedded to city ways and guided
by the values that rule the city. "Like Freddie she was an Ibo from
Eastern Nigeria, but when she spoke to him she always used pidgin
English, because living in Lagos City they did not want too many
embarrassing reminders of clan or custom. They and many others were

practically strangers in a town where all came to make fast money by faster means, and greedily to seek positions that yielded even more money." In the end Jagua goes home to her village to live, but this is the weakest part of the book and remains unconvincing. More likely, she, "like many women who came to Lagos [was] imprisoned, entangled in the city, unable to extricate herself from its clutches. The lowest and the most degraded standards of living were to her preferable to a quiet and dignified life in her own home where she would not be 'free'." And so with greed and lust comes also freedom for the individual to pattern his life as he himself may wish, not according to outdated customs and superstitions. The fact that some might use this freedom unwisely need not deter others from achieving a more meaningful emancipation.

The world of Jagua Nana is an authentic part of the African city, but it is only one part. At the same time Lagos is only one part of Nigeria. Beyond the city, for all its importance, its growth and its foreshadowing of the future, lies the country where the vast majority of the people of Africa still live under conditions far removed from what is to be found in the industrial, urban centres. If we are to understand the full dimension of the African personality, we must look into these villages where Onuora Nzekwu has set most of the scene for his novel, *Blade Among the Boys*. This is an interesting story which says much about the face of Africa. In the first place it deals with the African's deep sense of religion: a universal and timeless quality of traditional African society. Secondly, it poses the power of traditional African values and practices against Western "enlightenment," and concludes that the individual who chooses the latter and flouts the former does so at his peril.

The novel deals with the fortunes of a young Ibo, Patrick Ikenga. As a boy, Patrick is reared on a strict diet of Roman Catholic doctrine and practice and, not surprisingly, he early harbours ambitions of becoming a priest. His father dies when Patrick is only eleven years old and his mother brings him back to live in the village of his paternal uncle. The rest of the novel is concerned with the struggle between Christianity and paganism for Patrick's allegiance. Powerful psychological and material forces are brought to bear by both sides. The Church offers education—the necessary ingredient for worldly success—while standing for progressive ideas and modern thought. But belief in the traditional religious hierarchy of spirits and ancestors is deep-seated, and life in a village can be markedly uncomfortable for the non-conformist who makes light of time-honoured custom, and refuses to partake in accepted social and religious practice. Patrick displays unusual courage in finally turning his back on the village and entering a seminary to prepare for the priesthood. In the end, however, he is discovered to have committed adultery and is dismissed from the seminary.

Throughout this work the impact of modern Western ideas and standards as exemplified by the Catholic faith is blurred and softened by the virility of the traditional beliefs and customs. Patrick's father and mother are devout and active Christians. They are deeply involved in the affairs of their local parish, and they see to it that Patrick is early introduced to rigorous religious indoctrination so that by successive stages baptism is followed by first communion, regular church attendance, and service as an altar boy. Patrick's initially expressed desire to become a priest causes them no surprise or concern. But:

> had the priests gone behind the scenes they would have discovered . . . the numerous charms John Ikenga hid behind photographs hanging on the walls. . . . His was a different brand of Christianity . . . that accommodated . . . principles and practices of his tribal religion. For one thing, he never could drop the primary aim of tribal worship: to reinforce life by means of prayers, sacrifices and sympathetic magic. . . . He was certain that some envious ones were jealous . . . and were working magic on him. He . . . believed that the Church did not understand such matters and could not therefore give effective counter-measures. . . . To protect himself and his family he resorted to magic. . . . He consulted fortune-tellers, made and wore charms and even sponsored sacrifices to placate his tribal gods and his ancestral spirits.

As for Patrick's mother, his decision in favour of the priesthood eventually destroys her, despite her genuine devotion and loyalty to the Church. She pleads with him with growing desperation to meet his obligations to his family. "I am trying to save you from committing the worst crime anyone can commit in Ado—that of letting one's family fold up as if there is no one to keep it going. . . . I want John Ikenga's family to continue. It must continue. . . . I need a son to continue the work of reproduction in the family." When he refuses, she renounces him as her son and goes home to die.

Other pressures brought to bear on Patrick to make him conform to traditional ways give us further insight into the mind of the Ibo villager. Patrick is the ward of his uncle, Ononye, who supports him and pays for his schooling, and who will suffer no heretical Christian doctrine in his family. When Patrick falls ill with suspected malaria, Ononye forbids any utilisation of Western medicine. The boy is given hot baths and a concoction of herbs to drink. "His neck, wrists and waist were ringed round with charms which would keep witches, evil men and evil spirits from interfering with the efficacy of the treatment he received. A series of sacrifices, seeking the aid of his ancestral spirits in his recovery and warding off evil spirits . . . were offered." Some relatives, to be sure, suggest hospitalisation, but their advice lacks conviction for they basically mistrust Western medical practice. "Their desire to demonstrate that they belonged to the new generation of literate gentlemen had made them attend the hospitals . . . in which they themselves had little faith, for the old order still had a firm grip on them."

Patrick recovers and goes on to spend his adolescence and early manhood living in the traditional African world, learning its practices and absorbing its values. At the same time he continues his mission-school education for, as his uncle says, "Literacy is the hallmark of a gentleman these days. . . . The teaching of reading, writing and arithmetic . . . we have now learned to value as the passport to future wealth and power." Nonetheless, guided by his uncle's careful tutelage, he participates in the activities of appropriate age-groups in his lineage, attends religious ceremonies involving ritual purification and sacrifices to the ancestors, listens to detailed descriptions of the ways of spirits and the best means for detecting and combating witchcraft, is inducted into a masquerade cult, and on achieving adulthood begins building a large house in his home village. Through tribal custom it has long since been decided that he is to succeed to the headship of his patrilineal lineage and his training has therefore been unusually thorough. Though still harbouring a latent allegiance to the Church, Patrick comes to accept much of the traditional teaching. He abandons thoughts of the priesthood, and begins to think about marriage, possibly with the girl to whom he had been betrothed as a child. During the several years he had spent away from home working in the railroad system, he dealt heavily in bribary as a means for meeting the burdensome but proper levies on his resources made by his people in the village. "For in times of stress, and in his old age, he would fall back on the lineage whose bounden duty it would then be to minister unto his needs, the degree of ministration being determined by his contribution to their well-being now that he had the means to do so." After a brief exposure to the free-thinking ways of Lagos, he explains his philosophy and his reasons for abandoning Christianity and returning to his traditional faith:

"You realise . . . how enjoyable it is to be free. Gradually you stop going to church. . . . Simultaneously, you find that the traditional elements are gone too from your life, though not as distantly as the Christian ones. . . . Traditional religion, by virtue of its hold on the society in which you live, because it permeates all phases of the life of that society, and offers an explanation and a solution to the problems which confront you daily, appeals to you and attracts you to itself. . . . You find it easier to go back to traditional religion whose agents have not antagonised you the way the Christian missionaries have done. Traditional worship, in view of your nearness to nature, suits you. For even on sorrowful occasions it consists of ritual feasts held in a lively atmosphere which conjures up within you the right emotional feelings."

Somewhat inexplicably and unconvincingly, Patrick ultimately re-
vives his plans for the priesthood and breaks with his family and lineage. They are outraged by his heresy. Not only is he making a
mockery of their religious faith and way of life, but he is threatening
the very existence of the family—the ancestors and the living as well
as the yet unborn. Our children, observes Ononye, "are the links that
will carry our traditions, which distinguish us from all other peoples,
to future generations. If . . . they fail to take part in our rituals, time
will come when we can no longer identify one man from another. And
if, as we do believe, the dead do see and have power, I will be one of
those who will rise from the dead to take revenge on those who let
our traditions die away." Patrick is ostracised by his family and left to
defend himself as best he can against the inevitable wrath of the gods
and ancestral spirits. The girl to whom he was pledged years earlier
at the time of her birth manages to administer a love potion to him
and shortly thereafter he seduces her. When his action is discovered,
his clerical ambitions are brought to an abrupt end. Who knows what
caused his downfall? Was it lust or was it magic? As Patrick himself
observed on another occasion concerning another mystery, "Looks like
what a charm alone can accomplish. Or could it be mere coincidence?"

Religion, the ancient virtues, and modernity are themes which have
been brought together eloquently by Cheikh Kane in *L'Aventure
Ambiguë.* Here is another view of Africa which extols the simple traditional way of life, emphasises the fundamental religiousness of the
African people, and questions the validity of modern Western culture.
The conclusion is inescapable. If the world is to be saved, it can only
be done by cleaving to the basic verities revealed through love of God,
and it is Africa and not the West which has within it the power of salvation.

Samba Diallo is a young nephew of the chief of the Diallobé of
Senegal, and on him the future leadership of the tribe appears likely to
fall. He is given the most careful of religious instruction by his old and
wise Muslim religious teacher, and is then sent off to France to gain a
Western education, for the tribe is not prospering—its numbers are
decreasing, its people are sickly, and its properties are in disrepair.
After some years at the university in Paris, he returns to his people
only to find that he can no longer reach them: he has become too
Westernised. Finally, in effect, he kills himself.

The individuals in the book are types rather than flesh-and-blood
characters, symbols for a series of attitudes which reflect the African
view of the world. There is the old religious teacher who embodies
the belief that only ceaseless asceticism and total absorption with the
word of God can lead to a life of the highest attainment. Frail, and
emaciated from long years of fasting, his body is as feeble as his home

and property are run down. But his spirit is bright with the love of God:

> In many ways the master was a formidable man. His life was con-
> cerned with two occupations: cultivation of the spirit and the soil. To
> his fields he devoted the strictest minimum of his time and asked nothing
> more of the soil but what was needed for the barest nourishment for him
> and his family. . . . The rest of his time was given over to study, to
> meditation, to prayer and to the formation of the young people entrusted
> to his charge. . . . The master believed deeply that the love of God
> was not compatible with human pride. . . . Pride means a sense of
> superiority, but faith is above all humility, if not humiliation. The
> master thought that man had no reason to exalt himself except precisely
> in the adoration of God.

He was passionately serious and never laughed, at least not out-
wardly. But occasionally at prayer he found himself amused by the
rheumatic misery of his joints which no longer moved where and how
he wanted them to. "Was this impious? 'Perhaps it is some evil vanity
which fills me thus.' He thought for a minute. 'No . . . my laughter
is innocent. I laugh because my old friend jokes about his creaking
joints. But his will is better than ever. Even when he can't move, he
will keep trying, and he will continue to pray. I love him well.' "

The old master is afraid that the chief of the tribe is going to yield
to the desires of the people to send their best young men to France for
training and education. His apprehension is shared by Samba Diallo's
father who, like the master, can see no point to a life of material
prosperity if it lacks spiritual fulfilment. And Samba's father feels that
the West has lost sight of this ultimate objective in its pursuit of materialism. Work and its fruits need justification through God:

> If a man believes in God, the time he takes from prayer for work is still
> prayer. Indeed, it is a very beautiful prayer. . . . But if a life is not
> justified in God . . . it is in this case not a pious work. It is only a life,
> no more than what it appears to be. . . . The West is in the process of
> overturning these simple truths. It began, timidly, by putting God in
> quotation marks. Then, two centuries later, having gained more as-
> surance, it decreed, "God is dead". On that day began the era of frenzied
> work. Nietzsche is contemporary with the industrial revolution. God was
> no longer available as a measure and justification. . . . After the death
> of God comes the death of man. . . . Life and work are no longer in
> tune. . . . Formerly, the work of one life could only sustain a single
> life. . . . But now the West is on the point of being able to do without
> man as a producer of work. . . . And to the extent that work transcends
> human life, man ceases to be its ultimate goal. Man has never been so
> unhappy as in this moment when he has accumulated so much. No-
> where are these things more scorned than where they have been most ac-
> cumulated. Thus the history of the West seems to reveal the poverty of

the doctrine that man is an end in himself. Human happiness requires belief in the existence of God.

But the problem of survival for the Diallobé still remains unresolved, and the chief, however sympathetic he may be with the view that God must be served, still has the responsibility for the welfare of his people. They want to learn how better to build their houses, to care for their children, to increase their holdings, and gain the strength to re-establish their independence from foreign domination. These things can only be learned through western education, but is this to the ultimate advantage of the people? " 'If I tell them to go to the new school, they will go in mass. They will learn all the methods of building which we do not know. But in learning they will also forget. Will what they learn be worth what they forget?' " The master has no doubt; in his school they learn about God and forget about man. Another voice is heard, " 'Give them their chance, my brother. If you don't, I assure you there will soon be no more people in the country.' " It is the sister of the chief, the dowager princess whose practical energy and wisdom have long directed the affairs of the tribe through the nominal authority of her brother. Imposing in her full blue robes and the white veil wound voluminously about her head and neck, she is the essence of Fulani nobility and only her Muslim faith has ever succeeded in taming the imperiousness of her spirit. She goes on to point out that their royal grandfather and his warriors had been defeated by the foreigners a hundred years earlier. To defeat them in turn, " 'it is necessary to go and learn from them the art of conquest without justification. . . . The struggle has not yet ended. The foreigners' school is the new form of the war which we wage against those who came here, and we must send our élite to it, and eventually all of our people.' "

Samba Diallo thus becomes the instrument for reconciling the conflicting views of the master and the dowager princess, and in his success or failure lies personal survival and perhaps the salvation of his people. Certainly as he sets out on his journey he is much of the same opinion as his father and his master teacher. Under the master's guidance he has become a serious devoted Muslim, deeply involved in study of his texts, in prayer, in fasting, in mendicancy. He lives close to the soil and to God, and he finds this life rewarding. As his studies in France proceed, he gradually masters Western thought and culture. The process is an exhilarating intellectual adventure, but with it comes growing doubt as to the essential wisdom of Western values, and fear that he personally may lose touch with the truths he had learned during his childhood years. He still feels himself in close touch with nature. " 'The greatest dignity to which I still aspire today is to be her faithful son. I dare not fight her for I am part of her. Never do I seek nourishment from her breast without first asking humble pardon. I cannot cut down a tree and use its timber without begging its brotherly forgiveness.' "

Still, in Paris he feels strangely void, like the city which, for all its crowded busy streets, gives the impression of emptiness and lifeless-ness. Perhaps it is because Western culture has developed an artificial world which has buried nature and cut itself off from the primal source of life. Back home in Africa " 'the world was like my father's house: everything was revealed in its essence as if nothing could exist except through my experience. The world was not silent and sterile. It was alive. It was aggressive. . . . Here . . . the world is silent and I no longer vibrate. I am like a burst balloon, like a dead musical in-strument. I have the impression that nothing touches me any more.' "

The West may feel that it has much to teach the rest of the world, and some Africans may agree. To Samba Diallo this is a mistake. The West is different, not because the fundamental nature of its people is different, but because it has surrounded itself with artificiality. Those Africans who feel strangely uncomfortable while living in the West need not ascribe this sensation to the fact that they are not needed by the West:

> On the contrary, this feeling establishes our necessity and points up the urgency of our task which is to clear away the rubbish and excavate nature. This is a noble task. If we allow ourselves to be convinced that all we need is to acquire the West's mastery of the material world, we will fail. For the West has become a world of things, not people. In order to move from place to place, a vehicle is needed; walking is no longer sufficient. For eating, iron utensils are required; the fingers will not serve. Flesh and blood have disappeared.
>
> With the same action the West colonised us and gained mastery over the material world. If we do not make the West aware of the difference which separates us from this phenomenon, we will not be worth any more than it is, and we will never learn to master it. And our defeat would be the end of the last human being on this earth.

Samba Diallo sees Africa's destiny with clarity but at the same time he has become unable to play a personal rôle in carrying it out. " 'I am not clearly of the Diallobé, facing a clearly defined West, and ap-preciating with a cool head what I can take and what I must leave as counterpart. I have become both. I am not a clear head deciding be-tween two parts of a choice. I am a single strange nature, in distress at not being two.' " And so, repelled by Western culture but trapped by its teaching, wanting to return to the life of simple piety he once lived but unable to reach it, he returns home. He has learned how to teach his people to rebuild the houses they live in but he has forgotten how to live.

These four works present widely different aspects of the African personality, and in their very variety give some indication of the complexity of a vast continent and the differences that exist among the many people who dwell there. Consequently, generalities are risky; yet there seem to be certain qualities shared by the characters in these novels, as well as common reactions to forces in the world around them, which may constitute the essentials of the unique personality which many Africans insist is theirs. Alternatively, as other Africans maintain, these may simply be human beings acting characteristically in situations which could be, and are, reproduced daily in other parts of the world.

Let us look first at the backdrop. Here, one is struck immediately in all these works by the enormous influence which the outside world appears to have exerted on the traditional way of African life wherever contact has been made. More than any other continent, Africa had been isolated and inward-looking over many hundreds of years, but when outside influences came, their impact was far-reaching and their acceptance enthusiastic. For historical reasons these influences have varied widely from place to place. Thus in the South Africa of *A Walk in the Night*, the Westernisation of background and personality is virtually complete—the Capetown slums and their population are indistinguishable from what might be found in any industrialised city the world over. Even the race issue does not seem to be as fundamental as the struggle of human beings against the forces of poverty, ignorance, and psychic starvation.

Poised against the total Westernisation of the South African city, the Ibo village of *Blade Among the Boys* appears at first to have succeeded in its resistance to outside ways. Yet, despite the self-belief and self-satisfaction of traditional Ibo life, new ideas from the outside are gaining acceptance. Patrick Ikenga's uncle may belong to the old school but he sees the value of a Western education. Patrick himself is already profoundly affected by his mission training and his experience with urban living. His destruction comes not so much from personal shortcomings as from his inability to reconcile the old Africa with the West, and one is left at the end with the conviction that, though Patrick has failed, in welcoming ideas from the outside he has displayed a foresight superior to that of his elders.

As for the mystics of Cheikh Kane's tale, they are at least as much a product of Muslim ethics and metaphysics as of the traditional tribal way of life, while the pessimism and hostility displayed towards Western values reflects attitudes not entirely foreign to European existentialist thought. Finally, it is the modern Westernised Lagos of *Jagua Nana* which is the natural habitat of the novel's characters, and they cheerfully accept its perils and corruptions in return for the excitement, the novelty and the stimulation of taking part in the birth of a new Africa.

Though it is clear that outside forces have profoundly affected the African and his world, commanding his acceptance of alien ways, it does not mean that he has absorbed foreign ideas uncritically or turned his back on his own culture and traditions. The greater has been the influence from Europe, the more the African has felt compelled to reassert his own values. Onuora Nzekwu sets forth in precise detail the tough resilience of an ancient well-tried way of life with its ordered world and its tested solutions to human situations and needs. Patrick Ikenga's difficulty arises precisely from the fact that he can see the value of the traditional customs as well as the western concepts which he has come to respect and to need. Cheikh Kane goes much further than Nzekwu in arguing the moral superiority of rural traditionalism over the soulless materialism of a technically superior culture. The tragedy lies not in a confusion of choice but in the necessity for the sake of survival of accepting Western ways. When the chief of the tribe asks whether the new learning is worth what is lost in forgetting the old, the question seems rhetorical—the choice is forced and the result foredoomed. The world of Jagua Nana is populated with characters who are neither analytical nor introspective; yet their allegiance to the city is tempered by an inarticulate urge to go back to sources, to the simple village life where the real world and the ideal coincide in a romantic idyll.

The case of the protagonists of *A Walk in the Night* is more complex. All are rebels and failures in the world that surrounds them. All hate it and struggle against it. Yet none seems prepared to solve his problems by default in returning to the old life in the villages. In the end, death and moral destruction standing one's ground in the city are considered preferable. Once again the reasons are historical. In the first place, the Africans in the cities of South Africa have had a longer experience with urban life and are much more deeply committed to its ways and its possibilities than Africans in other parts of the continent. More important perhaps, they cannot afford to look back to the tribal ways, for it is precisely in this direction that the *apartheid* and Bantustan policies of the South African government are trying to force the people. In the effort to avoid being frozen culturally while the rest of the world moves on, they are compelled to turn their backs, at least temporarily, on values and viewpoints which otherwise might be treated more sympathetically. It may well require nothing less than a political revolution to persuade the Africans of South Africa to look to their traditional culture with a more kindly eye.

The reaction to outside forces, however, does not stop with mere resistance and the counterpoising of traditional values. The rise of in-

dependent states in Africa since 1957 has led to a search for an independence perhaps more subtle and difficult to achieve even than political freedom. Thoughtful Africans realise that political independence
and economic development must be accomplished sooner or later by a
true cultural emancipation which not only gives a fresh contemporary
definition to the African character and its aspirations, but also makes
possible a uniquely African contribution to world progress and civilisation. This is the basic meaning of the philosophy of *négritude* and
the concept of the African personality.

The search for cultural identity expresses itself in several ways am-
ply illustrated by the four novels under examination. First of all, there
is the need for historical roots and a modern culture based not on
foreign ideas but on native African values. This view is most clearly
expressed by Cheikh Kane, the only one of the four authors clearly
committed to the doctrine of *négritude*. The emotional appeal of
his whole argument is to the past—the beauty and simplicity of the
traditional life, the nobility of the ancestors and the glories of the old
empire, the sublimity of the ascetic man. Against the serene perfection
of this world, the West comes out a very poor second with its artificiality and ugliness, its amorality and godlessness, and its divorce from
the living pulse of the real world. Of the others, it is Nzekwu who
comes closest to Kane in allowing the traditional society to speak for
itself, though he leaves the reader uncertain at the end as to how the
modern Nigerian can make most effective use of traditional customs
and values.

A second aspect of African cultural identity is the need to establish
and express a sense of human dignity. Political freedom, satisfying as
it is, needs to be followed by a world-wide acknowledgment that the
new nation has earned its independence on its merits, not through
some hand-me-down charity arising from international politics. The
volumes we have been examining do not neglect this aspect of the
African psychology. It is not surprising that *L'Aventure Ambiguë*,
reflecting Gallic logic, is most precise in presenting characters of a
lofty moral and ethical superiority. Samba Diallo, his father, the old
master, the dowager, and the chief of the Diallobé all move through
the action with a stoic detachment and devotion to higher principles
that transcends the peccadillos of the everyday world, even while their
fates are being settled by these trivia. On the other hand, the few Europeans who appear are remarkable perhaps for their cleverness and
cynicism but never for nobility of character or largeness of spirit.

Alex La Guma treats the theme of dignity no less fully, if completely differently. His subjects meet the test on the white man's
ground, only dimly aware of the inevitability of their defeat, but in
refusing the sanctuary of the tribe and the village they succeed in
living out their lives as best they know how and so achieve their meas-

ure of human dignity. The humanity of *Blade Among the Boys* is realised primarily through the sympathetic treatment given to the traditional village life, while Jagua Nana, for all her moral shortcomings, is a warm, vivid, three-dimensional character.

The third element of cultural identity springs naturally from the search for roots and the wish for the approbation of one's fellow man. This is the desire to make some positive contribution to contemporary world culture. Again it is Kane whose *négritude* is most didactic—the African lives in close sympathy with the natural forces of the world, his religious instinct brings him into surer touch with the infinite, and his higher morality is the only hope for a world out of touch with its own rhythm, lacking faith in God, and apparently bent on self-destruction. Ekwensi and Nzekwu describe rather than instruct—their characters exhibit the earthiness, the religious sense, the quick humour, and the personal warmth of the African and by implication suggest that these are qualities worthy of emulation the world over. La Guma makes no effort to convert. His case study of the South African city slum is none the less an eloquent plea for a better way of life than what has been brought from Europe to that unhappy part of Africa.

One more comment might be added about these four novels. It may seem curious that the authors selected failure and personal shortcoming as their vehicle because the prevailing mood in Africa today is clearly one of great buoyancy and faith in the future. South Africa may be burdened with *apartheid* and urban slums but the African in that land gives no indication of being downhearted or beaten. Similarly, West Africans do not seem to be greatly disturbed by the many problems thrust upon them by their rapidly changing world; this is just part of the business of building new nations. As for the African villager, is he not the very person whose drive, shrewdness, and pastoral virtue will be enlisted to ensure the success of these new states? Finally, in French-speaking Africa, where the doctrine of *négritude* has received its widest support, there appears to be no doubt as to the importance of Africa's future in the world. We may conclude, therefore, that if these writers speak in sober tones, it does not mean despair, but only that the way may be difficult even though the goal is secure.

Chinua Achebe

by Anne Tibble

Chinua Achebe was born in Iboland, Eastern Nigeria, in 1930. He comes next to Tutuola in importance as a prose writer. Achebe as a novelist works not in imaginative fantasy but on the opposing basis of realism. With his three novels up to 1964, one of which is already translated into at least three European languages, he has built up a reputation. In each novel, in quiet, impartial-sounding prose that seems to be unemotional but isn't, Achebe gives a detailed, traditional, Iboland-village background that is also richly African. All three novels light up the struggle between values that linger longest in rural areas and the values of modernity.

First, see Achebe's description of the African dark as background:

The night was very quiet. It was always quiet except on moonlight nights. Darkness held a vague terror for these people, even the bravest among them. Children were warned not to whistle at night for fear of evil spirits. Dangerous animals became even more sinister and uncanny in the dark. A snake was never called by its name at night, because it would hear. It was called a string. And so on this particular night as the crier's voice was gradually swallowed up in the distance, silence returned to the world, a vibrant silence made more intense by the universal trill of a million million forest insects.

This background Achebe peoples with many characters, the chief of which have great weaknesses within great strengths. These weaknesses by which Achebe's characters outrage perennially-known and universally-understood human ethics tear apart and crush the slow flowering of lives important in the villages to which they belong. With both his African characters and his African background Achebe interweaves as passionately impartial a description of the strengths and weaknesses, also very easily recognizable, of the white invaders bringing a new god, a new wealth, new ways. Over both traditional and modern values he throws a fitful humour, a mildly comic irony.

In his first novel, *Things Fall Apart*, his African characters in their

"Chinua Achebe." From *African/English Literature: A Survey and Anthology* by Anne Tibble (London, Peter Owen Ltd., 1965), pp. 101–11. Reprinted by permission of the author and the publisher.

Ibo village life follow a ceremonious ritual by no means simple. Their code of virtue is not unbecoming to human beings of the continent from which some of our earliest ancestors may have set forth.

He describes the villagers of Umuofia. He tells about their feast of New Yam, about their communal rejoicing over a betrothal, about preparations of the *Ilo* wrestling ground for the Week of Peace that must precede the planting of the yams, about the village's fear of the pronouncements of the Oracle of the Hills and the Caves; he describes the mad Priestess of the Oracle (is she the Oracle itself?) carrying off a loved only child; he tells of an Ozo dance when a man of worth takes one of the Clan titles, the procession of the nine Egwugwus or masked Ancestor Spirits and of their dispensing of justice; he describes twin babies being put out to die, a superstitious practice that by no means all neighbouring tribes of the Ibos followed; he gives the song for a woman who died:

> For whom is it well? For whom is it well?
> There is no one for whom it is well;

This brings to mind Euripides' "Is there on God's earth one happy man?"

Humour is in Achebe's account of the rain-maker. We are left in no doubt at all that the rain-maker's magic claims come from acute personal weather-lore and from far-reaching rain-rumour in a dry land. The disguise of the *Egwugwu* "spirits" is pierced. Umuofia villagers' child-like, fear-thrilled acceptance of these Masks is comparable to the fear-thrill that a horror film gives to a Western audience. Deception and self-deception alike are seen through:

> Okonkwo's wives, and perhaps other women as well might have noticed that the second *egwugwu* had the springy walk of Okonkwo.
> . . . But if they thought these things they kept them within themselves. The *egwugwu* with the springy walk was one of the dead fathers of the clan. He looked terrible. . . .

Things Fall Apart is the tragedy of Obi Okonkwo of Umuofia, the ambitious, energetic son reacting against a father scorned by his fellows for being an idle "loafer" who didn't "get on." Obi made himself a person of substance, respected in eight of nine villages. This was just before the time of the first missionaries. The missionaries were quickly followed by soldiers and officers of foreign law.

Here is an instance of Achebe's perception of how Obi's weakness within strength, his lack of the integrity of real individuality, will bring about his undoing:

> Okonkwo ruled his household with a heavy hand. His wives, especially the youngest, lived in pereptual fear of his fiery temper and so did his little children. Perhaps down in his heart Okonkwo was not a cruel man.

But his whole life was dominated by fear, the fear of failure and weakness. It was deeper and more intimate than the fear of evil and capricious gods and of magic, the fear of the forest, and of the forces of nature, malevolent, red in tooth and claw. Okonkwo's fear was greater than these. It was not external but lay deep within himself. It was the fear of himself, lest he should be found to resemble his father. Even as a little boy he had resented his father's failure and weakness . . . and so Okonkwo was ruled by one passion—to hate everything that his father Unoka had loved. One of these things was gentleness and another was idleness.

In keeping with his bullying, Okonkwo outrages true village tradition by beating one of his wives in the Week of Peace that should precede yam planting.

Threat of war comes to Umuofia. One of their girls is murdered by a villager of neighbouring Mbaino. Why or by whom she was murdered does not seem clear to at least one reader. But Achebe may have meant to imply that this kind of murder could happen in Iboland—as it can happen anywhere. Lack of explanation is not necessarily a flaw in an otherwise clear story. Okonkwo, sent to obtain restitution from the elders of Mbaino, succeeds in bringing back a boy. Thus he wards off the need for Umuofia's making war on Mbaino. This kind of success in peaceful negotiation gives a man prestige in such a community. The boy Ikemefuna lives in Okonkwo's household as his son. He becomes his own son's soon-loved brother. But at the end of two years a majority of Umuofia's headmen consent to what Achebe surely wishes the reader to see as a cruelly primitive, implacable, eye-for-an-eye retribution, imposed by the Oracle and superstitiously believed in. Hadn't Obi averted just such cruelty by bringing the village the useful Ikemefuna? But the innocent boy must after all die. The men take him out into the forest.

Here seems the crux of Obi's—and Achebe's—story. A man should be individually strong by the traditional standard of the "God within": his conscience. This is the *Chi* of Ibo theology. Achebe seems to be saying that this standard of the "God within" is a perennial human standard: it is not one that has recently "evolved." But rather than seem weak by the superstitious standards of his fellows, and against the advice of the wisest old warrior-elder, Obi takes upon himself to deal the child who has called him father the fatal blow.[1]

At the funeral of that same old warrior-elder Obi's gun—symbol of the individual strength, the coveted technical prowess of the white man—"accidentally" explodes. The explosion kills the dead man's

---

[1] Austin J. Shelton's article (*Transition*, 13) "The Offended *Chi* in Achebe's Novels" takes insufficient account of the subtlety of Achebe's emancipation as a writer.

link with the living, his eldest son. Unless this "accident" is seen as inevitable because Okonkwo is what he is, it may seem merely an unconvincing incident. Actually it conveys the important statement that the ambitious Okonkwo wants more power but has not a strong enough *Chi*, a conscience of sufficient awareness and integrity, to hold it. He fails abjectly to control his modern weapon. Thereby he shows himself unfit not only for true, traditional responsibility but for the even heavier responsibility that further enlightenment and modern lethal instruments impose on men.

Obi accepts the seven years' banishment from the village for his crime. He must go to his mother's people. In Umuofia culture a mother's people will always help a son or a daughter in trouble. Here there is tacit comparison between this form of non-vindictive justice and the colder penalties both of the primitive Oracle and of modern legality. These penalties, Achebe is implying, are both of them often useless and, therefore, evil.

The first white missionaries have arrived in Iboland by Obi's return to Umuofia. One has been killed by the villagers of neighbouring Abame. Umuofia people well know that the killing of any stranger unless in battle is blameful. Killing this one is senseless as well. They have heard more and more of the white man's daring, knowledge, power, and weapons. They envy and desire all these.

More missionaries arrive, this time at Umuofia itself. They are given a piece of the Evil Forest on which to build a Church. This is to be a test of their god. Umuofia people are convinced that the watching Spirits of the Evil Forest will cause the missionaries to die and their power to make converts fail. These missionaries have condemned abandonment of twins, possessing of more than one wife, beating of wives; they have asserted their god to be the "only god on earth" and Umuofia gods to be "wicked heathen idols."

The missionaries don't perish. But their converts are the weak, the unfortunate, distraught mothers of twins, or social outcasts, *osu*. That this question of the Ibo social outcast, *osu*, is an important one for Achebe is clear from his second novel in which the story centres round the struggle of an educated Ibo who has to choose between Clara, the girl he loves, and his village which is outraged by his choice: for Clara is *osu*. Presumably *osu* are outcasts because of some crime or social misdemeanour one of their ancestors has been guilty of. The village Elders attempt to identify themselves with relentless "natural" laws of punishment: they, the guardians of the community's morals, cannot trust to present mercy and forgive the innocent descendant of an offender. They must hold to implacable logic of judgement. Simple human forgiveness would be thought weak and sliding.

By the missionaries' survival Achebe seeks to show how inevitable it is that cruelty and superstition, even the implacable judgement of

Elders, about *osu,* about twins, or about mystic powers of the royal python, must all go down when challenged. They may be challenged by more developed superstitions—as that forgiveness is commanded by the Son of the only God, miraculously born of a Virgin, who rose from the dead, and who will preside at a Judgement Day to decree eternal torment for wrong-doers. Compassion could never be a simple human good? But Christianity must mean more than its superstitions if it is to hold more of the elusive truth. All this indicates the depth of imaginative thought at which Achebe consistently works.

Because of Okonkwo's harshness as a father his son runs away from home. He joins the missionaries. Obi curses him. When the seven years' exile are up and Obi has been helped to rebuild his home in Umuofia, more trouble has arisen between the missionaries and the villagers there. Trouble often arose between missionaries and villagers. Hitherto we have had chiefly the English version. Now we have the African version.

Urged by Obi the villagers burn the Christian Church. The Christians allow themselves to be backed by their military. Messengers of the foreign District Commissioner take six villagers, among them Obi, to a discussion, beat them up, and free them. Obi urges war against the foreigner. Soldiers in numbers descend on the village, to uphold the *pax Britannica* by superior force of arms. Obi sees the villagers have lost heart against the colossus. They won't fight. Rather than give in he goes out and hangs himself.

Thus *Things Fall Apart* is a tragedy, the downfall of a man who was not strong enough to challenge cruel stupidity in his fellows; a man not courageous enough, and therefore not trusted enough, to stand alone for the age-old wisdom of not helping in the slaughter of an innocent boy accepted as a son. The novel illustrates, in Achebe's unadorned prose, not only the gulf that can yawn between the African point of view and the white man's, but also the hiatus that gapes between perennial standards of behaviour true and false.

Achebe's second novel, *No Longer at Ease* (1960), skips a generation. It misses out Obi Okonkwo's son, Isaac, who became a Christian for a reason that was understandable, even valid, but was certainly not strength of belief. *No Longer at Ease* takes up the story again at Obi's grandson, also called Obi. This Obi is a young man growing up in the nineteen-thirties and forties to a Nigeria ready to become independent with new towns, urban-industrial development and the irresistible prospect of material riches for more and more people.

Obi is being educated in the white man's knowledge. He is the hope of his village. He has been to England on the village's money. On his return he horrifies his parents and his benefactors, the Progressive Union of Elders, by having fallen in love, on the boat coming home, with Clara: Clara has been to England too and is a nurse. Innocent, she yet belongs to an *osu* family. By obscure, stupid, and surely unjust, village reckoning, she is an outcast.

Obi comes home to a modern Lagos. There emphasis on money, success, luxury, and class distinctions are of prime importance. There can be no denying that some Africans took to these so-called American and British values as easily as do most human beings. Desire for power in terms of rule or of having your own way, like desire for wealth and physical luxury is latent in people of most cultures judging by the ease with which opportunity for these things is passed on. (We must except cultures such as Bushman, Pygmy, Amerindian, Maori, and some Nilotes: these are relatively uninterested in technological advance and education. But they are said to be dying.) Yet hot on the heels of "advance" and "progress," writers like Chinua Achebe sense the need to think again; and—more insight gained—to speak for some "eternal" values that are to be preferred to some of civilization's more materialist ones. These perennial values are at once beyond, and at the same time part of, what we often, imprecisely, call the "natural."

Nigerian village cultures represent the greater extent of the country's life. They are not, of course, its vocal aspect or its growing-point. In Scotland, Wales and Ireland, as well as in many other parts of the Earth, a parallel could be made: rural cultures are far greater in extent than the most press-noisy urban ones. To think only from urban standpoints is to fall victim to many illusions. Thus, Obi's parents and the Elders of his village want him to be a splendid and prosperous man of the town. They have no inkling of what they are asking him to stand against.

Again, the crux of Achebe's second novel is of similar profundity to that of his first. Besides being, overtly, young Obi Okonkwo's story, *No Longer at Ease* is about the confusion of values, not only between "good" tradition and blind, ugly superstitious tradition, but also between new "advance" and new corruptions. First Obi gets into debt over taxes, then over his new car, then over sending money to his people. Next he takes bribes. The white leaders are not free from using personal pull in well-disguised, or "civilized," "innocent" forms: such as that you are most likely to gain promotion if you go to Church and say you are a Christian, if you let it be known that you have been to a well-known school, or even if your aunt slept with a king. As if unaware that any of these things are not in the deepest sense corrupt, they are supremely critical of the African new officials' form of corruption, their addiction to stark bribery, by money or gifts. Bribery of the overt kind whites feel they have outgrown.

Again and again, in his laconic, flat prose, Achebe shows up the new values. Again he stresses how clarity and charity and strength of mind are needed to keep one's head above the shifting morass of social change. Wisdom and strength of mind might be thought to belong to, to be derived from, bodily bravery. In reality they have only a little to do with physical courage. How can the traditional brave man of action become the modern man of insight? This is what Achebe seems to be asking. Sometimes it looks as if the complacent, white man's offers of progress and his religion have emasculated the black man.

And again, as backdrop to this novel Achebe paints a moving picture of traditional village life under the onslaught of modernity.

But in *No Longer at Ease* the detached, matter-of-fact, confident prose has become lighter: "We all have to stand on the earth itself and go with her at her pace": this is Obi thinking after his downfall towards the end of the book. Words put into a chief character's mouth or mind should never be confused with an author's own thought. But this philosophic outlook of Obi's may mean that his creator, too, has accepted the inevitability of modern change. It may also mean that the pitfalls of 'progress' need not be seen as wholly tragic.

In his third novel, *Arrow of God* (1964), Achebe returns to the Nigeria of 1931. This could be looked at as a retreat from facing the struggle at too close quarters in his own generation. But *Arrow of God* is Achebe's richest and most competently constructed novel to date. It may not be the great African novel that Ezekiel Mphahlele is waiting for. But it would not come altogether badly out of a comparison with novels like *Anna Karenina, Madame Bovary,* and *Middlemarch.*

Arrow of God has more resonance than Achebe's previous novels have. It has less comic sense. The chasm between perennial values and the cruelly superstitious, as well as those which are meretricious among the new, is returned to as mortal, tragic; superficial misunderstandings alone are treated as comic.

In a group of six Ibo villages called Umuaro, the ageing Eleuzu, headstrong, ambitious, prosperous, jealous of his power after years of wielding it, is the priest of the most powerful of Umuaro's lesser deities, Ulu:

> In the very distant past, when lizards were still few and far between, the six villages—Umuachala, Umunneora, Umuagu, Umuezeani, Umuogwugwu, and Umuisiuzo lived as different people, and each worshipped its own deity.
> Then the hired soldiers of Abam used to strike in the dead of night, set fire to houses and carry men, women and children into slavery. Things were so bad for the six villages that their leaders came together to save themselves. They hired a strong team of medicine-men to install a common deity for them. This deity which the fathers of the six villages made was called Ulu. . . .
> The six villages took the name of Umuaro, and the priest of Ulu be-

came their Chief Priest. From that day they were never again beaten by an enemy. How could such a people disregard the god who founded the town and protected it? . . .

Thus in their sore need of a god, not against circumstances but against human cruelty, the villagers united. Their Elders asked the *good* medicine-men, called by some "witch-doctors" but really diviners and often the village conscience, to set up a god. Then the Elders turned about and declared that the god himself it was who had created their union; the god it was who now protected *them*. Villagers' sense of community as well as their unity with natural forces is here brought out by Achebe. Such sense of community and of unity with nature can be paralleled, of course, amongst remote Welsh, English and Irish villagers. It is found in most rural areas of the Earth. In his book *The African Image* Ezekiel Mphahlele takes Dan Jacobson and Hannah Arendt lightly to task for asserting that African tradition in its unity with nature made no "human reality." Achebe seems to be saying that a self-aware, individual sense of this "human reality" is as relentlessly necessary for human living as is the modern, more scientifically connoted, community sense.

African creation-myths, like all creation-myths, are a patchwork of guesses both beautiful and crude. More fully than before Achebe outlines the Ibo ones. Umuaro believes in Ani-Mmo, the spirit-world, in a High God or Creator, and in an Earth Mother. The High God of Umuaro took little interest in his creatures. Earth Mother could not protect her children's lives or change their fates. Each Umuaro man's and woman's *Chi*, his "god within," gave him his knowledge of good and ill; a man's *Chi*, therefore, might be said to be the personality made out of his inherited traits, even his destiny. With a man's *Chi* we may compare that difficult Christian assumption "free will." Achebe makes us ponder on all that we do not know about, as well as what we know about. He persuades us, as novelists and poets do set out to persuade, towards clearer thought about what we are all doing here.

Umuaro's gods, lesser than the High One, are like Greek gods: they are not above jealousy and spite as men are not above these. In dramatic action Achebe illustrates disagreements, greeds, jealousies, and fears among Umuaro men and women. He gives dialogue without mincing and proverbs in abundance, revealing the richness of Ibo culture. By the "arrow of God," presumably, he means to indicate the killing by Christianity of Ibo superstitions. But can, Achebe seems again to be asking, God's Christian creatures solve the problem of how to live more wisely?

The god of Umuaro's rival village of Okperi is Eru the Magnificent. Eru personifies the universal desire, latent in some maybe, for riches. Eru is the "one who gives wealth to those who find favour with him." We are not told how riches are got in traditional West Africa. No doubt riches are got as they are got elsewhere and have been got since the days of the Pharaohs—by prolonged endeavour and by shrewd and sharp long-term plans. Eru's rich priest, Nwaka, excites the jealousy of Eleuzu, priest of Ulu.

When the white man first came to Umuaro, the district, like many another, but by no means like all African regions, had no king. The man "who aspired to be king must first pay all the debts of every man and woman in Umuaro." The council of Elders decided that such social responsibility must be the sign of fitness to be a king. No man was found to be as generous with his personal gains as all that. Umuaro remained kingless. Thus, Achebe seems to imply, if rich men cannot shoulder responsibility as heavy as this for their fellows, better no king.

The white man, "who turned everything upside down," interfered and decided in favour of rival Okperi's land-claim against Umuaro. Eleuzu stood out against his village. In the cause of what he then saw as truth, Eleuzu sided with the white man, agreeing that the land was originally Okperi's.

But as time went on Eleuzu grew, as power makes so many grow, more and more overweening in pride and obstinacy. Achebe draws Eleuzu's character, with its strengths and its weaknesses, in more loving detail and with more warmth than he has yet expended on any of his creations. He shows again the interplay between Umuaro's ceremonies, rivalries, quarrels, cruelties, and the power Umuaro men and women attribute to their gods, ancestor spirits, and priest. Humour is seen in what the black man admired in the white besides his wealth, his weapons, his strength and his knowledge—an ability to "write word with his *left* hand."

Blindly the Umuaro villagers fear, as well as admire, the white man's knowledge and force. They conclude all comes from the white man's god. Madly pretending—interpreting—their own god, priest Eleuzu declares it is Ulu's decree to postpone the people's yam harvest; he locks them in the old year for two moons. This haughty cruelty brings famine to his village and his own family.

But not even Eleuzu the priest of a powerful god can stand as a stiff-necked individual. Eleuzu's son dies. The people see this as an unmistakable portent; Ulu has turned against his overweening priest. They abandon Eleuzu. They offer yams to the Church in grovelling hopes that the Christian god will bless the new harvest. Eleuzu in his last days is still haughty and arrogantly opinionated. But he is demented, almost a laughing-stock, though spared knowledge of any "final outcome." Does the white man have the "last" word again? Achebe indicates that—only temporarily, and not by moral superiority—the white man does.

But he does not try to offer any larger-than-life or any over-simple solution to the mortal conflict among human values. The sifting of these issues, his packed and dramatic stories seem to suggest, forms part of life's perpetual challenge to our race.

The Idea of Assimilation:
Mongo Beti and Camara Laye

by Jeannette Macaulay

I shall start first by giving a background to what everybody loosely terms a cultural conflict because the more "familiar" we are with these terms, the less they become representative of actual situations. If we can assume that when two cultures come into contact, the people whom they influence form comparisons between the two and have to choose between values as they are put in practice and their effects, and assume one or other form of synthesis of the two cultures, one can say that there are only three alternatives.

In the case of the Negro in North America or in the West Indian Islands where the coloured populations have socially often evolved by themselves, one finds that, as they lived in a country dominated by foreigners (in those cases, representatives of the Western European culture) they could not ignore this culture because they had to assume it in some form in order to achieve posts in the administration and so on. Because of racial discrimination, these people, within the confines of territories which had been allotted to them by the government, have not been able to lose the dominant aspects of their culture which, later on, fused with the dominant aspect of the foreign culture to form a synthesis. This synthesis may be an unconscious evolution, as comes out in forms of jazz or the calypso.

I think that in the Union of South Africa one has a similar situation which is in the process of crystallization, where the people are becoming more and more separated from smaller aspects of traditional life and have to adapt themselves very rapidly to the advancing influences of the white population. In such circumstances, you are going to have a people retaining only those stronger aspects of their cultural heritage. Now, in the rest of Africa, newly independent Africa, south of the Sahara, the situation is not so clearly defined. One has a young generation clearly in the process of making a fundamental cultural choice—

"The Idea of Assimilation: Mongo Beti: and Camara Laye," by Jeannette Macaulay. From *Protest and Conflict in African Literature,* ed. Cosmo Pieterse and Donald Munro (London: William Heimann, Ltd., 1969), pp. 12ff. Reprinted by permission of the author.

the politician, the musician, the artist, the writer is free to choose in which direction he can direct the evolution of his work. This is what we are going to discuss in the works of Mongo Beti and Camara Laye who are from French West Africa. Mongo Beti is from the Cameroon Republic. His real name is Alexander Biyidi. Camara Laye is a Guinean.

I'll start with Camara Laye. His novel *L'Enfant Noir*[1] caused a great stir in Paris when it came out in 1953. In 1954, it won the Charles Brilliant literary award, and immediately became a very important novel because the African élite began to study this work in the light of their own political and social background, interpretation of life or world view. One has a very sharp criticism coming out against *L'Enfant Noir*—that of being a very simplified Utopian Africa, a portrayal of life that is not realistic, only pandering to the desires of a sophisticated French society.

L'Enfant Noir is the story of young Camara Laye in the background of upper Guinea where he lived with his family and friends. It's a very self-centred novel. One is surprised to see that there is nothing in that novel which comes from outside; there is no influence of the conflicting cultures in the background which must have existed in Conakry at the time. There is no shock of impact between the consciousness of the child and his environment in Laye's relationship to his surroundings. His psyche is very much a product of the young boy's growing up in a very well organized traditional society. The main issue flowing from this is a criticism that Camara Laye has not at all dealt with the problems created by the French system of colonization. But, on the other hand, one wonders whether this criticism can be just. There is a quotation which I have here from "Présence Africaine" number 16 which was published in 1957. It was signed A. B. which are the initials of Alexander Biyidi alias Mongo Beti. It is interesting to study the works of the two authors in the light of this criticism. It reads:

> Any one who has read the touching *Black Boy* by Richard Wright and who will consequently be tempted to compare the two novels, will immediately be struck by the shocking lack of scope and of depth in the Guinean's book. This book will disappoint all those who find that in this century, it is of categorical importance that the writer defend himself against literature which justifies itself against art for its own sake. Actually, the point in question here is not so much the book as the mentality of which it is the unfortunate product. Since the choice of title also implies a sort of challenge, Wright disdains the slightest pandering to the public taste. He poses the problems however crude. He avoids all that is commonplace, futile, naïve. Laye, on the other hand, is stub-

---

[1] Camara Laye, *L'Enfant Noir*, Libraire Plon, 1954. Trans. as *The African Child*, Fontana, 1955.

bornly satisfied with the anodyne, facile, and picturesque and also the most lucrative. Does this Guinean, a fellow African, who was, as he would have us believe, a highly intelligent boy, never see any but the tranquil, beautiful, eternal Africa? Is it possible that Laye was not even once witness to the smallest trial of colonial administration? [2]

The funny thing about that quotation is that Biyidi has chosen to dictate what an author should write. Should he not comply with the accepted critical ideas, whether they be of Negritude or anti-clericism? One feels this man should not have written! He is not conforming. And yet somehow, one would have thought that the novel *L'Enfant Noir* by its very closed atmosphere, by the fact that it excludes all talk about a foreign culture, by the fact that there isn't a single European in it (there are no elements of antagonism, culturally speaking), would be the strongest justification for Negritude and for its advocates to welcome the book in that it states that there is a stable society existing independent of Western influences and in that it demonstrates that. This is a viable system: the society within itself caters for every aspect of the social life of the village.

L'Enfant Noir is followed up by Camara Laye's second novel *Le Regard du Roi*, which is translated as *The Radiance of the King*.[3] Here we meet Clarence, a European who is bankrupt—and this, for a white man in Africa, is a terrible thing to happen. He finds that he hasn't any means of earning a living, and the only hope for him lies in working in the court of the king. But this is not as easy as one would have thought, because every task has its spiritual significance. Being a foreigner, he finds that he has not got the understanding, the feeling for simple tasks like, for example, being a drummer. He says, "Well, that's nothing. I could do that myself!" [4] And the beggar to whom he addresses himself says, "No, but you see that man is not only a drummer, he's a griot and the task of drumming has been hereditary in his family for generations." [5] This is the sort of thing that Clarence comes up against all the time. He has to adapt himself to a new society, a society which does not need him in any way, a society whose conceptions of life, of the value of life and the values in life are completely different from his own. In the end, Clarence's search for the king with whom he hopes to hold an audience becomes an obsession. It's the mirage which lures him on through dark forests with people he doesn't feel anything for, with people who do not understand him. I think that Clarence is destroyed in the course of the novel. At least the man we see at the beginning of the novel doesn't exist at the end

[2] *Présence Africaine*, no. 16.
[3] Camara Laye, *Le Regard du Roi*: in English *The Radiance of the King* trans. James Kirkup, Collins Fontana, 1965.
[4] *The Radiance of the King*, p. 39.
[5] *The Radiance of the King*, p. 40.

of it. When the king finally comes to the village, Clarence happens to be waiting for him. Clarence finds that he is unprepared. He would like to offer something, but he has nothing to give. He realizes he has lost everything—not only materially, but also spiritually. He has nothing to which he can belong.

This is a very significant part of Camara Laye's thought if we follow it from *L'Enfant Noir*. There is this very dense atmosphere of self-sufficiency in his traditional African location. We feel that the European is shocked by the fact that there is a self-sufficient society and that he has to conform to *it* within its limits if he is to survive. When the king holds an audience with him, Clarence says:

> "Oh Lord, my Lord, is it true that you called me? Is it true that the smell of my body does not make you recoil in horror? And yet, no one is more vile than I, and none more lonely. And yet you, my Lord, are willing to let your glance follow me. Or, was it perhaps because of his very nakedness? 'Your very nakedness,' seemed to say the glance of the king, 'this frightening vacuum in you which kneels to me, your hunger which fills mine, your very abjection which could not exist without my permission, and the shame it arouses in you.' " [6]

The whole novel becomes mystical in tone, and Clarence seeks redemption. He waits for the king, not so much for the potential wealth which the king signified for him at the beginning, but because he feels that this is the only thing to which he can attach himself. It is the only future he knows of. When, in a state of semi-consciousness, he either dreams or sees the king and talks to him, one feels that he dies. This is the end of the novel; it doesn't continue. Either he dies or he wakes up a new man with new hope and a new understanding of life. I think that this new understanding is part of Clarence's process of rehabilitation. He goes through a whole cleansing and purging of his prejudices and the things he takes for granted in his society, for example, that a man has certain rights just by being human—he has a right to be given a job; that sort of thing, basic concepts of Western philosophy—are put in question. He realizes that there can be another side. In the end, Clarence is constantly drowsy. He's always falling asleep. He can't keep his eyes open. His constant drowsiness is a symbol of incomprehension, of inability to cope and understand the strange culture, the strange people among whom he lives. Also, there is a suggestion that perhaps this tendency to sleep signifies Clarence's inability to be anything positive, to take a hold of himself and get out of the nightmare in which he lives. Also, this sleep, suggesting darkness, might be part of the interplay of light and shade which goes on all through the novel. It's a very beautiful choice of colour which really emphasizes the latent antagonism between white and black,

[6] *The Radiance of the King*, p. 283.

between Western civilization typified by Clarence and the immortal Naba who is the African king and who stands for Africa in general.

Camara Laye's third novel *Dramouss*,[7] which has just come out, is mainly a diatribe against the political errors of President Sekou Touré, and I don't think it concerns us very much here. We can see his first two novels are a very positive assertion of his own identity. He lays open a challenge to anyone who is foreign to it to accept this identity for what it is, to try to understand it, and then to seek to merge the two—as when Clarence is finally received by the king.

One could suggest that Clarence is going to be absorbed into the society. That could mean Western civilization is going to be absorbed into Africa—which I rather doubt—or that the spiritual development of a being is the ultimate factor in judging humanity, and not race, colour, religion or political ideology. I think it would mean more likely that Camara Laye did not talk about hunger just accidentally. He meant, probably, that there is a lot that is complementary between the two cultures. Unless one is prepared to see the African traditional heritage for what it is, as something separate, independent, self-sufficient, and, unless from that point of view, one tries to understand, and co-operate with, the African, unless this is done, there is no hope of there ever being a fruitful meeting point between the two. From the point of view of assimilation, it is suggested that there should be an assimilation in reverse. The European has to become, to a certain extent, a part of the African society in order to understand it; whereas in the actual political situation, the African has always had to become a part of the European mainstream in order to understand it and create the synthesis, the balance.

This is more in line with Mongo Beti's writing because he's a very sceptical author, very amusing—and not as profound and majestic perhaps as Camara Laye. His first novel *Le Pauvre Christ de Bomba* (which I don't think translates very well—*The Poor Christ of Bomba*[8]) is a violently anti-clerical work. The novel opens with Reverend Father Superior Drumont finding out that his following his thinned out considerably, and he begins to wonder why. And he asks a question:

"Why do you think everybody has stopped coming to church? Do you think that I've done anything wrong in the last twenty years?" [9]

The cook Zachary replies:

"Here's the real reason, Father. It's like this. Those of us who first rushed to receive your religion came expecting a revelation. Yes, that's it! a

[7] Camara Laye, *Dramouss*, Librairie Plon, 1966. Trans. James Kirkup as *A Dream of Africa*, Collins, 1968.
[8] Mongo Beti, *Le Pauvre Christ de Bomba*, Paris, Stock, 1960.
[9] *Le Pauvre Christ de Bomba*.

form of revelation, a school from which they would have the explanation of your secret, the secret of your force and the force of your aeroplanes, your railways and the rest, the key to your mystery really. Instead of that, you started telling them about God, the soul, eternal life, etc. Do you really think they did not know of all this before, long before your arrival? Indeed, they had the impression that you were hiding things from them. Later on, they noticed that money could provide them with a lot of things like record players, cars, and, perhaps one day, aeroplanes. And there you are—they abandon religion. They hurry elsewhere that is, towards money and more money." [10]

And there Mongo Beti creates the first problem—a society which did not deal in currency is disjointed, is thrown into a state of imbalance with the coming of not only the Catholic religion but of the colonizer. This is part, perhaps, of the particular situation in the former French Cameroons, and in the Belgian colonies, where the administration had been, to a great extent, in the hands of the Catholic Church so that, to the ordinary man, the priest was very much a sort of Governor-General or High Commissioner and he had tremendous powers.

It seems in Mongo Beti's first novel that he is not against the ideology of the Catholic Church, but what he disagrees with is its dogmatism and its institutions, which he thinks are not really all that much better than those of the old days. For example, the sixer which is supposed to be a home for young girls and women preparing to become converts is in actual fact a source of cheap labour, and the priest finds, to his great disgust, that it is run by the catechists who use the sixty girls for a fairly well-organized brothel: all this at about sixty yards away from his home! [Everything following signified to the people of Bomba who seem to be slipping away.] He realizes that his converts have been very superficially Christian, that he has been dealing with a people who are really very unified and very closed in their own ideas. They are not going to be any better for being Westernized. Towards the end of his trip round the small constituencies and congregations of his mission, Father Drumont realizes that he has not done anything to improve the life of these people. He is the only man, his mission is the only thing representative of Western civilization in that area. There is nothing against which Father Drumont could test the validity of his decision and, because of this, he made mistakes which it took him twenty years to recognize. In the end, he confesses to the Administration Officer:

"As for me, I am a complete failure. These good people have also worshipped God without me whether by eating men, dancing in the moonlight, or wearing around their necks fetishes made from tree barks. Why must we insist on imposing our methods of worship on them?" And

[10] *Le Pauvre Christ de Bomba.*

later he adds, "You see, I prefer never to have to answer to God for
colonialism. I would not like to be in your shoes, Mr. Pitain. You will
say I am the exception among missionaries. It's true, and I'm deeply
hurt because of this." [11]

Father Drumont realizes that he's part of a big network. He realizes
he's as much an Administrative Officer as Monsieur Pitain is, and
resigns from his position.

But Mongo Beti's novel is not one-sided. He does not only criticize
Father Drumont; he laughs at the chief who has too many wives; he
laughs at the sorcerer; he laughs at the old people; and, in *Ville
Cruelle*,[12] he makes a lot of fun out of the situation of two cultures
from which the young man has not very much to choose. Banda goes
to the city to sell his cocoa crop in *Ville Cruelle*. There he is cheated
by the Greek merchant who condemns his crop, only to retrieve it
later and sell it at a better price. He comes up against hooliganism,
and becomes involved with a theft. All the characteristic traits of city
life which would confuse and which would be completely beyond
the comprehension of a boy who had grown up away from that situation in a tribal village are portrayed here. And yet, when Banda thinks
of it, he has nothing to which he could return. He dislikes city life
and he goes back home. He realizes that there is nothing to choose
between the two because as soon as he comes back, there's the old man
Tonga who bores him to death with his sententious egoism. He says
here:

"It's true. There is not much difference between the two—white man
and old man. In fact, it's the same thing. No, that's not exactly true.
With the white man it's primarily money, more money, and yet more
money; but with an old man, it's even more difficult. You must listen
to him all day. From morning to night you must for ever admire and
approve of what he says. No, it's not true. The white man is not exactly like the old man."

Mongo Beti is a very sceptical writer, and his characters—Tundi,
the houseboy in his first novel *Le Pauvre Christ de Bomba,* and Banda,
the hero of *Ville Cruelle*—are young people, rather naïve, hesitating
between two cultures, the first being the traditional heritage from
which they are progressively separated, and the second the Western
influence signified by city life with which they are not fully in tune.

I think that the problem with Mongo Beti's novels—particularly
in his last two—*Mission Terminée*[13] and *Le Roi Miraculé*[14]—is that

[11] *Le Pauvre Christ de Bomba.*
[12] Mongo Beti, *Ville Cruelle* (short story) in *Trois Ecrivains Noirs*, Présence Africaine, 1954.
[13] Mongo Beti, *Mission Terminée*, Paris 1957, Corrêa.
[14] Mongo Beti, *Le Roi Miraculé*, Paris 1958, Corrêa.

he laughs at both sides of the question. He is too amused by it all ever to get down to the problem of seeing a way out of the whole situation. His main characters—Tundi, Medsa, Christophe of *Le Roi Miraculé*, Medsa from *Mission Terminée,* and Aoanda—are very young. They are between fifteen and eighteen; they have all had some education; and yet they are very immature. We cannot judge from these people and their evolution in the situations through which they pass what the author thinks. We cannot draw conclusions about the conflict of culture in the society he portrays because the characters hover between the city and the village. We hesitate between these two poles, we smile a bit over the discrepancies, but we are not a part of the events, and we do not ever really see this village in conflict. We do not see on which side the author is going to be.

This is the main difference between Mongo Beti and Camara Laye— one of attitude. I think that Mongo Beti is a very sophisticated writer. He's a little bit more divorced from the situation as it is in the Cameroon Republic than is Camara Laye, and he has a very ready pen for burlesque. He seems to lapse into comedy as soon as he gets away from a tricky situation. One never takes the whole thing seriously. Yet he is the more realistic of the two authors because altogether he may be suggesting that there is not a clear cut line of demarcation between the young "assimilé" and the village boy. There is no clear pattern of choice. Perhaps, there is no choice. There are students like Christophe who go home on holiday, and find that the old people are quite as funny as the school-teachers. Christophe will probably grow up choosing what he would like to copy from the two heritages. Thus perhaps Mongo Beti portrays a simpler way out. He shows us the modern society in Africa as it would appear to a boy who goes away to school, returns home, and finds that unconsciously he compares the village with what he has been taught, and does not know what to do in life— whether he is going to become a doctor or a labourer. He has not become anything yet, and perhaps this is what Africa is at the moment.

We are at the stage where we look forwards and backwards, and we consider the problem of assimilation. It is a problem, but there is no ready solution. There is no crystallization for the time being, nor is there in Mongo Beti's novels.

It seems that he has much more feeling for his subject than Camara Laye. Camara Laye is a very intense writer, but when he puts across his society and the force of it, one cannot but wonder how one can apply the ideas implicit in the novel to the present-day situation, whether it is possible for the West to reassess it's prejudices and ideas about Africa; whether it is still true that the old Africa is a compact and well-unified, harmonious society. Mongo Beti shows that it is not a compact society, things are falling apart. The young generation goes to school, they are taught different things. They come back and they size up their villages and they find there is a lot to be done. How should, how do they go about doing this? The question remains unanswered.

And yet, from a literary point of view, Camara Laye has more to offer because he would symbolize the whole process of development that has taken place between the African and the West but in reverse. He has shown the rather painful process through which a young or old man has to adapt himself to the smallest item of life in a Western society. It does not matter to what extent he has to make sacrifices in order to achieve this; it is taken for granted in the West. This is one of the most striking points of Camara Laye's novels—the fact that everything is taken for granted. He does not explain why things should be so. He does not explain why, for example, the smith who is trying to hammer out an axe never gets it quite perfect, but is compelled to strive hopelessly after perfection, so his gift will, perhaps, because of the effort put into it, be worthy of the king. He doesn't explain why there should be this mystery around the king, and he doesn't explain, for example, why Clarence should not be able to do anything in this society. One never knows where this novel is situated. It is a very timeless, open locality. Clarence and his two guides go through endless villages and endless forests. Everything is dark and there is a chance that nothing lies at the end of the journey, just as perhaps there is nothing at the end of the whole problem of adaptation. To what is Clarence going to adapt himself? Is he going to become an African? That is not possible. He was not born in that society, he cannot be a part of it. The only way he can contribute is as part of the chief's harem and in helping take care of the wives and add mulatto children to the king's already large family. His function is purely animal, to breed. He has finally been stripped of every prop of his European society.

Camara Laye may be a very positive writer. He may be saying, "Look, there is nothing in this. You and I are completely different, and I don't need you. But if you want to know me, come to me, come and see what I think and how I react." There is no bending down, there is no concession.

Mongo Beti is very much more rational about the problem of assimilation. He takes it for granted, for example, that there should be white school-teachers whereas there is not a single European teacher, there is not a single religious mission house in Camara Laye's two novels. In Camara Laye's second novel (and in his first) where the school is run by coloured teachers the school does not symbolize a foreign culture as such so a confrontation is avoided.

The process of assimilation imposed by Europe on Africa was only a superficial phenomenon, Mongo Beti implied in *Le Pauvre Christ de Bomba*. The things that are apparently Western in Africa are only so for a time. They are only so because they have had to be so. But with a certain lapse of time, there is going to be a shedding of all that is not true, of all that has no significance in the life of the African. There will be a co-operation, as Sénghor put it; there will be a communion between two cultures; but there will not be this painful choice of which way to turn. Mongo Beti's suggestion that there is no going back is the better one. There should be no constraining forces to keep the developing younger generations in check. They must be allowed to evolve and grow in the direction indicated by their individual personalities.

Camara Laye: Another Interpretation

by Janheinz Jahn

J. A. Ramsaran has given an interpretation of Camara Laye's symbolism in *The Radiance of the King* in which he relates Laye's symbolism to Kafka, and he looks to Christianity and Islam for further comparisons. But I think that we could find a more convincing explanation nearer home, in *African* thinking. I should like to consider here Camara Laye's two books, because the first is a key to the second. In *The Dark Child* Camara Laye shows his understanding and respect for African traditions, and in *The Radiance of the King* he makes this tradition work on a stranger.

In *The Dark Child* Camara Laye shows the new spirit of French West Africans towards tradition. He did not consider his African childhood as something remote, primitive, something to be ashamed of. On the contrary: looking back on it from a distance, and having learned the technical skills European education had to offer, he discovered these skills had been animated, and had been more closely related to man, in his native civilisation. In his novel he describes lovingly the work of his father, a goldsmith, who was in his way a technician, but who is helped by the praise-singers while he works.

See how Camara Laye describes the actual smelting of gold:

> My father used to utter actual words at this time, I know that he was uttering them in his mind. I could see it by his lips. What were the words my father's lips were forming? I do not know, I do not know for certain: I was never told what they were. But what else could they have been, if not magical incantations? Were they not the spirits of fire and gold, of fire and air, of fire born in air, of gold married with fire—were not these spirits he was invoking? The operation that was going on before my eyes was simply the smelting of gold, but it was something more than that: a magical operation.
>
> During the whole process of transformation the praise-singer had kept on singing his praises, accelerating his rhythm, increasing his flatteries, as the trinket took shape, and praising my father's talents to the skies.

"Camara Laye: Another Interpretation" by Janheinz Jahn. From *Introduction to African Literature: An Anthology of Critical Writings from "Black Orpheus"*, ed. Ulli Beier (Evanston, Ill.: Northwestern University Press; London: Longmans, Green & Co., Ltd., 1967), pp. 200–3. Reprinted by permission of the publishers.

Indeed, the praise-singer participated in a curious—I was going to say direct, effective—way in the work. He too, was intoxicated with the joy of creation, he declaimed his rapture, and plucked his harp like a man inspired: he warmed to the task as if he had been the craftsman himself, as if the trinket had been made by his own hands.

This scene illustrates and emphasises the importance and the quality of the word in Africa, the effective power of the creative word, which has such importance in Africa philosophy. Sénghor, the famous poet and philosopher from Senegal, in one of his essays comments on the scene:

> Laye's father is forging a golden jewel. The prayer, or rather the poem, which he recites, the song of praise which the Griot sings as he works the gold, the dance of the smith at the end of the operation, it is all that—poem, song and dance—which, more than the gestures of the craftsman, accomplish the work, and make it a work of art.
>
> Thus finally all human doing and creating is a kind of magic, and a formula of chemistry, a calculation of statistics, what else is it than a magic formula, the right word in the right moment to accomplish a creative mystery? Camara Laye, although an engineer, remained related to his African tradition and thus did not lose his soul in the technical environment because he was able to give to those abstract formulas a spiritual meaning, the living meaning of a symbol.

In his second book, *The Radiance of the King*, he does even more. The whole book is full of symbolism. It is usually considered as an ingenious allegory about man's search for God. But I think that the book cannot be seen in this sense only; it is ambivalent, even multivalent, as Sénghor says of all African art. Clarence, a European, finds himself without the help and support of his countrymen in an African environment. He is without money, without hope of outside help. He is thrown exactly into that position in which many Africans often find themselves in the European world. He has to conform. And thus he gradually becomes initiated. The whole book can be considered as a lesson in African wisdom.

Clarence concentrates his hopes on the African King. He stands in the dust of the street and watches the King pass. A beggar who is also watching promises to put in a good word for him, so that Clarence might get a job. When the beggar reappears, Clarence was trying to read the beggar's face, but he could make out nothing at all: he had been too short a time in this country to be able to decipher the expression on the black men's faces:

> "Well," he asked.
> "I am sorry," said the beggar, "there is no post available for you."
> "But I would have accepted any post whatsoever!"
> "I know, but there are no posts available."

"I should have been satisfied with the humblest situation," said Clarence. "I could have . . ." he said. But what could he have done? Had he the least idea? "I could have been a simple drummer boy . . ."

"That is not a simple occupation," said the beggar. "The drummers are drawn from a noble caste and their employment is hereditary. Even if you had been allowed to beat a drum it would have had no meaning. The white men think they know everything, and what *do* they know, when all's said and done? Perhaps I should not have announced that you were ready to accept any kind of employment whatsoever, perhaps they were suspicious of a man who was ready to accept just *any* kind of employment feeling that such a one would be incapable of doing anything."

Thus is the beginning of this European's education. He gets one lesson after the other, most of them painful. At a Law Court he is treated like Africans were at times treated in colonialist Law Courts: his evidence has no value and he cannot get justice. Only the beggar helps him on: his art of begging supplies enough food while they go South where the King is expected. Clarence does not see that they move on; he believes he is tricked, that they go the same way every day, so unchanged is the landscape to him, the forest that never ends. In a village Clarence does not want to go on; the beggar sells him there, getting a woman and a donkey for him. Clarence does not know that he has been sold, his life is comfortable, he is not supposed to work and gets a nice companion to sleep with him in his hut. But sometimes he has the impression that his woman is different, that the woman he has in the night is not his woman. He worries; he wants to find out, though he is told that it is better for him not to know. But as a white man he cannot leave any secret untouched, he wants to know the truth. He finally finds out that he is used as a stallion to mate with the wives of the *naba*, the chief. Knowing it makes him more unhappy than before, seeing his pride in his white race reduced to nothing but a biological difference whimsically used by a *naba* to make his offspring look different from other offspring.

Even his humanitarian ideals, his Christian pity, are shown to be worthless and harmful. The Master of Ceremonies has done wrong in letting Clarence into the secret, and as a punishment the Master of Ceremonies gets whipped. Clarence, attending the scene, is torn by his conscience, mutters "Savages!" and stops the whipping. But not even the whipped Master of Ceremonies thanks him for his interference, because the Master of Ceremonies will enjoy no respite now. If the display had been allowed to pursue its rightful course, he would have been able really to enjoy the respite, the sense of relief that the conclusion of a well-regulated torture always affords. Whereas now he has to drag himself around as if he had never received a single stroke.

Clarence's preconceived ideas are altered, his prejudices torn. None of the persons who surround him is wholly reliable, but all are human, neither good nor bad but both.

Noaga and Nagoa, the two boys who accompany Clarence all the time, are neither good nor bad. At any time they take their chance; they steal where there is an opportunity. Clarence is often worried about them, at times he is shocked, at times compelled to admire. They never consider life too seriously. There is no question whether they are to be redeemed by the King or not. "Tomorrow we go with the King," they say. Their redemption is not a question of good or evil, they cannot be rejected by the King, because already they live life as a unity. Clarence on the other hand can only be redeemed after he has learned that his moral problems are not essential. This is one of the strongest arguments against the Christian interpretation of the end of the book.

Clarence learns, and learns gradually, to become one of those around him; human himself, humble at last when all his preconceptions are gone. It is again a smith, Diallo the blacksmith, who gives him the most worthy lessons. One morning he learns about the essence of African art: Diallo's reflections on the axe he is making for the King, which Mr. Ramsaran has quoted, make clear that not the purpose of the axe is important, but its meaning. The process of creation is more important than the created object. In itself it is not worth much, its worth lasts as long as the artist creates it, doing his best to justify his own life. And as soon as it is finished he starts to forge a new one, a better one again, and each one is the sum of everything he has ever learnt. And the former axes are destooled works of art, they are of no value to him, they become mere tools which now the farmer may use.

Finally Clarence is redeemed after he has learned that all his former scales of values are wrong. When finally he has learned to have visions, when he has understood that what he thought to be sin is not sin but life, that by all his errors there is nothing that really counts but his good will, then the king draws him to his breast. Like everything in this novel this king is a symbol too. He is fortune, merit, favour, mercy, he is king and redeemer. Camara Laye gives the sum of all religion, of all humanity, in this novel. And he shows that here, finally, all religion is one. Various symbols of different religions are used to fuse them into a unified concept of religion.

Mr. Ramsaran sees the novel as a "strange mixture of two qualities, the sensual and the spiritual." But the sensual and the spiritual are one in African thinking. It is Clarence, the European, who separates the two. For Clarence the mixture is strange. He tries to split these forces, until he is redeemed and has learned that there is no split. Unity is not a final synthesis for Laye, it is the original state.

The end of the novel, often misunderstood, means that even the white man in Africa can be redeemed and accepted when he shows his will to learn and not only to teach. And that Camara Laye in all his lessons does not consider the African way of faith and redemption the only one imaginable and superior. He wants to say that it is the only right way for Africa and that it is of equal value with an other way of mankind.

Discovery

by Gerald Moore

So I shall voyage no more from home; may I speak here.
Derek Walcott

It was to the islands of the New World that the first dark voyagers came. There is reason to believe that at least one officer of African descent sailed with Columbus on his first voyage. And long before the sixteenth century was out Africans both slave and free had been carried to many of the Caribbean islands, whilst the indigenous Arawaks of the Greater Antilles were already far gone towards extinction. But though Africans may have been present at the very first landfall on the islands and were certainly prominent in their exploration and early settlement, that is not the sort of discovery with which we are concerned in this chapter. Discovery in the cultural sense comes with the realization that one is neither a rootless being devoid of identity, nor a lost son of Africa or Asia, but a man made and shaped by this island now. In West Indian literature this species of discovery has come about only during the past twenty years, some four and a half centuries after Columbus landed in Jamaica. And it was in Jamaica that the first announcement of the discovery was made, with the publication of V. S. Reid's novel *New Day* in 1947.

This novel rests upon a single proposition: that Jamaica has a history. This history is distinct from that of its various racial groups separately viewed. No group of people, however polyglot, can inhabit an island through four hundred and fifty years of turbulence and change without forming a history and culture uniquely their own. It follows that there is such a creature as a Jamaican, and that we can only get to know him by looking at his island and following its story.

This central proposition is built into the structure of Reid's novel, for the life of a single man, his narrator, bridges the bloody Morant Bay Rebellion of 1865 and the new constitution of 1944. The first event signalled the abolition of representative government after more than

"Discovery." From *The Chosen Tongue* by Gerald Moore (New York: Harper & Row, Publishers, 1969), pp. 3–20. Reprinted by permission of the publisher.

two hundred years, the second announced its return. As the old man
compares these events in his mind, relating them to one another and
to the larger history of the island, the lineaments of Jamaica begin to
emerge. For the constitution abolished in 1865, though offering a
measure of local autonomy, gave government into the hands of the
white plantocracy. Slavery, which had effectively ended only twenty-
seven years before, still left its mark upon every aspect of society, still
manipulated attitudes and motives, still pushed events towards the
culmination of the Rebellion itself. The constitution which returned
in 1944 held the promise, at least, of government based on consent;
the consent of that vast despised majority which had been as powerless
under the intervening eighty years of crown colony rule as it was under
the old regime of the planters.

Reid's book, written so soon after the latter event, is not concerned
to ask whether that promise has been fulfilled. It announces by its
very title a hope only, but a hope which had not been there before at
any time in the island's history.

Yet the importance of *New Day* does not rest only on its central
concern with Jamaica and its people. The same new confidence that
dictated its theme extends into the style itself, for the whole book is
couched in the form of a long monologue by the aged narrator as
the crowds celebrating their new measure of freedom surge under his
window. Hence it is written throughout in a style approximating to
Jamaican country dialect of the mid-nineteenth century. To use this
style of speech even for dialogue, except to produce comical "quashi"
(country bumpkin) effect, was effrontery enough to the delicate colonial
sensibility which rotated around wistful connections with "Home" and
garden parties at King's House. To write an entire book in this
despised dialect, albeit spoken habitually by nine-tenths of the population, and in off-moments by the rest, was radical indeed.

Here is the old man beginning to carry us back into the menacing
atmosphere of the Parish of St. Thomas a few days before the Rebellion broke out. Yet what he recovers first from the debris of memory
is the breaking of a bright morning over that sodden impoverished
earth. We notice the characteristic repetition of the verb root, trans-
posed from West African speech, and the use of English archaisms
like "a-drown," "day-cloud" and the delightful "kitty-up" which remind us that the English settlers of seventeenth century Jamaica and
Barbados have left many distinctive regional marks upon the popular
speech of the islands:

> I remember I remember one August morning when rain was a-drown
> the earth. For two weeks now the sun had no' shone. Black is the morn-
> ing, black the evening, and Mas'r God's heaven does no look on us at all.
> Yallahs and Morant Bay and Plantain Garden rivers heavy so, until you
> do not know where rivers end and land begins. That was the time when

an alligator swam clear up to the barrack and took away my friend Timothy's bro'. Then there was dirging down at the barracks. Day in, day out, you heard it through the rain, a mark-time with the drip, drip, drip of *guinep* and mango trees weeping.

Then one morning when day-cloud was peeping, I woke and did no' hear the rain. Creeping out o' my kitty-up, I went to the door and pulled the latch-wood—Wayah!

Look there! Is no' that Mas'r God's heaven looking down on us again? [1]

The extent to which Reid has modified his rendering of dialect, so as to reduce visual irritation and slowness in apprehension for the general reader of English, may be seen by looking at a passage of any typical Jamaican country story recorded, not in phonetic script, but in ordinary Roman:

Ol' Witch razor mout' tu'n over. Ol' Witch gi' out, "Bway, whe' you come from, torment me so?" Boy said "Hi, Nana! When me to home, when me yawzy bite me, it is de bigges' barrow me mamma got, kill him an' tek de blood wash me." An' Ol' Witch kill a barrow an' wash him, an' de boy gone to bed, gone sleep. [2]

Such a comparison makes it clear that Reid has in effect composed a musical script with dialect features. For the purposes he set out to achieve, anything more documentary would have been self-defeating and might well have reinforced the existing prejudice against the literary use of dialect rather than diminishing it.

Obvious though it may be to date the appearance of a new West Indian literature from the publication of *New Day*, it is probably just also. Recognition is due to some earlier works such as Mittelholzer's *Corentyne Thunder* (1941), but it was with *New Day* that a new generation of West Indian writers really began the task of breaking free from the colonial cocoon and flying with wings of their own, in a distinctly tropical sky.

There are, of course, dissentients even now. It is not entirely surprising that it was those of negro extraction who led the movement towards a new regional consciousness centred in the West Indies themselves, and not in some dim anterior condition alleged to be Africa, India, China or England. Not only are those of African descent an overwhelming majority of the area's population, especially in Jamaica and all the smaller islands, but by and large they have been there longest, thereby shedding most of the associations, other than colour, which might tie them to an identifiable culture, religion or language rooted elsewhere. Hence it is equally unsurprising to find a writer like V. S. Naipaul ridiculing the whole idea of a West Indian history, or a West Indian anything else. For Naipaul is a Trinidad

[1] *New Day*, English edition (London, Heinemann, 1950), p. 37.
[2] "Andrew and his Sisters" in *Memoirs of the American Folk-lore Society*, Vol. XVII, 1924.

East Indian who grew up in a community whose older members
still spoke, thought and worshipped in terms of India, remembering
the very villages from which they came. Massive Indian immigration
continued into Trinidad and Guyana until 1917, so that many are
still living who remember another life and another land. Yet Naipaul
himself admits that this dense pattern of associations with India is
rapidly disappearing among the younger generations. Indeed, this
process of "Creolization" is one of the principal themes of his novels
and it is a process he generally laments, since he sees it as one of
loss rather than transition. The positive point about this transition
had already been made by another Trinidad Indian writer, Samuel
Selvon, in his very first book. In *A Brighter Sun* (1952), Selvon shows
how his young hero Tiger and his bride Urmila, East Indians both
and of orthodox Hindu background are quite naturally befriended by
their Creole (African) neighbours, Joe and Rita, when they move into
a new district, away from the strict social rituals of their own family
groups. Visiting relatives may glower and protest, but Tiger is not
prepared to reject those who have shown him real generosity, who
share his youth and his poverty. Hindu religious rituals and social
taboos have less and less meaning for him. The English dialect of
Trinidad has become his language, and his life is shaped by its brash
energy and jazzy tempo, rather than by any real consciousness of
Mother India. Their parents merely live in Trinidad, but Tiger and
Urmila have become Trinidadians.

Yet Naipaul does not seem to recognize that people like these will
soon need to define a West Indian existence, call it nationalism or what
you will, quite as urgently as their Creole compatriots. For he has
written as recently as 1961:

> How can the history of this West Indian futility be written? . . . The
> history of the islands can never be satisfactorily told. Brutality is not
> the only difficulty. History is built around achievement and creation;
> and nothing was created in the West Indies.[3]

Here Naipaul is surely confusing a purely personal rejection with a
historical fact. Many might think that this kind of total rejection of
what and where one is, once so common in the West Indies, can only
become a sickness of the spirit. From this sickness the society as a
whole seems to be making a slow but miraculous recovery. The salient
impression upon the outsider who looks at West Indian achievement
in literature, music, dance, drama and art over the past twenty years is
precisely of intense creativity. But Naipaul also challenges the product:

> Living in a borrowed culture, the West Indian, more than most, needs
> writers to tell him who he is and where he stands. Here the West

³ *The Middle Passage* (London, Deutsch, 1962), pp. 28–29.

Indian writers have failed. Most have so far only flattered the prejudices of their race or colour groups. With two or three exceptions, the West Indian writer has so far avoided the American Negro type of protest writing, but his aims have been equally propagandist: to win acceptance for his group.[4]

The charge is singularly unfair. It is possible to read an early novel of Selvon's without even guessing the race of the author himself. The same cannot be said of early Naipaul, the Naipaul of *The Mystic Masseur* (1957) or *The Suffrage of Elvira* (1958), which, witty and accomplished as it is, remains firmly rooted and confined in a Trinidad East Indian society. But even if the charge were justified, would not the writer's aim to "win acceptance for his group" look rather different if that group happened to be the vast majority of his island's population, as with the black Jamaican for example? Here was a majority whose claim to be in any way representative of Jamaica had been constantly ridiculed by the tiny coloured and white élite, clinging to the coat-tails of colonial officialdom. It was this élite, and not the Jamaican masses, whose culture was truly "borrowed" and provincial. Surely for the black Jamaican to win acceptance for his group was, in these circumstances, to win acceptance for the reality of Jamaican life itself? Any true West Indian nationalism must ultimately learn to ignore colour, but before it can do this it must take cognizance of the objective fact that most West Indians are more or less black. This fact alone, the implications of which were so long ignored, will influence decisively the nature of the culture now emerging. For, even if the West Indies had created nothing else, they have certainly created a people; a people, moreover, forged from the most diverse of elements in the most tragic of circumstances.

New Day taught West Indians to look at their past in more positive terms; to see it as one of constant struggle and protest rather than of passive endurance. Jamaica alone experienced dozens of courageous slave rebellions, as well as two substantial and protracted wars against the Maroons. The suffering and privation of rural life also gave rise to violent movements in more recent years. Such a movement forms the subject of Andrew Salkey's first novel *A Quality of Violence,* set in a remote district of Jamaica in 1905. Here it is drought which is driving the peasants to extremity and many of them seek the outlet of violent religious excitement in the syncretic cult of Pocomania. Ma Johnson, the leader of the cult, finally dominates the action of the novel by her willingness to die, stoned by her own followers, in order that the kind of power she represents may live. Writers like Reid, Salkey and Roger Mais (in his last novel, *Black Lightning*) have given a strong rural dimension to the Jamaican novel, reminding us

[4] *Ibid.,* p. 68.

how explosions of terrible energy can pass across the face of those verdant, peaceful-looking hills. In its totally different way, another novel published soon after *New Day* contributed to the exploration of West Indian reality. Whereas the action of *New Day* is rooted in the life of the newly-emancipated black peasantry of nineteenth century rural Jamaica, Edgar Mittelholzer's *A Morning at the Office* (1950) is concerned with a cross-section of contemporary Trinidad society in the urban, commercial world of Port of Spain. Compared with the warm romanticism of Reid's hero and treatment, Mittelholzer's method is deliberately clinical. He confines his narrative to the events of a single morning in the office of Essential Products Limited, but he constantly escapes from these limits both spatially and temporally by giving us glimpses of the past lives of his characters, their daydreams, aspirations and sneaking fears. Furthermore, he adopts the technique of "telescopic objectivity" propounded by one of them, a writer who visits the office during the day and is perhaps to some extent a flattering self-portrait. His formula requires the novelist to explore the history of certain selected objects which surround the lives of his characters. These can be "dynamic" objects, like the table-leg which sends out a rough hand to clasp Miss Henery's thigh in the midst of her erotic reverie; or "static" objects, which are only important because of their past significance in their owners' lives, like Sidney Whitmer's nib, which has left the realm of his personal affairs but continues to trouble the relationship between Jagabir, the East Indian accountant, and Mary, the Creole cleaner. Tracing the careers of such objects is another of the devices by which Mittelholzer escapes from the strait limits of his morning.

This clinical approach enables him to be didactic from time to time about West Indian society, since he is laying it bare for our enlightenment. Thus Mittelholzer, as omniscient author, weaves together the separate anxieties of the fearful Jagabir, the ambitious young Creole office boy Horace Xavier and the tearful, loquacious Mary. Their common insecurity does not unite them; often it sets them tearing at each other in dumb hatred and mutual contempt:

> His [Jagabir's] ears were perpetually on the alert, for the fear was always with him that, despite his efficiency as a book-keeper, he would one day be thrown out. He had been brought up to feel that an East Indian's place was in the Field. . . . An office was meant for white people and good-class coloured people. He considered his officiousness justified, it was his defence against possible attack and the ejection that might result from such an attack.
>
> Horace, who had merely glanced up at his approach continued to read. He too, did not like Mr. Jagabir. From the first day he had come to work at the office Mr. Jagabir had begun to nag at him. Horace considered him a mean, quarrelsome man.

"You might say morning, Xavier," said Mr. Jagabir. Horace, prepared for this, looked up. "Who? Me? I thought it was your place to say morning. You come in and find me here." There was no respect in his voice as would have been the case with another member of staff.

Mr. Jagabir hesitated, unsure of himself, then said: "I'm your superior."

"If you were the king it was your place to tell me morning when you come in and find me here." Mr. Jagabir did not argue. He suddenly knew he had erred. The boy was probably right. . . . Frowning heavily, he went to his desk. . . . On his way he gave Mary a swift sideways glance. Horace's rebuke still moved like a pebble in his chest, and he was very much aware that he was guilty of a second breach of good manners in refraining from saying good morning to Mary. A feeling of frustration and resentment tightened his inside, and he told himself he had every right to ignore Mary. She was an insolent woman. She hated him—as all the rest of them hated him. Because he was an Indian, because he was the son of indentured coolies, they all looked on him as dirt.[5]

This jangling of enclosed fears, hostilities and anxieties continues throughout the morning. Occasionally Mittelholzer as commentator is even more specific about the categories within which virtually all his characters feel compelled to operate. Thus he interrupts an account of Miss Henery's contemplation of a suitor and his claims to remark:

as a member of the West Indian coloured middle-class, she conceived of human hair in terms of "good" and "bad"—sometimes "good" and "hard"; "good" hair is hair that is European in appearance; "bad" or "hard" hair is hair of the kinky, Negroid type.[6]

The emergence of Mittelholzer as lecturer introducing West Indian society to a supposedly foreign public is sometimes irritating. Nevertheless, he never steps from lecturing into preaching: his comment on this farrago of hair-splitting prejudice is confined to the single word "human," which can be left to set up its own reverberation. He does not protest, he describes. Consequently, such words as "kinky," "Negroid," "black," "coloured," "coolie," "white," occur in almost every paragraph, like some kind of dreadful stammer which must be employed before any person can be registered by his neighbours as existing at all. It is true that Mittelholzer gives us a two-layered map (in full-colour and class) of Trinidad society which would be of assistance to any enterprising tourist. But by being ruthlessly direct in the description of what many West Indians take for granted, and assume to be so taken everywhere, he prepares that groundwork of reality from which alone any new integrated vision of West Indian

[5] *A Morning at the Office* (London: Hogarth, 1950; Penguin edition, 1964), pp. 27–28.
[6] *Ibid.*, p. 59.

humanity can spring. The effect of the novel is not ultimately depressing, partly because Mittelholzer is a compassionate surgeon, who pities as he dissects; partly because a strong vein of humour flows through the whole book. And the novelist does offer us one character, the gentle Miss Bisnauth, who refuses to think ill of anybody, who transcends the anxieties which confine everyone else to their own shade of skin and insists on living in a world of people. In this way, she serves to show us how dreadfully imprisoning such a social order is, how it restricts acquaintance, corrupts judgement, limits choice, dictates action. Another character, Mrs. Hinckson, has glimpses of this truth also, but is unable to grasp it. In her quiet style, it is Edna Bisnauth who points the way towards a new definition of personality which only a rejection of these old categories, by setting people free, can make possible.

The nature of Mittelholzer's purpose in this book dictates a spare, analytical style, confining itself to the exposure of motives, the linking of people with objects, and the bare bones of a narrative structure. His tone is deliberately cool and carefully detached. But his purpose also enables him to register the various levels of speech within the office, and how these are imposed as much by the expectations of others as by differences of opportunity and education. Thus Mary plays her "black-momma" part in the accepted manner with lines like these:

> "Ow boy! It's not for want o' trying. You know how often Ah talk to Richard! Oh, God! Ah weary talking, weary, weary. And he leading his brudder astray—dat's de hurtful part." [7]

The "posh" coloured folk like Miss Henery, Mrs. Hinckson and Pat Lorry sedulously avoid anything that savours of dialect, especially in the presence of their supposed inferiors. Jagabir hovers linguistically, as he does socially, uncertain where to settle. But he puts on a special East Indian voice when he is in his most insinuating and ingratiating manner, as when he mutters to Miss Henery, *à propos* of Horace:

> "Dat boy got too much on his mind that he shouldn't got. . . . Lil' half-penny black boy like dat to mek out he in love wid a big-family lady like Mrs. Hinckson. He properly rude." [8]

Language, then, is one of the instruments with which people try to plot their own positions on Mittelholzer's map of Trinidad society. Along with skin-colour, it is the focus of some of their strongest taboos, tensions and patterns of inhibited response. This is especially true in an urban office like the scene of the novel, which throws together people who might successfully avoid much social contact outside, and so be relieved of the necessity to demonstrate continually their precise social station to those imagined as above or below them.

[7] *Ibid.,* p. 22.
[8] *Ibid.,* p. 84.

Novels set in a more socially and racially homogeneous environment open up to the writer an easier prospect of escaping from realistic rapportage and a freer use of language, since he is not concerned with making discriminations within his group. This freedom is fully exploited by George Lamming in his first, semi-autobiographical novel *In the Castle of My Skin* (1953), which centres around his growth from the ages of nine to eighteen in a small Barbados village.

Lamming's discovery of his childhood world, which forms one of the most beautiful and original books yet produced by the West Indies, is not effected by the sort of clinical analysis offered by Mittelholzer. Rather, he shows us the gradual unfolding and flowering of an adolescent sensibility, interwoven movement by movement with changes in the life of the village around. These changes are felt and observed by others even more than by the narrator himself. Thus it is not only the process of growing that distances the boy from the innocence of childhood, but the actual disintegration of his childhood world as he moves through and beyond it.

This poignant intricacy of effect is achieved partly by Lamming's deliberate crumbling of time into fragments, which are then rearranged by association with particular objects or experiences, not in accordance with any strict chronological scheme. We are often not sure, if we pause to ask, just how old the narrator is at a particular moment, or how much time has gone by since the last cluster of memory was explored. Each moment enjoys an autonomy and completeness of its own, like a movement in music. One sequence in the novel begins with his burying a pebble in the beach sand, in the hope of finding it there next day and achieving one victory over "envious and calumniating Time." But on the morrow, although he finds the marked place and burrows there, the stone has gone. His desolation at this images the sense, growing ever stronger through the book, that life is a continued process of goodbyes to moments and people that we shall never see again. So he writes, following upon the discovery of the pebble's disappearance:

> I tried to recall when this feeling had started, but that seemed useless. . . . You couldn't bear the thought of seeing things for the last time, and things included people, objects and situations. . . . I remembered vaguely that something used to happen when as a small boy I rode in a bus and reviewed the objects and people as they glided by. The shop and that lamp-post and the man who stood at the corner blank and impersonal. It seemed that the bus was steady while they slipped past, and I wondered whether I would see them again. . . . I experienced the feeling in a high degree when I left the village school; and in the circumstances there was no reason to be sorry. . . . Yet the feeling was there. I was seeing the village school for the last time. The teachers shook my hand and wished me the best of luck. And I was left

with the intolerable feeling that they had somehow gone for ever. I recalled the lamp-posts and the shops and the man at the corner, and I knew that the feeling was not new. . . .

Later, when Trumper came to say that he was going to America I couldn't bear to look him straight in the face. . . . He left on a wet morning three years before I left the High School; and although an important difference in our fortunes had forced us apart I went to see him off. We stood on the pier together and watched the ship which was anchored in the distance. There were hundreds of them leaving for America, and I saw them all less real than Trumper but with the same sickness, which the feeling brought on. It seemed I wasn't going to see any of those faces again. . . . I started to think of the High School and what had happened to all of us in the intervening years; and suddenly as if by an inner compulsion my mind went back to the spot under the grapeleaf and the pebble which I had seen for the last time. I ducked my head in the water and come up wet and refreshed.

It was a year or two after the riots and I was eleven. . . .[9]

These few paragraphs, growing out of a single moment of time to which the last sentences return us, roam backwards to a childhood recollection of the writer's first awareness of this intense mortality within experience, then forwards to the leaving of the village school; forwards again (beyond the pebble's moment) to his friend Trumper's departure, then back to the central episode of the vain search for the pebble. Only then, four pages into the new chapter, does Lamming establish the period of this episode ("a year or two after the riots"), for the pebble's importance as an object resides not only in itself but in its ability to set memory and imagination moving freely in time. Mittelholzer had attempted an evocation of the history and significance of certain objects in *A Morning at the Office,* but did not sustain it through the book. Lamming, by rooting their power to move him and us in the rendering of certain childhood experiences, is able to trace the progress of time's sickness through objects as well as through people. He does this not only with the pebble but with the dark mysterious woods around the white landlord's house, which were later felled to leave a bare and startled landscape; or with the railway where the boys once took their nails to be beaten into blades by the passing trains, which was later torn up for wartime scrap.

It is an elegiac childhood on which change has cast its sadness from the first and which sustains its note into the last sentences of the book:

The earth where I walked was a marvel of blackness and I knew in a sense more deep than simple departure I had said farewell, farewell to the land.[10]

[9] *In the Castle of My Skin* (London, Michael Joseph, 1953), pp. 215–16.
[10] *Ibid.,* p. 303.

The book begins with a great flood, announcing the ninth birthday of the fatherless only child who looks out upon the waste of waters carrying everything away. So the flood becomes the first great climacteric announcing change. We are told nothing of what preceded it. At this time the social and physical geography of the village still reflects the age of plantation slavery in which Barbados was founded. The house of the English landlord on the hill, shrouded by its woods, looks out over the little field-patches and hovels of its tenantry. To them the landlord is still the only real source of power and authority, but the flood costs him money and begins the slow process of his disengagement. As the landlord's power wanes it is replaced by that of Mr. Slime, an ex-teacher who builds up his position through a Penny Bank, a Friendly Society, a trade union, and finally in island politics. The village has supported Slime without really comprehending his goals, but he uses their painfully-saved pennies to buy them out and sell off the land under their feet to the "big-shot Coloureds" from the neighbouring and expanding suburbs. Slime is the type of every corrupt popular demagogue who had risen to power in the modern West Indies. He knows how to exploit the resentments of others because he is himself genuinely resentful. His type of leadership, even when crooked, may have something to offer the urban worker in need of organization, but it holds nothing for the ruined peasantry. Abandoned by their old paternal overlords (who also feel abandoned, because their former pre-eminence is going) and betrayed by their new leaders, the emigrant ship is all that awaits them now.

The flood is followed by the waterfront strike, the strike by the riot and British naval intervention (we are now in the late 'thirties), the riot by the war with its tree-felling and metal-scrapping, the war by the big landgrab and the enforced departures. Around these events George Lamming and his friends Trumper, Bob and Boy Blue, weave their own pattern of adventure—swimming, running, exploring, hunting for crabs, creeping into the landlord's garden by night to watch the white folks dancing. George's admission to High School gradually forces the four friends apart, Trumper departing to America and the other two into the police force. At the end of the book, George is leaving for a teaching post in Trinidad; but it is Trumper, newly returned from America, who already has a larger experience of the world to offer. Trumper had discovered his race by leaving the obscuring intimacy of the island for the impersonal jungle of America. In Barbados the whites are few and aloof, unable to penetrate the dense solidarity of the black masses; hence overt racial insults are kept to a minimum. Being black is almost a condition of being Barbadian, scarcely needing definition in terms of an opposed system of power and values. America has changed all that. Trumper plays George a record in the local rumshop:

"You know the voice?" Trumper asked. He was very serious now. I tried to recall whether I might have heard it. I couldn't.

"Paul Robeson," he said. "One o' the greatest o' my people."

"What people?" I asked. I was a bit puzzled.

"My people," said Trumper. His tone was insistent. Then he softened into a smile. I didn't know whether he was smiling at my ignorance, or whether he was smiling at his satisfaction with the box and the voice and above all Paul Robeson.

"Who are your people?" I asked him. It seemed a kind of huge joke.

"The Negro race," said Trumper. The smile had left his face and his manner had turned grave again. I finished my drink and looked at him. . . .[11]

Lamming's many English voices in this story of "Little England" embrace not only the tender evocative prose of his narrative and the groping dialogue of the boys as they struggle with new levels of experience, but the free surrealistic flow of Pa's dream and the vigorous dialect of the shoemaker threatened with eviction. The old man called Pa is not only the oldest person in the village and the repository of its vague traditions, but a link with Africa itself, the original home of its people. Dreaming on the night of his wife's death, he speaks of the land his imagination has painted to cradle itself in; here the highly alliterative and rhythmic language introduces a new theme in the complex musical structure of the whole work:

> time was I see by the sun how the season sail and the moon make warn-ing what crops to expect. . . . Far and near there were neighbours who keep gods like my brother rear rabbits, and the answer was obedience to a question never asked. Sometimes they was glad and sometimes they was sad, but the gift of the gods was always good. When life leave the body and the corpse keep contract with the grave in the jungle the soul sail away above or below as the gods find fit. And the rest who remain give praise. In the land of the tribes 'twas the way of our neigh-bours. . . .[12]

But to a younger generation, modern Barbados was the only reality that imagination could compass. Even the sharp pain of slavery had faded to the extent that the schoolboys debate whether it ever really existed on the island. And when the shoemaker, the village philosopher and a man born and bred there, is told to get himself and his shop off the land now suddenly and mysteriously bought by a total stranger, he can only round upon the bailiff in wounded incredulous rage:

> "Respect for who?" . . . "I've respect as when as I've got to have it, but for you, a two-colour shit-smelling bastard like you, what you' talkin' 'bout respect. An' if you don't get off this blasted land before

[11] *Ibid.*, p. 295.
[12] *Ibid.*, p. 210.

I count ten, if by the time I count ten you ain't off this spot o' land
they'll hang me, the law'll hang me!" [13]

Thus Lamming fills his story with the sound and rhythm of his
people's speech, but he also exploits his freedom to escape from it into
a personal narrative style of great flexibility and beauty. His presence
in the book is more often as narrator than as actor; many scenes are
described in which the young Lamming does not himself figure, and
this assists the equality of balance between a story of individual
growth and one of historical change objectively observed, a balance
which lies at the heart of the book's whole structure.

Although Lamming often evokes moments of boyhood experience
with great clarity and freshness, the aspects of his book which dwell
upon the poetry of time and the processes of island history draw upon
the consciousness and literary skill of the grown man. Alongside his
book we may lay a more recent chronicle of boyhood, Michael Anthony's *The Year in San Fernando* (1965). Anthony's may seem the
less ambitious of the two, since he attempts to describe the events and
feelings of a single year in the life of a twelve-year-old boy. We learn
virtually nothing of the hero's past life and nothing whatever of his
future, yet this twelfth year is clearly of such importance in the discovery of himself and his world that there is no sense of our wanting
to know more. The young Francis is one of several children of a poor
widow in the seaside village of Mayaro, in Eastern Trinidad. He
has never travelled far from his home and knows no one outside his
village circle. Mr. Chandles, an arrogant and spoilt young man from
San Fernando, is courting a local girl and suddenly proposes carrying
Francis back with him to be a sort of servant-companion to his
mother and to have schooling at his expense. Naturally the idea is
fallen upon at Mayaro, although Francis himself has very mixed
feelings about leaving home. In the big "upstair" house at San
Fernando he is baffled by the mysterious conduct and hidden motives
of the adults around him. Mr. Chandles and his mother have frequent
and bitter quarrels, centring upon the division of her inheritance
between him and his brother Edwin. Francis is also shocked to discover
that Chandles is having an affair with a beautiful girl called Julia,
whilst also sleeping with his fiancée Marva, from time to time, under
his mother's roof. Francis is himself fascinated by Julia, who plays
upon his own dawning sexuality with light and tender flirtatiousness.
The geography of the strange city is soon charged with meaning for
him; the street where Julia lives is by turns a magnet and a route to
be shunned, according to his present feelings for her. The dark space
underneath the Chandles' house is his refuge whenever he is bruised
by life, until one night he disturbs Julia and Chandles kissing there.

[13] *Ibid.,* p. 234.

Mount Naparima, which broods over the town, also has its moods,
changing ever as the seasons shift. The length of a childhood year
is fully measured by the cycle of ploughing, growth, harvest and burning in the great canefields which stretch for miles around the city.
Anthony's simple but alert style of narration captures all the hero's
bewilderment and insecurity, the slow growth of his affection for his
moody and mysterious employers, his growing conviction that his
year of momentous, trivial events is to be unique and that, at its end,
he will return to Mayaro for good.

In the midst of the year his mother comes to see him, but her visit
is soon over. After escorting her to the Mayaro bus he walks slowly
homewards, all the landscape of city, land and season strangely or-
chestrating with his mood:

> The pavement along Romaine Street rose very prominently from the
> road and I was just faintly eased of my sadness and I stepped up onto
> the pavement then down to the pitch again and I walked right down
> the street like that. In the little spaces between the houses I could see
> red flickers. They were "burning-out"—the estate people were. I stood up
> to watch the fire whenever I came to a little space, and I could hear the
> crackle and the way the flames roared in the wind. This was the last of
> the cane-fires, for the crop was nearly ended. Watching the fires had been
> a great attraction for me through all these months. They had started
> from far away in that great expanse of green. Now the fires were blazing
> out the last patch, near the town. I stood up at the big gap between the
> school and our house, and the fire I could see here stretched over some
> distance, and the flame-tongues licked the air, and they reddened a large
> part of the sky between the houses. Away over the brown open field I
> could see the dusk coming.[14]

Writing like this, never striving for big effects or *post hoc* finger-
wagging, demands tact and imaginative integrity. These qualities are
constantly displayed in Anthony's writing, though the apparent small-
ness of his themes has caused him to be attacked by many West
Indian reviewers, looking perhaps for riots, sultry affairs and deeds
of violence. Yet *The Year in San Fernando* does move towards a
climax of its own. At the end of the year Chandles is to marry Marva
and Francis is to go home for Christmas. But the old lady falls ill
and dies, bringing the struggle between the Chandles brothers to a
head. Edwin appears and tells Francis that it is he who will have the
house now that his mother is gone. Francis, already sure that San
Fernando has taught him all he is yet able to learn, senses that
the adventure is over, and perhaps the first innocence of childhood
ended with it. He goes to the bedroom to bid farewell to the dying
Mrs. Chandles and, as he goes towards the bus, forces himself to
remember what he saw there:

[14] *The Year at San Fernando* (London, Deutsch, 1965), pp. 94–5.

In my mind I kept seeing what was stretched out there on the bed. That was what Mrs. Chandles looked like. Although she wasn't dead yet. They had already swept the room and arranged it so people could come in to see the dead. There was a white cloth bandaging her chin and tied in a bow at the top of her head. That was done so she wouldn't die with her mouth open. Then they wouldn't have to break it shut. But she was still gasping breathlessly.

I had not stayed long in the room. I had just looked at what was on the bed. The room had been clean and tidy and sweet with the smell of lavender water. I had told Mrs. Princet goodbye and I had watched Mrs. Chandles and said goodbye just for the sake of saying it. The elderly lady had come in then and she had said, "Shake Mrs. Chandles' hand, you wouldn't see her again." I had hesitated, and Mrs. Princet had said, "Go on, shake it, shake hands," and I had gone up to the bed and held Mrs. Chandles' hand. It felt just like any other hand. Only bony and small and very hot.[15]

Francis never seems more than twelve, but his year in San Fernando has taught him to look with less fear and more compassion at the unpredictable behaviour of adults. His discoveries, despite the excitements of travel, have been largely human ones.

[15] *Ibid.,* p. 186.

The Ironic Approach:
The Novels of V. S. Naipaul

by Gordon Rohlehr

About Naipaul's first three novels George Lamming writes in
The Pleasures of Exile:

> His books can't move beyond a castrated satire; and although satire
> may be a useful element in fiction, no important work comparable to
> Selvon's can rest safely on satire alone. When such a writer is a colonial,
> ashamed of his cultural background and striving like mad to prove him-
> self through promotion to the peaks of a "superior" culture whose
> values are gravely in doubt, then satire, like the charge of philistinism,
> is for me nothing more than a refuge. And it is too small a refuge for
> a writer who wishes to be taken seriously.

This is an important and damaging criticism which merits examination. Lamming, Selvon and Naipaul are equally preoccupied with the
West Indian social scene and with what it means to them, as individuals, to be West Indians. Yet Lamming criticizes Naipaul's presentation of the West Indian experience and the nature of his personal
quest to discover where he stands. There is the assertion that mere
irony is irrelevant to West Indian society at this stage. Thus satire
is a means of running away from the sordid truth, by seeking refuge
in laughter, whose basis is an assumption of one's own cultural superiority to the world one ridicules.

Yet Naipaul's "Englishness" does not manifest itself, as Lamming
suggests, in a crude and overt striving to attain the dubious standards
of the metropolis. In fact, his ironic awareness uncovers all that is
drab, petty and humourless in English life, as we see in *Mr. Stone
and the Knight's Companion*. It manifests itself, rather, in his unconscious acceptance of a typical European view of Third World
inferiority, a view which is now being attacked from several quarters.

"The Ironic Approach: The Novels of V. S. Naipaul" by Gordon Rohlehr. From
The Islands in Between: Essays on West Indian Literature, ed. and with an
introduction by Louis James (London & Ibadan, Nairobi: Oxford University Press,
1968). Reprinted by permission of the publisher.

It shows itself in his contemptuous rejection of all things West Indian, which at times breaks through even the geniality of *The Mystic Masseur* (1957). The conviction of an anarchic society which the author must reject lies also behind *Miguel Street*. Here, however, the rejection is not done in contempt, but with considerable sympathy. This book, like *A House for Mr. Biswas* (1961), forces one to reconsider Lamming's criticism to see what it misses of Naipaul's subtlety, and to see what it does not say about the complexity of his situation.

Naipaul is a Trinidad East Indian who has not come to terms with the Negro-Creole world in Trinidad, or with the East Indian world in Trinidad, or with the greyness of English life, or with life in India itself, where he went in search of his roots. After these two books Naipaul wrote *The Middle Passage* (1962), which manifests all the new depth and astringency which his irony has assumed, and at the same time demonstrates all the superficiality which one thought he had left far behind. This book makes one feel again the justice of Lamming's criticism, and realize how true a comment it is on one very real aspect of Naipaul's attitude, as it appears in some of his books.

The position of the ironist in colonial society is indeed a delicate one. Lamming can see little that is risible in a society whose history is one of underprivilege. One appreciates his point. The early Naipaul is at times the irresponsible ironist, subtle, but lacking in a sensitive participation in the life he anatomizes. If one says that the exercise of irony precludes sympathy, one is merely defining the limitations of irony, and the limitations of any of Naipaul's work which depends solely on irony. So far one agrees with Lamming.

Satire is the sensitive measure of a society's departure from a norm inherent in itself. Since Naipaul starts with the conviction that such a norm is absent from his society, his task as satirist becomes doubly difficult. Not only must he recreate experience, but also simultaneously create the standards against which this experience is to be judged. This explains the mixture of farce and social consciousness which occurs in the two early novels. In 1957 Naipaul's first novel, *The Mystic Masseur,* was published. It is about an Indian, Ganesh Ramsummair, who begins his career as a secondary school teacher and then becomes a masseur. He only achieves success, however, when he becomes a "mystic," and attends to Trinidad's spiritual problems. His brilliance as a mystic helps him to become a successful author, politician, diplomat and eventually gains him an M.B.E. In 1958 followed Naipaul's second novel, *The Suffrage of Elvira.* It deals with the farce of elections in an unsophisticated part of Trinidad, beset by superstition and ignorance, where everyone is conscious only of the profit he can make out of this new game.

The tone of these two books is almost the same. A situation of

superstition, ignorance, absurdity, knavery and self-interest, is presented as the reality in Trinidad social and political life. Naipaul consciously presents his real world as farcical. The reader is invited
simultaneously to recognize the degree of distortion and to share in
the author's grin as he insists that the situation is perfectly normal.
"I myself believe that the history of Ganesh is, in a way, the history of
our times." It is the Chaucerian pose; the genial elevation of the absurd
and the constant pretence on the part of the satirist that he fully
condones the behaviour of the rogues he satirizes. Chaucer's rascals
are always the best fellows in the land. "Ganesh elevated the profession
by putting the charlatans out of business." Naipaul's humour here
awakens Chaucerian echoes.

It is only when one reads *The Middle Passage* that one realizes
how completely Naipaul has accepted anarchy and absurdity as the
norms of his society. If in the early farces an absurd world is presented
as real, in *The Middle Passage* a real world is presented as tragically
futile and absurd. The deeper implication of the first two books is that
West Indian society, emerging from ignorance and superstition, is
peculiarly susceptible to depredation by the fraud and the politician,
and by all opportunists who are prepared to exploit the social unease
for their personal ends. That Ganesh and Harbans are treated so
genially conceals Naipaul's seriousness of purpose. Ganesh, who poses
as the defender of Hinduism while it is politic and profitable to do so,
completely rejects Indian dress and changes his name to G. Ramsay
Muir once he becomes a successful politician. This change of name
and dress is always used by Naipaul to symbolize the acculturation of
the East Indian to pseudo-western patterns of life, which is something
he writes of with bitterness, despair and regret. One should not be
misled by his genial tone to overestimate his admiration for Ganesh,
the successful fraud.

Yet even in a book of the geniality of *The Mystic Masseur* Naipaul
can lack sympathy. His hero approaches his nadir in such scenes as
the dinner at Government House, where Naipaul depicts an imaginary
confrontation between the most unsophisticated members of Creole
and Indian society, and the hypercivilized governor's wife. All that
Naipaul finds ridiculous in Creole society is paraded here: the bad
grammar, lack of taste or social grace, complete unawareness and the
struggle to be white. A black man, of whose blackness Naipaul makes
a special point, is dressed in a blue suit, with yellow gloves and a
monocle, which eventually falls into the soup. Several of the guests
have some difficulty in manipulating their knives and forks. One can
accept this as farce intended, in its distorted way, to show the Creole
and Indian on the painful and ridiculous road to whiteness. But
the suspicion persists that Naipaul himself regards these people with
more contempt than compassion. These are the same people whom he

describes in *The Middle Passage* as being "like monkeys pleading for evolution." The incongruity of his position here, as Lamming points out, is that while he laughs at his Creoles crudely aping standards of pseudo-whiteness, he can only do so assuming these very norms himself.

In 1959 came *Miguel Street*, a series of short stories about an urban slum in Trinidad, told by a boy who speaks in the first person. The "I" in this book is not merely an autobiographical "I." To discover Naipaul, one must get past the voice that tells the tale to the narrator behind the narrator. One must appreciate all the nuances and shifts of irony, of which the boy could not possibly be conscious. The boy-narrator is not Naipaul, but a device exploited by Naipaul the artist who operates in detachment. If these stories are autobiography, they are autobiography set at a distance through irony.

Early on a theme of futility is established:

> Popo's workshop no longer sounded with hammering and sawing. The sawdust no longer smelled fresh, and became black, almost like dirt. Popo began drinking a lot, and I didn't like him when he was drunk. He smelled of rum, and he used to cry and then grow angry and want to beat up everybody. That made him an accepted member of the gang.

It is such a careful selection of detail that makes these stories less slight than appears on the surface. The whole pattern of the book is to depict the inevitable movement from freshness to dirt, and from laughter to tears. Moreover, at every point the boy judges and measures this degradation, until he finally rejects a society which reduces every-one to its own level of amorality. But while the boy hints at a norm by saying that he does not like Popo drunk, Miguel Street accepts him fully. So that when Popo goes to jail, the mecca of Miguel Street, the verdict of the street is, "We was wrong about Popo. He is a man like any of we."

The statement serves two functions. It links the world of *Miguel Street* to the world of *The Mystic Masseur* by suggesting the distortion of accepted moral values as the norm. At the same time the claim is being made that all the eccentrics of Miguel Street are men "like any of we," that Yahoo-land is a real place. As I have suggested, in a society which is seen as having no true standards, irony is bound to operate in reverse, the ironist starting with an abnormal situation and hinting at a sanity which is absent from his world. However, if the impulse behind *Miguel Street* is similar to that behind *The Mystic Masseur*, the whole tone is more serious. The farce has become a nightmare. Here one finds it difficult to accept Lamming's description of Naipaul's satire as a refuge and escape from experience. If satire is a means of running away, it is equally a means of fighting; an act of bravery, not cowardice; the confrontation of a nightmare, not the seeking of a refuge.

This passage is an example of how Naipaul's larger ironic awareness controls the boy's naïve account of the facts:

> And once Hat said, "Every day Big Foot father, the policeman, giving Big Foot blows. Like medicine. Three times a day after meals. And hear Big Foot talk afterwards. He used to say, 'When I get big and have children, I go beat them, beat them'. . . ."
>
> I asked Hat, "And Big Foot mother? She used to beat him too?"
>
> Hat said, "Oh God! That woulda kill him. Big Foot didn't have any mother. His father didn't married, thank God!"

What Naipaul is aware of here is a lack of family life and a heritage of brutality passed on from father to son. Miguel Street accepts this as normal and ideal.

One of the main themes of these stories is the nature and complexity of laughter in Miguel Street. Hat constantly points out how apparent laughter conceals tears. The laughter of Miguel Street is sometimes crude and cynical. But whenever this occurs, the boy points out the need for a greater sensitivity. "And all of us from Miguel Street laughed at Big Foot. All except me. For I knew how he felt." At most other times, however, there is propriety about the street's laughter. It is silent when Laura cries "all the cry she had tried to cover up with her laughter." Contemptuous laughter is always frowned upon, limits are placed on cynicism. This is why Nathaniel can never belong to the street, and Hat relegates him to a lower world.

" 'I don't know why he don't go back to the Dry River where he come from. They ain't have any culture there and he would be happier.' " There are the several occasions when Hat threatens to thrash Boysie if he dares laugh at the latest Miguel Street misfortune. Because of Naipaul's sympathy, Miguel Street comes across to the reader not merely as a jungle, but as a place where people in the face of insuperable frustration still preserve an intimacy and humour which is almost a new type of maturity.

In 1960 Naipaul revisited Trinidad after an absence of ten years. Born in Trinidad in 1932, he had left at the age of eighteen for England, where he went to Oxford and has lived ever since. In *The Middle Passage,* a travel-book written about his return to the West Indies, he attempts to assess his relation to the world which he has been treating in his fiction. Although this book was published in 1962, one year after *A House for Mr. Biswas,* one feels justified in considering it first, since in the latter book Naipaul presents his experience with a completeness and conclusiveness which is absent from *The Middle Passage.* Naipaul shows in his direct examination of Trinidad a superficiality which he has outgrown in his novels.

It has been pointed out that *The Middle Passage* is not written from the standpoint of a professional historian or sociologist and that

Naipaul's reactions are those of imaginative sensibility. This is true and this is where the difficulty lies. To this author's sensibility, Trinidad represents a nightmare, and one has constantly to differentiate between his sensitive examination of history and his honest expression of hysteria. He confesses a pathological dislike for Trinidad:

> I had never wanted to stay in Trinidad. When I was in the fourth form I wrote a vow on the endpaper of my Kennedy's Revised Latin Primer to leave within five years. I left after six; and for many years afterwards in England, falling asleep in bed-sitters with the electric fire on, I had been awakened by the nightmare that I was back in tropical Trinidad.

It is a nightmare which, nurtured through a decade of absence, and reinforced by the literature which Naipaul has read about the West Indies, has now become an obsession. "As soon as the *Francisco Bobadilla* had touched the quay. . . . I began to feel all my old fear of Trinidad. I did not want to stay."

The book, however, is written with a conscious nobility of purpose. It purports to be an assessment of Naipaul's West Indian experience and an apology for his self-chosen exile. The important first two chapters of the book are carefully written. One notes, for example, the appropriateness of all the quotations which Naipaul uses as epigraphs to these chapters. First there is the general epigraph to the book, a quotation from Anthony Froude's *The English in the West Indies*:

> They were valued only for the wealth which they yielded, and society there has never assumed any particularly noble aspect. . . . There are no people there in the true sense of the word, with a character and purpose of their own.

Or one may consider the two quotations from Thomas Mann and Tacitus, at the beginning of the chapter on Trinidad. The quotation from Mann is particularly apt. What one notices is that these three quotations are about three entirely different peoples: West Indians, Israelites and Britons. The impression conveyed is one of the timelessness of the process which Naipaul observes at work in the West Indies today. It is to his credit that he chooses his epigraphs from three different sources, and thus places the West Indian experience against a backcloth of universal experience. It is regrettable that this impression of universality could not be maintained.

The name "Middle Passage" is a symbol at many levels. It is symbolic of that original journey which was the beginning of a slavery and which Naipaul sees existing in spirit. At the same time it is a symbol of the West Indies today in that transitional middle stage between the cultures which her peoples lost and the new sense of cultural identity which they have not yet gained. Like Thomas Mann's Israelites, they are seen to be "in a transitional land, pitching their tents between the houses of their fathers and the real Egypt . . . un-anchored souls wavering in spirit and without a secure doctrine." Like the Britons under Roman rule, they are seen to speak of "such novelties as 'civilization' when really they are only a feature of en-slavement."

The name "Middle Passage" also refers to the new journey which the West Indian emigrant makes to England. The first chapter is a sensitive record of certain very real aspects of West Indian life. There is the emigrant who abandons a perfectly good job to go to a land of which he is completely ignorant, but which even as a child he has known to be the Mother Country. There are the tourist-class petty bourgeois West Indians with their values of colour and money, who demonstrate every feature of insularity, ignorance, vulgarity and self-contempt in their society. These people refer to the immigrants as "the wild cows" and the "orang-outangs." But as is suggested by the sentence beginning, "Like monkeys pleading for evolution," Naipaul is himself capable of the denigratory comparison. His contempt is the result of superior intellectual awareness; the tourists' contempt is self-contempt, the result of ignorance. It is difficult to say which is worse. There is also the English-woman, completely perplexed at it all, an apt representative of the society towards which the emigrants travel.

One of the questions which the book poses is, "What explains the West Indian emigrant?" The answer which it suggests can be found in the themes on which it is written. Those themes are stated in the epigraphs. West Indian history has bred "no people in the true sense of the word, with a character and purpose of their own." The West Indian experience, as Naipaul has expressed it, is not a fusion or coalition of cultures to enhance their separate excellences, but their degradation to a new norm of anarchy. Naipaul uses Trinidad as an example of all that is degrading in the West Indian experience and, because of this, is in a sense not writing about Trinidad at all. He is writing an essay on the horrors of acculturation, and an explanation of why he had to escape. He sees only what was destroyed in the West Indies:

> How can the history of this West Indian futility be written? . . . The history of these islands can never be satisfactorily told. . . . History is built around achievement and creation; and nothing was created in the West Indies.

Naipaul sees the West Indies as a rubbish-heap. It is a despairing image to choose. This explains the sublimated bitterness which lies behind his laughter whenever he observes the East Indian conforming to the pattern of West Indian history; joining the Negro-Creoles in their quest for "whiteness." Perhaps the most delicate and ruthless of his stories is the *Christmas Story*, where an East Indian is made to describe the process of his acculturation and, supremely ignorant of the fact, becomes the mouthpiece of his own degradation. He is a teacher who adopts the Christian faith when he realizes that this is the only way to gain promotion in a school managed by the Church. He is not given the cynical awareness of a Ganesh as he outlines the stages of his acculturation, but naïvely declares that he has buried his East Indian past, and refers to other Indians as "these people" or "the others." Behind the *Christmas Story* and *The Middle Passage* is a bitter despair of the whole colonial process and an implicit rejection of the colonial experience, which expresses itself in irony and in contempt for all things West Indian:

> The city throbbed with steel-bands. A good opening line for a novelist or travel writer; but the steel-band had long been regarded as a high manifestation of West Indian culture, and it was a sound I detested.
> The land of the Calypso is not a copy-writer's phrase. It is one side of the truth, and it was this gaiety, so inexplicable to the tourist who sees the shacks of Shanty Town and the corbeaux patrolling the modern highway, and inexplicable to me who had remembered it as the land of failures, which now, on my return, assaulted me.

It is apparently beyond Naipaul to be able to understand why there is music in spite of the rubbish-heap, and to recognize in such merry-making not merely cynical indifference to the dung-hill, but evidence of an affirmation and vibrancy of life, however crude. Such recognition requires not brutality and subtlety, which he points out as the special gifts of the satirist, but the entirely different talents of delicacy, tenderness and a quality of intimacy. In *Miguel Street,* in spite of the fact that the boy eventually rejects the rubbish-heap, there is a sympathy for its inhabitants, and an implicit recognition of the positives of this world. This is why parts of *The Middle Passage* strike one as superficial, and a retrogression in sensibility.

Sometimes one wonders at Naipaul's hypersensitivity and asks oneself whether the neurosis is completely controlled by the irony. Is not this complete acquiescence with Froude that there are "No people there in the true sense of the world," a formula for evading the complex sympathy which the West Indian experience seems to demand? I stated above that what appears to Lamming as a conscious struggle on Naipaul's part to adopt the standards of a "superior" metropolitan culture, is explicable as a too easy acquiescence with European historians; they assumed that the "native" was an inferior animal and consequently failed to look for positives in his society. Perhaps it is easier to see Trinidad as an historical rubbish-heap and a sociological abstraction; easier to see evidence in every observed and carefully chosen detail of some deep-seated social malaise which justifies one's neurosis; easier than to see the country as a vast Miguel Street of individuals, people in a truer sense of the word than Froude seems to have been aware of, each making demands on one's imaginative sympathy, because of the unique history which each has endured.

Naipaul's hatred of the steel band and all it indicates is no mere rejection of West Indian culture, but a rejection of the single common ground where Trinidadians of all races meet on a basis of equality. Carnival in Trinidad, dominated by steel band, calypso and costume, is more than a time of general merry-making. One can, without naïvely propounding a West Indian version of the myth of the happy Negro, recognize Carnival as one of the few symbols, however tenuous, of a oneness in the Trinidadian people. Naipaul can show us how both Indians and Negroes despise each other in a monkey-like struggle to ape standards of pseudo-whiteness. But he rejects as crude, noisy and unsophisticated the sole symbol of their miscibility, the one sign that the people themselves are reconstructing something to take the place of the personality which history destroyed.

A similar shortcoming manifests itself in what Naipaul has to say about the Negro. He is able to recognize Negro self-contempt as a product of history, to see the historical inferiority complex as the central dilemma of Creole culture. But he does not understand the Negro's attempt at reconstructing something to take the place of his lost dignity:

> The involvement of the Negro with the white world is one of the limi-tations of West Indian writing, as it is the destruction of American Negro writing. The American Negro's subject is his blackness. This can-not be the basis of any serious literature, and it has happened again and again that once the American Negro has made his statement, his profitable protest, he has nothing to say.

The obvious comment is that where one's blackness means something very definite, it can become the basis of the most serious literature. And much as one accepts Naipaul's point that protest literature can become a sterile and stereotyped posturing in the name of blackness, one also realizes that protest against the past is a vital transitional stage in the reconstruction of a sense of personality. Naipaul does not realize that in treating the theme of East Indian acculturation, and the reconstruction of the Indian personality in the New World, he is at one with Negro writers who are also trying to reconstruct per-sonality, and is writing a most vital portion of the sensitive history of the West Indies. Naipaul's Mr. Biswas rebels because his society denies him personality and forces him to live with an inferiority complex and a sense of nonentity. Negro writers, in the Caribbean or America, protest because their society annihilated identity. Both in the case of Mr. Biswas and the Negro of the New World, underprivilege is struggling to build its symbolic house against overwhelming odds.

A House for Mr. Biswas is more profound than anything else Naipaul has written because, for the first time, he is able to feel his own history not merely as a squalid farce, but as an adventure in sensibility. Mr. Biswas has nothing to recommend him except a talent for sign-painting, and the fact that he is a Brahmin and therefore an accessible target for Hindu snobbery. These qualities together land him in trouble. For it is while he is painting decorations at the Tulsi store, that he is detected passing a love-note to one of the Tulsi daughters. When summoned before Mrs. Tulsi and her right-hand man Seth, he allows himself to be brow-beaten into marriage and spends the rest of his life fighting to be independent of the Tulsis. His ambition is to build a house of his own.

The book can be interpreted on several levels. There is the obvious surface level where Biswas can be seen as a second-generation Indian who, although rebelling against his own decaying Hindu world, cannot come to a meaningful compromise with the Creole world of Trinidad. This Creole world comes in only by implication and allusion. The Tulsis refer to it with contempt, although Biswas is quick to point out to them just how degrading a concession they make to it by sending their sons to a Roman Catholic school. Naipaul himself is aware of acculturation in the bilingualism which is now imposed on the East Indian. Hindi remains the language of intimacy but, by the end of the book, Mr. Biswas has for years been a journalist writing in English, and the readers and learners all speak Creole.

In *An Area of Darkness* Naipaul writes thus of the East Indian confrontation with the Creole world:

> Into this alienness we daily ventured, and at length we were absorbed into it. But we knew that there had been change, gain, loss. We knew that something which was once whole had been washed away. What was whole was the idea of India.

The Hindu world soon becomes the world Naipaul describes in *The Middle Passage*:

> an enclosing self-sufficient world absorbed with its quarrels and jealousies, as difficult for the outsider to penetrate as for one of its own members to escape. It protected and imprisoned, a static world, awaiting decay.

Since the society offers him two equally terrible nightmares, isolation and non-identification are the only alternatives left to Biswas. The two houses which he builds and has to abandon are built in inhospitable waste-lands far from society. "He had built his own house in a place as wild and out of the way as he could have wished . . .

not seeming to invite habitation so much as decay." But rejection of
his Hindu roots proves a formidable task, and the Biswas who, as a
boy contemptuously spurns this dead ritualistic life, mutters "Rama,
Rama, Sita, Rama" during the storm. At the most acute moment of
crisis the old ritual is what reasserts itself. It is a sign of Naipaul's
complete control that even in this little detail he is not found wanting.
A House for Mr. Biswas moves far beyond preoccupations with race
or the Hindu world in Trinidad, and depicts a classic struggle for
personality against a society that denies it. But the book is only able
to do so because this narrow, enclosed Hindu world has been established with such fidelity and completeness.

Naipaul establishes this world with such consistency that it becomes
symbolic of darkness, stagnation and decay. Hanuman House, the
home of the Tulsis, is an

> alien white fortress, bulky, impregnable and blank . . . windowless
> . . . slightly sinister. . . . The kitchen . . . was lower than the hall and
> completely without light. The doorway gaped black . . . blackness
> seemed to fill the kitchen like a solid substance.

Every other Tulsi home is like this. There is the shop at The Chase
where "the walls were black and fluffy with soot as though a new
species of spider had been bred there," the barracks at Green Vale,
"The trees darkened the road, their rotting leaves choked the grass
gutters. The trees surrounded the barracks." The Tulsis soon reduce
the house at Shorthills to a ramshackle decay; round the house in
Port-of-Spain they build a symbolic wall.

The term "barracks" suggests the regimentation of life which Biswas
fights until he builds a house of his own. Biswas's rebellion can be
read as the rebellion of an individual against a communal way of
life. Hanuman House, symbolically presided over by the monkey-
god, is described as a "communal organization" whose maintenance
depends on a recognition of authority by, and a denial of personality
to the ruled. As soon as Tulsi autocracy becomes weak, the whole system disintegrates, and one has the anarchy of the Shorthills episode,
where the naked self-interest behind Tulsi ritual manifests itself, and
life returns to the law of the jungle as the beauty and luxuriance of
the land are wantonly despoiled.

In this decaying paradise of totalitarianism, Biswas the individualist
is described as "serpent" and "spy." As he appears before "the family
tribunal" Seth describes the nature of the crime which he has committed. "This house is like a republic already." The argument which
the Tulsis employ against him is the eternal argument of totalitarianism; namely, that the individual is meaningless if he tries to be independent of the system. The Tulsis try to make Biswas aware of the
fact that he has come to them with no material possessions and argue

that he is therefore a nonentity who can only gain significance if he surrenders to them. Tulsidom depends for its existence on the psychic emasculation of the men and on the maintenance of their sense of inferiority. At the most humiliating moments of his struggle, Biswas nearly surrenders to this sense of inferiority. It is seen by Naipaul as a surrender to darkness and chaos.

It is worth pointing out that the traditional Hindu custom requires the bride to join her husband's household and become almost a servant of her mother-in-law. The complete humiliation of Biswas's position is that he has to assume the ritualistic role of the newly married Hindu girl. Thus his is a rebellion against complete humiliation in the eyes of society, and against nonentity in an entire and comprehensive sense. It is interesting to note the honesty and care with which this rebellion is depicted. Initially Biswas enjoys it. It exhilarates him. But it soon becomes a vicious and bitter struggle, fought with invective, saliva and scorn. Indeed, Biswas is at times petty, cowardly and contemptible, and part of the book's triumph is that Naipaul has been able to present a hero in all his littleness, and still preserve a sense of the man's inner dignity.

As the rebellion progresses, Biswas finds that "All his joy had turned into disgust at his condition." This happens one morning as he realizes his irrelevance to the Tulsi scene. If he were to disappear, the ritual would still go on. He therefore realizes that rebellion for rebellion's sake is not enough, and must coincide with the positive act of constructing something new to take the place of the old life one repudiates.

For the present, however, he merely seeks to emancipate himself from Hanuman House, and is sent to The Chase, a Tulsi outpost in a remote area. But when, for the first time since marriage, he confronts life outside Hanuman House, Biswas finds himself afraid of the freedom which his rebellion has won him. Like so many protest politicians, he fails initially when required to be constructive—"How lonely the shop was! And how frightening! . . . afraid to disturb the silence, afraid to open the door of the shop, to step into the light. . . ." *A House for Mr. Biswas* can be read as a book which probes the relationship between rebellion and independence. True independence, it is revealed, does not immediately follow rebellion; true personality does not immediately follow emancipation, but must be constructed in a lifetime of painful struggle and retrogression. What does follow emancipation is a dark "void" which Biswas must learn to face before he can "step into the light." It takes him all his life to fight the void and whatever graciousness life has to offer comes late, when he has almost lost the capacity to enjoy it. His victory lies in the fact that he has remained himself.

The house, which Mr. Biswas determines to build as soon as he sees the Tulsi barracks at Green Vale, is more than a place where he

can live. It is his personality symbolized, the private individuality
which he must both build and maintain against the rest of the world.
The development in Mr. Biswas's house parallels at all points his
development as a person. We are reminded of the destructive power
of the Tulsis in the scene where Shama, acting as the agent of their
malice, smashes the doll's house which Biswas buys for his daughter.
It is described as if it were a body torn apart:

> None of its parts was whole. Its delicate joints were exposed and useless.
> Below the torn skin of paint . . . the hacked and splintered wood was
> white and raw.
> "O God!"

The scene is rendered with complete naturalness and sensitive force
and its point is clear. Anything which manifests individuality and
difference causes dread, envy and hostility in Hanuman House. The
reaction of the Tulsis to the doll's house is a measure of the terrible
revenge which this "communal organization" can take on one who
dares to be individual.

The book can be interpreted on a metaphysical level, since it questions the basis and meaning of personality. An interesting ambivalence
emerges from the book. Firstly there is the dependence of the individual upon society for his sense of being; where by society one
means not only other people, but a whole concrete world with which
the consciousness establishes some deep intimacy, and claims as its
own. As soon as Biswas "stepped out of the yard, he returned to nonentity." Outside Tulsi society he is lost. Secondly there is the necessary
rebellion which the individual must make against society and the
void which must be confronted. In the void are meaninglessness, nonentity, fear, lunacy, and chaos, the storm within and the storm without. It is out of this confrontation that the new personality grows.

In many ways Biswas is an archetypal figure. He is described as
stranger, visitor, and wanderer. Weak, and frequently absurd, he is
recognized in Hanuman House as a buffoon, and the role of fool is
one which he at times accepts in humiliation and at others rejects
with bitterness. But Biswas the clown is also Biswas the rebel. He is
also man the artist, and his art is the only aspect of him that the
Tulsis really admire, not realizing that it is an expression of the very
personality they detest. Whenever Biswas is attacked by the sense of
life as meaningless void, he immediately turns to his paint brushes
and tries to create something against the emptiness. Perhaps he himself
gives the best definition of his significance. To his bewildered son who
asks him, "Who are you?" he replies, "I am just somebody. Nobody
at all. I am just a man you know." Biswas is Everyman, wavering between identity and nonentity, and claiming his acquaintance with the
rest of men.

The book is powerfully symbolic, but it is never crudely or obtrusively so. If Biswas represents all the things I feel he does, it is because he is fully presented as a person whose every quirk and idiosyncrasy we know, in a world whose every sight, sound and smell is recorded with fidelity and precision. Whatever is suggested of the numinous and universal, is conveyed through a fidelity to the concrete and particular. Landscape and life are not treated as isolated, but both conform to the artist's unity of purpose. Description is organically employed to reinforce theme. In the end, nature which, when associated with the Tulsis, took the form of jungle, nettle and weed surrounding The Chase, or decaying leaves on half-dead trees surrounding Green Vale, or the landslide at Shorthills, manifests itself in the coolness of the laburnum, and the scent of the lily in Mr. Biswas's yard. His house may be dangerously cracked in places, but because it is his own, there is grace in its grotesqueness.

Ostensibly preoccupied with the present, Naipaul observes acculturation as a timeless feature of the West Indian experience which he never really accepts. Like the boy in *Miguel Street,* he rejects the rubbish-heap. Like Mr. Biswas, he rejects Hanuman House. Rejecting Hanuman House and Miguel Street as two sides of the greater nightmare of being an Indian in Trinidad, he seeks the freedom of the independent personality, and makes the difficult choice of exile and dispossession. There are few pleasures in his exile. Yet out of it grow irony and a necessary detachment from the nightmare:

> So later, and very slowly, in securer times of different stresses, when the memories had lost the power to hurt, with pain or joy, they would fall into place and give back the past.
> How can the history of this West Indian futility be written? [1]

This finally is the question which Naipaul, and which perhaps every serious West Indian writer, asks, as he wonders what qualities of mind and feeling are necessary in order to face the West Indian experience. The answer which Naipaul ventures in *The Middle Passage* relates to the problem of West Indian creative writing, as well as to the writing of West Indian history as an academic pursuit. West Indian history can never be satisfactorily told, he says, because nothing was created in the West Indies, where there is neither achievement, nor a tradition of accepted values. Yet in *Miguel Street* and *A House for Mr. Biswas* he tells a vital part of West Indian history, for the books are a sensitive presentation of the history of underprivilege. The worth of his irony is that it enables him to examine his past without any sentimental self-indulgence. We see Biswas as a full human being who is as weak and contemptible as he is forceful and admirable. Irony

[1] *The Middle Passage.*

enables Naipaul to get down to the bare humanity beneath his history. Because he is dealing with his own personal past, his irony does not preclude sympathy but reinforces it. He is able to answer in terms of creative sensibility a question to which he could find no satisfactory academic answer.

The Fugitive in the Forest:
Four Novels by Wilson Harris

by John Hearne

It is from Yeats's great phrase about "the unity from a mythology that marries us to rock and hill" that we may, justifiably, begin an examination of Wilson Harris's singular exploration of his corner of the West Indian experience. To Harris, this sacramental union of man and landscape remains the lost, or never established, factor in our lives. We enjoy, we exploit, we are coarsely nourished by our respective Caribbean territories—but illegitimately. We have yet to put our signatures to that great contract of the imagination by which a people and a place enter into a domestic relationship rather than drift into the uncertainties of liaison. No other British Caribbean novelist has made quite such an explicit and conscious effort as Harris to reduce the material reckonings of everyday life to the significance of myth. It is useful to consider first the geographical matrix in which his imagination was fashioned.

The people of the Guyana coastland inhabit a narrow boat filled with carefully nurtured earth and anchored at the middle of the boundary lines between two oceans. For the savannah and the forest at their backs make up, really, another ocean, as severe, beautiful and monotonous as the huge Atlantic onto which they look. The bulwarks of this "boat" are the anxiously maintained erections of sea-walls, dikes and sluice gates which, on both sides, protect them from the creeping intrusion of the ocean or from the mass attack of flood water from the jungle rivers. The coastland itself, with its wide, dead flat perspectives of sugar cane, rice or scrub, its horizons of great palms, its ruler-straight reaches of grey-brown canals, its long villages on stilts, is a sort of tropical parody of the painter Hobbema, enlarged and harsh under the ferocious light of the equator's sun. The ocean before them is not the inviting and familiar meadow that it is for the people of the Eastern Caribbean for whom, despite all its dangers, it has become a

"The Fugitive in the Forest: Four Novels by Wilson Harris" by John Hearne. From *The Islands in Between: Essays on West Indian Literature,* ed. and with an introduction by Louis James (London & Ibadan, Nairobi: Oxford University Press, 1968). Reprinted by permission of the publisher.

cherished part in the design of their life. The forest, the savannah, the great and dangerous black rivers of the interior behind them are the significant other part of the Guyanese landscape. To stand, for example, on a ridge in the Pakaraima Sierras and look south and west is to realize, faintly, the tremendous and terrifying weight which a sensitive Guyanese must carry on his imagination; an endless, regular surface of tree tops, broken occasionally by a loop of brown river, stretches unbearably to the edge of the world. And beyond that, another vast, unfathomed reach. And beyond that, another. And so on for two thousand miles that are nearly empty of human life, in which the most powerful assertions of human life can drown almost overnight in a ravenous flood of wood and water. This is one of the great primary landscapes of the world, and it can crush the mind like sleep. Like sleep, it inspires the dreams by which we record the progress of our waking life.

It is important to remember this element of the dream, and of the dream's sister, death, if we are to come to any understanding of these four Wilson Harris novels—*Palace of the Peacock* (1960), *The Far Journey of Oudin* (1961), *The Whole Armour* (1962) and *The Secret Ladder* (1963). For the quartet opens with one dream of death, and closes with another dream of creation. Between these two dreams lies an evocation of being not accessible to any reviewer's summary. If we are to share the writer's experience, we must accept possession of the living by the dead; we must accept the resurrected man and the fact that "the end precedes the beginning" and that "the end and beginning were always there." Harris's world is not only one of prosaic action, but one of rite and mythical formation. "The first condition for understanding the Greek myth," said Gide, "is to believe in it." And it is not improper that Harris makes belief the condition for entry into his Guyanese world.

In *Palace of the Peacock,* the first of the quartet and Harris's first novel, we are immediately presented with this pattern of interwoven dream and waking. It opens with a horseman shot from his saddle as he gallops, the discovery of the corpse by the elusive figure who is to become the narrator, and the narrator's dreaming conviction after the discovery that, somehow, he the living has lost his sight and can see only with a dead man's "open and obstinate" eye. This symbol of the eye recurs frequently in the four stories of the quartet. It is, I think, the clearest hint that Harris gives us of the structure and methods we must expect to find throughout his work. The human eye, living and dead, serves something of the same purpose as the mirror on the wall in a Dutch interior painting. Both reflector and captor, it enhances the material vividness of the foreground figures, yet its troubling duplication reminds us of the other life it holds captive in an infinite and shrinking series. Nor are the diminished figures in the glass—or in the eye—any less real for being reduced. What disturbs us is their jewel brightness, their sense of independent life, their possession of a separate but complementary world.

Again, in *The Far Journey of Oudin,* as in *The Whole Armour,* we are introduced early to this concept of the equal inheritance which the quick must share with the dead. The death of Oudin is first conveyed to us by the image of "the match-box world" he holds in the corner of his staring eye. He has taken possession rather than suffered exile, and it is not until his wife cries out *"Oudin dead. Oudin dead. Oudin dead"* that we, as readers, realize how completely we have come to acknowledge the miniature but potent version of life held in Oudin's eye. It is not until the woman's wail breaks into the stillness of our fascination that we can make the conventional response and see Oudin as just another old Guyanese peasant dead on the floor of a hut on the coastal savannah. In *The Whole Armour,* Abram (whose death precipitates the actions and conflicts of those who survive him) recognizes his dying and contorted self in the mirror of his son's eye almost before he is aware of the heart seizure that is killing him with furious speed.

If I have given priority to this analysis of Harris's reflecting and imprisoning "eye," it is because his use of it does serve to introduce us to the fictive world his persons inhabit. The passages in which he assembles, in our nerves, the power and meaning of the eye are intricate and compelling; we are sensuously convinced before we cerebrally grasp. And if, as I have suggested, he sees his mandate as one of creating a mythical framework, then his use of the "eye" is legitimate. For the imperceptible shuttle system from dream to waking and death to life, the dogmatic *possibility* of causal relationships between these states, give the essences of much of myth. Harris does not, like the naturalistic novelist, offer us the demonstrable proofs of observation; he simply throws himself on our willing agreement. And this, for Harris, is the only way for the artist in the modern world where he is deprived of his traditional assurances. "The creative human consolation," he wrote in *Tradition and the West Indian Novel* (1965), "—if one dwells upon it meaningfully today—lies in the search for a kind of *inward* dialogue and space when one is *deprived* of a ready conversational tongue and hackneyed comfortable approach." [My italics.]

This is one of the most fruitful obsessions any novelist can carry into his study of the human heart today; it is also an extremely dangerous one. For in so doing, he offers his artistic throat to the knives of ridicule, inattention and misunderstanding. Obversely, his mendicant's role imposes a certain limitation on his own freedom of aesthetic venture. He must work, in short, within an extremely limited frame and convince us by his intensity rather than by his generous scope.

C. L. R. James and other critics have made much of Wilson Harris's relation to the existentialists, but his technique seems to me to lie in the symbolist tradition. One that relies, in Edmund Wilson's words, on "a complicated association of ideas represented by a medley of metaphors" and is designed "to communicate unique personal feelings." Or, in the words of Rilke, as a bee, it gathers "the honey of the visible" for storage in "the great, golden hive of the Invisible."

On the surface, the plot of *Palace of the Peacock* seems simple enough. It describes the struggles of a boat's crew as they forge a passage up a nameless Guyanese river, through rapids, between walls of forests and under towering battlements of cliff face, to the great falls at the head of the stream. What they are seeking is never explicitly defined, except, perhaps, in the title; the *Palace of the Peacock,* the home of the God King, El Dorado, the City of Gold. The second stage of the journey takes seven days—the days of the Creation—and death by misadventure, exhaustion and murder attend their passage up the river. They hope to make contact with a fugitive and sensibly suspicious "folk," who, while accompanying their passage along the banks of the river, never appear, but send them only the shy and enigmatic missives of the forest; a wounded tapir or a parrot with a silver ring around its leg. At the end all are dead. The last is transfixed, or translated, at the moment of his death by a knowledge of a loving communion between the living and the dead that completely obliterates the hope of the treasure he had come to seize for the purchase of vulgar consolations he can now barely remember.

On this level it is a mere morality and, to borrow Harris's adjective, a rather "hackneyed" one at that. But we are early relieved of this possible banality by the realization that the crew's names match, man for man, those of another legendary crew who had all perished many years before in the rapids near the beginning of a similar venture into the interior. At this point, it becomes the reader's pleasure, as it must have become the writer's excitement, to determine the extent to which each crew possesses the other; to decide at what moment the anguish of one group is simply that of commonplace muscle and endurance pitted against the immediate pressures of a river's current, or is the accumulated reflections of the greed and love, cruelty and faithfulness which another body of men had once imposed on those among whom they had lived, on the land they had once tried to dominate.

The narrator "I" of the story, and also dreamer of the dead horseman, is evidently skipper of the "real" crew. But he becomes, as his little party penetrates further and further into the claustrophobic heartland of the continent, not only the poet Donne of the punning lines "When thou hast Donne, thou hast not done . . . ," but the other long dead captain, Donne, a fierce, driven, cruel man. He begins to recognize that it is not only their equipment and their boat that his crew are hauling so painfully up to the great waterfall of their journey's end. They are dragging with them, also, the multiple reverberations of the past and are suffering the consequences of future action which they have already committed in their dreams, or seen in dreams, through the eyes of the dead. The extract that follows may give some idea of Harris's method of approach, of "fixing" the frontier between the two zones of reality:

> The change in Donne I suddenly felt in the quickest flash was in me. It was something in the open air as well, in the strange half-sun, in the river, in the mysterious youthful longing which the whole crew possessed for Mariella and for the Mission where she lived above the falls. The murdered horseman of the savannahs, the skeleton footfall on the river bank and in the bush, the moonhead and crucifixion in the waterfall and in the river were over as though a cruel ambush of soul had partly lifted its veil and face to show that death was the shadow of a dream. In this remarkable filtered light it was not men of vain flesh and blood I saw toiling laboriously and meaningfully, but active ghosts whose labour was indeed a flitting shadow over their shoulders as living men would don raiment and cast it off in turn to fulfil the simplest necessity of being.

It should be remarked here that Mariella was the mistress of the dead Donne; she was a gentle and untutored creature of the high savannahs, whom Donne had abused, beaten and ultimately crushed by his violent pride. Nor is our work of full apprehension made any simpler when we discover, further on, that the Mariella of the Mission, for whom the crew is longing, *is* in fact the mission and the land around it and not a material woman at all.

Harris is not an "easy" writer, as the extract just given should demonstrate. The contending experiences he is attempting to resolve in a finished, persuasive work of art do not really yield to the methods and syntax of, say, Naipaul. But it is worth joining battle with him, even when he fails to carry off his attack. His effects are cumulative. Images, metaphors, incidents and assertions which, at the beginning of any of his stories, may at first seem examples only of a wilful and unrelated vividness will suddenly, by a process of duplication in a new setting, become clear and powerful factors in an orderly poetic statement. He is very seldom self-indulgent.

So, the nameless boat, with its twice-named crew, continues to beat up the nameless river towards the Palace of the Peacock. With a quite astonishing coolness of nerve, almost, one might say, with arrogance, Harris continues to shift his characters from phase to phase of reality and of Time. His transitions are often so abrupt, so arbitrary, that we are, momentarily, confused, until we learn to accept the use to which our sensations are being put. This is a world of hallucination, or rather, a world in which hallucinatory apprehensions of Time's circular and organic wholeness is a commonplace of existence. Quarrels between the crew occur, and they die by accident, exhaustion or murder. Sometimes the dead ones are replaced, for a second or for a day, by counterparts from the other crew who were swallowed by the river at the beginning of *their* venture. But even those who die in the present follow the progress of the boat along the enormous heights of cliff face above the river, for they too are forever reflected in the undying eye; they too survive on what Harris terms "the elastic frontier" which stretches to and fro to enclose whole provinces of the territory of death and the territory of life. The "folk," the indigenes, remain unapproachable. They live, unconsciously, in harmonious relationship with the organic body of a land through which Time moves like blood, carrying action, dream and death on an unending circulatory voyage of nourishment, salvage and renewal. Finally, the survivors in the boat reach the waterfall:

> They saw in the distance at last a thread of silver lightning that expanded and grew into a veil of smoke. They drew as near as they could and stopped under the cloud. Right and left grew the universal wall of cliff they knew, and before them the highest waterfall they had ever seen moved and still stood upon the escarpment. . . . Steps and balconies had been nailed with abandon from bottom to top making hazardous ladders against the universal walls. . . .

It is up these "hazardous ladders" that the narrator Donne figure now climbs to the Palace of the Peacock on the escarpment. And it is as he stands at a window of the palace looking out onto the high savannahs that he realizes the nature of the treasure he has come so far and at such mortal cost (for he too is now dead) to seek:

> He had stopped a little to wonder whether he was wrong in knowledge and belief, and the force that had divided them from each other—and mangled them beyond all earthly hope and recognition—was the wind of rumour and superstition, and the truth was they had all come home at last to the compassion of the nameless unflinching folk. . . . [I] felt the faces before me begin to fade and part company from me and from themselves as if our need of one another was now fulfilled. . . . Each of us now held at last in his arms what he had been forever seeking and what he had eternally possessed.

The expedition which had begun as a pedestrian, rather sordid, gold rush has ended as an argosy, because of the suffering, and because of the surrender of the primal solitude of the landscape and to the implacable occupation of their dreams. They are dead men, to be sure, but by their deaths they have won admittance to the antique, beautiful and imperishable palace that, in each year of our obsessive enslavement of the earth, is moved beyond yet another horizon. The Golden Palace that they can bring back to us in our dreams is the knowledge that all the territories "overwhelmed and abandoned [have] always been ours to rule and take."

Inevitably, such a brief critical reduction of so dense, intricate and active a work as *Palace of the Peacock* must do the book a disservice. Harris's vision is too subtle, and his technique too sculptural, for us to do other than to enter his work and try to join the highly idiosyncratic celebration he is conducting. Once we accept the ritual stages, without necessarily committing ourselves, we begin to understand what he is trying to communicate. This is straightforward enough. It is the conviction that, in his time, in his corner of the world, a people must learn not only the gross and monotonous facts of their immediate history but must assemble, from the exchanges of their daily lives, the assurances and inspiring reverberations of myth. It is a uniquely difficult commission to execute. For they must do this in a self-conscious age of technology in which there are fewer and fewer effective symbols —a multiple furrow tractor, for instance, can never become the key to that door of perception which we can make out of a horse, a plough, and a man behind the plough. They must do it at a time when they are living at the beginning of a history. *Palace of the Peacock* is one of the few pieces of evidence we have that success in this task is possible.

If I have given to *Palace of the Peacock* a great deal of the space allowed me in this essay, it is because this first book in the quartet seems to state most of the themes which are later developed in the others. Like many other novelists who rely heavily on the use of symbol to give resonance to their work, Harris tends to find a symphonic design best suited to his purpose. The images employed in the several stories depend for their final "proof" on the manner in which they are later reworked and given new moulded structures by the author.

It is therefore a pity that limitation of space prevents a detailed study of *The Far Journey of Oudin*. In this story, we are returned to the crafty, suspicious and greedy peasant world of the coastal savannahs. The basic theme is one of Harris's constant preoccupations, that of dominion, of tyrannical and thus sterile authority which is hardly distinguishable from rape. The savage relish with which the first Donne maltreats his tender, fertile Mariella, is only a reflection of the unimaginative waste he has made of the high savannahs which he could have transformed into incalculable fruitfulness by the exercise of humility. In *The Far Journey of Oudin,* the concern appears in the sad, vulgar Mahommed, who sees himself becoming a "new kind of ruler" on the profits he has accrued from buying up the abandoned frame houses of the old-fashioned sugar plantations. It also appears in the main plot of the book in the duel between the sexually impotent Ram, a predator who is gradually acquiring a dominant wealth by theft, usury and cold manipulation of his neighbour's frailties; and

Oudin, a vagrant, who gradually acquires some wealth and power while in Ram's service.

This book, the most complex of the quartet, is also the least satisfactory. The main fault lies in failure of nerve on the author's part. Faced with the drab and mercenary domestic exchanges of a *khulak* community, the author panics, becomes rhetorical, pretentious and sometimes nearly bombastic. He robes his innocent and uncaring people in philosophical vestments which they wear about as comfortably as would a navvy dressed in a duke's full coronation regalia. Unlike any other stories in the quartet, this one also seems to preach a message, and the message is in the end platitudinous: "all that glitters is not gold," "you can't take it with you," and so on.

With *The Whole Armour*, we see Harris restored to the heights of his impressive powers. It is perhaps the most accomplished work of the series. Plot, image, character, architecture and language all fuse into a whole that is as compact, shapely and penetrative as a bullet. In it, he returns to that ideal frontier which is as much a spiritual as a geographical boundary—the line between the challenging wilderness and the cultivated sensibility—and which is the setting in which he always moves most confidently. Once more the plot is austere; an undecorated stage on which the principals are the foci of our total attention. In this story, too, Harris undertakes the portrayal of a relationship which seems to be beyond the powers or outside the interest of most West Indian novelists; the complexities of love between a man and a woman who is a *person* in whom the subtleties of erotic response can be kindled or who is approached, as a new-found land, with awe, delight and a careful sounding of the shoals. Sharon, the young girl in *The Whole Armour*, is such a one, and the relationship between her and Cristo, the fugitive accused of murder, gives a lyric immediacy and profane disturbance that is very rare indeed in West Indian fiction.

With none of Harris's novels is it easy to chart all the fabulous and mythical meanings which are concealed beneath the deceptive simplicity of his plots. *The Whole Armour* starts with the boy Cristo, son of the whore Magda, as a fugitive. He is accused of murder and forced by his mother into the care of Abram, an inscrutable and determined recluse who lives in a cabin on the wild shore near the mouth of the Pomeroon. Abram dies of a heart attack and Cristo returns up river to his mother. She insists that they go back to Abram's hut, and there find that a jaguar ("tiger" in local speech) has dragged the dead man out into the bush and half eaten the corpse. In a scene of great power, Magda compels Cristo to strip the festering remains and reclothe them in his own garments. Cristo sets off for the Venezuelan border and Magda stages a grotesque wake for her "dead" son, during which a man is stabbed accidentally by the drunken Peet.

The community begins to settle back into the rhythms of its agricultural assault on the surrounding jungle. There are rumours of the nightly appearance of a great tiger. It is Cristo returned, hiding by day, and emerging at night clad in a tiger skin. He and Sharon, Peet's daughter, have a brief exchange of love. By chance, he is seen and reported to the river police. The book closes with the police advancing on the house in which he and Sharon have probably brought a new life into being.

Violent or improbable as the events and characters parsimoniously outlined above may seem, they are perfectly credible in the context of the scarcely touched littoral and backlands between Western Guyana and the Orinoco basin. It is a peculiar, insulated territory of scarcely yielding nature and Victorian civilities. It is a territory where the individual can, by the exercise of endurance and courage, put a lot of space between himself and bureaucratic disciplines. It is the territory, also, where the Singer sewing machine and the omen, the outboard motor and the ancestral admonition in a dream, are all of equal relevance. It is not a territory of schizophrenics, but a community of souls where double vision, an acceptance of the two worlds of reality, is a condition of survival.

It is with this double vision, this flank attack on the material exchanges of everyday life, that we must approach the significance of Cristo's (Christ's) forty days and forty nights in the wilderness before his return to Sharon (earthly fertility); and his conviction that, from his child in Sharon's womb, a new race will spring, uncontaminated by the mean and bloody exploitations of the sugar lands but "reborn into Guiana's first aliens and arrivals," a kind ready to move out and explore the continent from the only area of Guyana where there was never established the "grand sugar estate and absentee proprietor."

It is an explosive statement because here, for the first time in British West Indian fiction, we are faced with a serenely confident charter of liberation from the immediate past. Cristo not only thinks what he says but lives it. He is freed from the squalid commercial transaction between white and black, aborigines and conquistadors, which is most of West Indian history. It is at this point that the symbolic trappings which the characters have been asked to bear become necessary uniforms. His proximate responsibility for the death of his putative father Abram, his assumption of the skin of "Christ, the tiger," his return to the coastlands, his fathering of a child, his legacy to that child of a more audacious understanding and use of the land, are all part of a carefully fashioned, artistic criticism of a system that for too long nourished itself on the cycle of parturition, forced labour and the flesh's surrender, but which never acknowledged the reality of holy dying.

The Secret Ladder confirms the sense one had in reading *The*

Whole Armour that Harris was developing a new assurance in han-
dling the techniques of fiction. The story is perhaps the most interesting of any in the quartet. A surveying party led by the deeply introspective but highly articulate Fenwick comes to measure the rise of
water along the Canje River on the line where the coastal savannahs
begin to merge into the forest. They are the advance guard, the scouts,
for a flood control and land development scheme. Their purpose is
sensed rather than rationally comprehended by the inhabitants of the
district; a gentle and diffident colony of bush Negroes, descendants of
runaways, who have not so much been abandoned by history as opted
out of it. Poseidon is the leader, or more exactly the revered father
of this tribe; he is so immensely old, so intractably withdrawn, that he
has become almost a legend. Even the hardbitten, sophisticated tech-
nicians who make up Fenwick's crew regard him with a curious mixture of awe and ownership, as though he were already more god than
man. For days, the tribe under Poseidon conduct a sly, almost timorous
campaign of sabotage against Fenwick's work. There is an unseasona-
ble dry spell and the river will not rise enough to give the average
readings necessary for any future development plans. Finally, the tribe
is driven by their terror of dispossession into an act of pathetic and
uncertain violence against one member of the crew and his lover,
the girl Catalena. In a scuffle that would hardly have marked a
younger man, old Poseidon is accidentally struck and falls dead in
the shadow of one of his own horses. The tribe is by now quite dazed
with shock and terror, not only by Poseidon's death but because they
believe, wrongly, that two of their number have killed one of Fenwick's crew in a quarrel over the purchase of a turtle. As they flee the
territory, the first rains begin.

Simply on the level of a drama played out between the invading,
often impatient forces of material progress and the dispossession of a
timid, uncomprehending folk, this would be a fine story. The characters of the crew are distinct; the tension of wills (between Fenwick and
his men) in the heavy atmosphere of a jungle just before the rains,
the lack of communication between the tough, Faustian surveyors and
the frightened, dream-burdened people of the river are both sustained
with great skill. So is Fenwick's mingled guilt and exasperation over
his failure to convince Poseidon of their good intentions; his recognition that the magnificent and inconsolable old man has a part of the
truth that the planners must recognize if their future of material
plenty is to give them nourishment.

But there is another exploration of meaning carried in the current
of the social conflict for, in *The Secret Ladder,* Harris returns to
many of the themes and symbols of the first book. The action takes
place over seven days. Fenwick's boat is named *Palace of the Peacock.*
To him, the rivers of Guyana are "the curious rungs in a ladder on

which one sets one's musing foot again and again, to climb into both the past and the future of the continent of mystery." The crew, although more substantial and prosaic than the first crew, are yet seen, through Fenwick's eyes, as actors in an inward drama of his dreams. And these dreams are inspired by—or, if you prefer, are the other side of—what Harris once called "the material structural witnesses" of history. For Fenwick, as for Wilson Harris, the experiences of the day must be revised in the language of dreams, of free association, so that in the end, by the potent magic of image, all the fragments of our strange, broken heritage may begin to act one upon the other, become whole within our instinctive grasp. It is only when this has been achieved that we will enter into an active, conscious possession and use of the West Indian inheritance.

The Road to *Banana Bottom*

by Kenneth Ramchand

Claude McKay's *Home to Harlem* (1928) is set in the group life of the American Black Belt; *Banjo* (1929), more loosely constructed, assembles a pan-Negro cast on the Marseilles waterfront called the Ditch. In both novels, McKay's preoccupation with the place of the Negro in white civilization takes the form of a celebration of Negro qualities on the one hand, and attacks upon the civilized white world on the other:

> For civilisation had gone out among these native, earthy people, had despoiled them of their primitive soil, had uprooted, enchained, transported and transformed them to labor under its laws, and yet lacked the spirit to tolerate them within its walls.
>
> That this primitive child, this kinky-headed, big-laughing black boy of the world, did not go down and disappear under the serried crush of trampling white feet; that he managed to remain on the scene, not worldly wise, not "getting there," yet not machine-made nor poor-in-spirit like the regimented creatures of civilisation, was baffling to civilised understanding. Before the grim, pale rider-down of souls he went his careless way with a primitive hoofing and a grin.
>
> *(Banjo,* p. 314)

The cultural dualism towards which McKay developed raises problems of three kinds for the artist. Characterization of the primitive Negro would run close to the White man's stereotype; the polemic novelist might be tempted into passionate statement at the expense of imaginative rendering; and the celebration of one race in exclusive terms could harden into a denial of the possibilities of life and of our common humanity.

Home to Harlem and *Banjo* are not exempt from weaknesses along these lines. But the novels are more dramatic and more tentative than they are usually held to be. In a significant passage in his autobiography, McKay wrote that it was impossible for him to take D. H. Lawrence seriously as a social thinker. Yet Lawrence was the modern

"The Road to *Banana Bottom*" (excerpt). From *The West Indian Novel and Its Background* by Kenneth Ramchand (New York: Barnes & Noble, Inc.; London: Faber and Faber, Ltd., Publishers, 1970), pp. 247–73. Reprinted by permission of the publishers.

writer he preferred above any: "In D. H. Lawrence I found confusion
—all of the ferment and torment and turmoil, the hesitation and
hate and alarm . . . and the incertitude of this age, and the psychic
and romantic groping for a way out." [1] I take this as an unconscious
declaration of affinity, and I wish to see *Home to Harlem* and *Banjo*
as part of a "romantic groping for a way out." The life was to end
in disillusion, poverty and despair, with a pathetic conversion to a
scavenging Roman Catholicism in 1944: the art was to achieve a
splendid resolution in the serene pages of *Banana Bottom* (1933),
where a surer grasp of technique matches a sudden access to understanding.

Disillusioned by the "white folks' war," and seized by loneliness after
two years in England, Jake Brown of *Home to Harlem* (1928) returns
to the joyful place where he immediately strikes it up with Felice a
"little brown girl" at a cabaret called the Baltimore. His exultation
at being back in sweet-sweet Harlem where there are such "pippins for
the pappies" (p. 14) carries over into authorial amplifications: "Oh to
be in Harlem again after two years away. The deep-dyed colour, the
thickness, the closeness of it. The noises of Harlem. The sugared
laughter. The honey-talk on its streets. And all night long, ragtime
and "blues" playing somewhere . . . singing somewhere, dancing
somewhere! Oh the contagious fever of Harlem. Burning everywhere
in dark-eyed Harlem. . . . Burning a jake's sweet blood. . . ." (p.
15). The disappearance of Felice is the device by which McKay gives
the novel the appearance of a plot, allowing Jake to taste other joys in
Harlem while he looks for the missing girl:

> The pianist was a slight-built, long-headed fellow. His face shone like
> anthracite, his eyes were arresting, intense, deep yellow slits. He seemed
> in a continual state of swaying excitement, whether or not he was playing.
>
> They were ready, Rose and the dancer-boy. The pianist began, his
> eyes towards the ceiling in a sort of ecstatic dream. Fiddler, saxophonist,
> drummer and cymbalist seemed to catch their inspiration from him. . . .
>
> They danced, Rose and the boy. Oh they danced! *An exercise of
> rhythmical exactness for two. There was no motion she made that he
> did not imitate.* They reared and pranced together, smacking palm
> against palm, working knee against knee, grinning with real joy. They
> shimmied, breast to breast, bent themselves far back and shimmied
> again. Lifting high her short skirt and showing her green bloomers, Rose
> kicked. . . .
>
> And the pianist! At intervals his yellow eyes, almost bloodshot, swept
> the cabaret with a triumphant glow, gave the dancers a caressing look,
> and returned to the ceiling. *Lean, smart fingers beating barbaric beauty
> out of a white frame.* Brown bodies, caught up in the wild rhythm, wig-
> gling and swaying in their seats.
>
> (*Home to Harlem,* pp. 92–4)

---

[1] *A Long Way from Home,* p. 247.

In the first of the italicized phrases, McKay's power of expression flags, and in the second there is a self-conscious straining for a polemic effect. But there is something to be said for this passage. Impressionistic syntax creates a rhythmic quality; the vividly seen pianist's transport is all the more intense for being confined by the ceiling; and McKay's tactic of shifting the focus from pianist to dance and back to the inspired medium communicates the infectious quality of the music. The description is not an exotic *tour de force*: the capacity for joy and life which McKay projects as Harlem's priceless instinctive possession is the novel's central value. McKay is not always as tactful as this in his presentation of Harlem's and the Negro's rhythmic qualities. Sometimes indeed there is no presentation, only authorial romanticizing, as in the following passage from another point in the novel:

> The piano-player had wandered off into some dim, far-away ancestral source of music. Far, far away from music-hall syncopation and jazz, he was lost in some sensual dream of his own. No tortures, banal shrieks and agonies. Tum-tum . . . tum-tum . . . tum-tum. The notes were naked, acute, alert. Like black youth burning naked in the bush. Love in the deep heart of the jungle. . . . The sharp spring of a leopard from a leafy limb, the snarl of a jackal, green lizards in amorous play, the flight of a plumed bird, and the sudden laughter of mischievous monkeys in their green homes. Tum-tum . . . tum-tum . . . tum-tum . . . tum-tum. . . . Simple-clear and quivering. Like a primitive dance of war or of love . . . the marshalling of spears or the sacred frenzy of a phallic celebration.

> *(Home to Harlem, pp. 196–7)*

And in another jazz passage, from *Banjo*, McKay loses all artistic instinct to make his point against civilization:

> Shake to the loud music of life playing to the primeval round of life. Rough rhythm of darkly-carnal life. Strong surging flux of profound currents forced into shallow channels. Play that thing! One movement of the thousand movements of the eternal life-flow. Shake that thing! In the face of the shadow of Death. Treacherous hand of murderous Death, lurking in sinister alleys, where the shadows of life dance, nevertheless to their music of life. Death over there! Life over here! Shake down Death and forget his commerce, his purpose, his haunting presence in a great shaking orgy. Dance down the Death of these days, the Death of these ways in shaking that thing. Jungle jazzing. Orient wriggling, civilised stepping. Shake that thing! Sweet dancing thing of primitive joy, perverse pleasure, prostitute ways, many-colored variations of the rhythm, savage, barbaric, refined—eternal rhythm of the mysterious, magical, magnificent—the dance divine of life. . . . Oh, Shake That Thing!

> *(Banjo, pp. 57–8)*

Jake, like Banjo, is an exponent of values McKay sometimes artlessly propagandizes. So I would like to turn for a while from problems of the authorial voice to problems of characterization.

"*Home to Harlem* for the most part nauseates me, and after the dirtier parts of its filth I feel distinctly like taking a bath. . . . It looks as though McKay has set out to cater for that prurient demand on the part of white folk for a portrayal in Negroes of that utter licentiousness which conventional civilisation holds white folk back from enjoying—if enjoyment it can be called." [2] So wrote the high-minded W. E. B. du Bois. Reviewing *Banjo,* another Coloured conservative advised: "If you like filth, obscenity, pimpery, prostitution, pan-handling and more filth you ought to be enthusiastic about *Banjo.*" [3] Although he celebrates the unfettered joy that lower-class Negro life has to offer, McKay does not sentimentalize either the Ditch or Harlem. This is implicit in the characterization of Jake. Jake's capacity for a life of sensations is his uncorrupted legacy, but McKay also makes him a romantic spirit yearning for transcendence. "I love you, I ain't got no man," says Congo Rose, and Jake yields like Tom Jones. But the affair proves unsatisfactory because "her spirit lacked that charm and verve, the infectious joy of his little lost brown. He sometimes felt that she had no spirit at all—that strange elusive something that he felt in himself, sometimes here, sometimes there, roaming away from him . . . wandering to some unknown new port, caught a moment by some romantic rhythm, color, face, passing through cabarets, saloons, speakeasies, and then returning to him. . . . The little brown had something of that in her, too. That night he had felt a reaching out and a marriage of spirits" (pp. 41–2). Jake stands for the best that Harlem has to offer—he is its natural exponent, but by the end of Part I his need for relief has been established: "Jake had taken the job on the railroad just to break the hold that Harlem had upon him. When he quitted Rose he felt that he ought to get right out of the atmosphere. If I don't get away from it for a while it'll sure git me he mused" (p. 125).

In Part II of *Home to Harlem,* McKay introduces Ray, a Haitian intellectual with literary ambitions, a man exiled from his native islands by the American occupation. Two processes begin at this point. The first is the education of Jake. When Ray honours both Wordsworth and Toussaint by quoting the sonnet on the great revolutionary:

> Jake felt like one passing through a dream, vivid in rich, varied colors. It was revelation beautiful in his mind. That brief account of an island of savage black people, who fought for collective liberty and were strug-

[2] W. E. B. du Bois in *Crisis Magazine.* Quoted by Stephen Bronz in *Roots of Negro Consciousness,* p. 84.

[3] Dewey Jones in the Chicago *Defender,* quoted by Bronz, p. 84.

gling to create a culture of their own. A romance of his race, just down
there by Panama. How strange!

Jake was very American in spirit and shared a little of that comfortable Yankee contempt for poor foreigners. And as an American Negro he
looked askance at foreign niggers. Africa was a jungle and Africans bush-
niggers, cannibals. And West Indians were monkey-chasers. But now he
felt like a boy who stands with the map of the world in colors before
him, and feels the wonder of the world.

(Home to Harlem, p. 134)

Although McKay does not develop Jake's educative process farther
than race consciousness, the character remains conscious of a defi-
ciency to the end, and becomes critical of his way of living. In the
mainly North American criticism of McKay's work, it is customary to
blur the circumstantial distinctions between Jake and Banjo as fictional characters and concentrate on their identical symbolic functions. Bone,[4] for instance, describes Jake as "the typical McKay protagonist—the primitive Negro untouched by the decay of Occidental
civilisation . . . Jake represents pure instinct." This implies a simple-
minded view of the connection between authorial philosophy and
characterization, especially hazardous in a case like McKay's where
the philosophy is changing, and changing so often as a result of clarifi-
cations achieved through fictional airing. But the mistaken view begins
with and depends on misreading. After meeting Ray's girl Agatha and
admiring her poise and her simple charm, Jake becomes reflective.
The passage is explicit:

His thoughts wandered away back to his mysterious little brown of the
Baltimore. She was not elegant and educated, but she was nice. Maybe
if he found her again—it would be better than just running wild around
like that! Thinking honestly about it, after all, he was never satisfied,
flopping here and sleeping there. It gave him a little cocky pleasure to
brag of his conquests to the fellows around the bar. But after all the
swilling and boasting, it would be a thousand times nicer to have a little
brown woman of his own to whom he could go home and be his simple
self with. Lay his curly head between her brown breasts and be fondled
and be the spoiled child that every man loves sometimes to be when he is
all alone with a woman. *That* he could never be with the Madame
Lauras. They expected him always to be a prancing he-man. Maybe it
was the lack of a steady girl that kept him running crazy round. Boozing
and poking and rooting around, jolly enough all right, but not altogether contented.

(Home to Harlem, p. 212)

Although Jake is easy-living, it is in the novel *Banjo* that we meet
the complete insulated vagabond hero, the folk artist linked by his
instrument to the improvising unconventional world of *jazz.* The

[4] Robert A. Bone, *The Negro Novel in America* (N.Y., 1965), p. 69.

meeting with Agatha inspires Jake to articulate his discontent with
the vagabonding life. It is in reaction to the same girl, however, that
Ray recognizes the menace of respectability: "He was afraid that
some day the urge of the flesh and the mind's hankering after the
pattern of respectable comfort might chase his high dreams out of
him and deflate him to the contented animal that was a Harlem nigger
strutting his stuff. 'No happy-nigger strut for me' he would mutter
when the feeling for Agatha worked like a fever in his flesh. *He saw
destiny working in her large, dream-sad eyes, filling them with the
passive softness of resignation to life, and seeking to encompass and
yoke him down as just one of the thousand niggers of Harlem. And
he hated Agatha and, for escape, wrapped himself darkly in self-love"*
(p. 264).

Ray's quest for a *modus vivendi* is the second process that begins with
the meeting of Ray and Jake. Ray in *Home to Harlem* and in *Banjo*
is a portrait of the Negro intellectual in western civilization. He is a
figure of *malaise,* and through his tortured consciousness, a set of
social and racial dilemmas are expressed. There can be little doubt
that the discomfort and dilemmas of McKay himself inform the
presentation of the fictional character in direct ways. But there are
still distinctions to be made. A look at the chapter "Snowstorm in
Pittsburgh" from *Home to Harlem* will facilitate matters. Jake and
Ray have just returned from an all-night bar:

> Jake fell asleep as soon as his head touched the dirty pillow. Below
> him Ray lay in his bunk, tormented by bugs and the snoring cooks.
> The low-burning gaslight flickered and flared upon the shadows. The
> young man lay under the untellable horror of a dead-tired man who
> wills to sleep and cannot.
>
> In other sections of the big barn building the faint chink of coins
> touched his ears. Those men gambling the hopeless Pittsburgh night
> away did not disturb him. They were so quiet. It would have been bet-
> ter, perhaps, if they were noisy.
>
> *(Home to Harlem*, pp. 151–2)

This is a precisely rendered description of sleeplessness, and from
it we move into the troubled consciousness of the character counting
up to a million, thinking of love and then thinking about home:

> There was the quiet, chalky-dusty street and, jutting out over it, the
> front of the house that he had lived in. The high staircase built on the
> outside, and pots of begonias and ferns on the landing. . . . All the
> flowering things he loved, red and white and pink hibiscus, mimosas,
> rhododendrons, a thousand glowing creepers, climbing and spilling their
> vivid petals everywhere, and bright-buzzing humming-birds and butter-
> flies. . . .
>
> *(Home to Harlem*, pp. 152–3)

It is not difficult to recognize that McKay's own nostalgia is being
expressed here, but it is relevant as part of the character's mental
effort to induce sleep. The author's sense of the dramatic situation is
strong, moreover, so there is no question of this plausible nostalgia
getting out of hand:

> Intermittently the cooks broke their snoring with masticating noises of
> their fat lips, like animals eating. Ray fixed his eyes on the offensive
> bug-bitten bulk of the chef. These men claimed kinship with him. They
> were black like him. Man and nature put them in the same race. . . .
> Yet he loathed every soul in that great barrack-room except Jake. Race.
> . . . Why should he have and love a race? Races and nations were things
> like skunks, whose smells poisoned the air of life.
>
> *(Home to Harlem, pp. 153–4)*

Thus smoothly do we move with the character, and with the implied
author, from particular sleeplessness and particular reactions to people, to larger questions of race and nation. But even at this point,
McKay's sense of Ray as a particular character with a particular past,
and his awareness of his fictional creature as a troubled being remain
in tactical control. Ray's thoughts about race and nation dart back
and forth, with his own island always in his mind. The American
occupation has thrown him into being one with the "poor African na-
tives" and "Yankee 'coons,'" but he agitatedly slips out of such an
affinity only to be faced again by the returning thought:

> Some day Uncle Sam might let go of his island and he would escape
> from the clutches of that magnificent monster of civilisation and retire
> behind the natural defenses of his island, where the steam-roller of
> progress could not reach him. Escape he would. He had faith. He had
> hope. But, oh, what would become of that great mass of black swine.
> . . . Sleep! Oh, sleep! . . . But all his senses were burning wide awake.
> Thought was not a beautiful and reassuring angel. . . . No. It was suf-
> fering. . . .
>
> *(Home to Harlem, pp. 155–6)*

McKay does not hesitate to use Ray as a means of grinding the authorial axe, but the grinding is done by a character convincingly presented as a man aggrieved, and as a man debating with himself.

The effect of such a dramatic presentation may be felt in the well-
known chapter 15. Here, Ray thinks like McKay about the art and
raw material of fiction, supplies what is virtually a bibliography of
intellectual influences upon McKay, and then registers the two events
that shook McKay's life—"the great mass carnage in Europe" and "the
great mass revolution in Russia." Ray, we are told, realized that he
had lived through an era:

And also he realised that his spiritual masters had not crossed with him
into the new. He felt alone, hurt, neglected, cheated, almost naked. But
he was a savage, even though he was a sensitive one, and did not mind
nakedness. What had happened? Had they refused to come or had he
left them behind? Something had happened. But it was not desertion
nor young insurgency. It was death. Even as the last scion of a famous
line prances out his day and dies and is set aside with his ancestors in
their cold whited sepulcher, so had his masters marched with flags and
banners flying all their wonderful, trenchant, critical satirical, mind-
sharpening, pity-evoking constructive ideas of ultimate social righteousness into the vast international cemetery of the century.

(*Home to Harlem,* pp. 226–7)

A reading of McKay's autobiography *A Long Way from Home* might
indeed suggest that Ray is nothing but the author's mouthpiece, but
here it is necessary to make a theoretical distinction of some consequence. We have to discriminate between, on the one hand, a character who is simply an author's mouthpiece or embodiment of a consciously held theory, and on the other, an independent fictional character who happens to be modelled upon an author's own life. Ray in
Home to Harlem is modelled upon McKay. Because Ray's dilemmas
are presented, crucially, in dramatic terms in the novel itself, the
authorial urgency intensifies that of the character. It is like hitting
with the spin. There is a loss of concentration in the next novel.

Banjo has even less of a plot than *Home to Harlem*: the sub-title
declares it to be "a story without a plot." The setting on the Marseilles
waterfront is less cohesive than the Harlem of the previous novel. The
group of international Negroes McKay assembles hardly live together
—they meet like delegates at a conference for the Negro stateless.
Long stretches of the novel are turned over to debating and discussing
Negro questions: Sénghor is mentioned a few times, and Garvey
haunts the conversations, but every shade of Negro and every shade
of Negro opinion is represented. The loss of concentration on characters is met by a heavy reliance upon speech-making.

When a Martiniquan student refuses to accompany Ray to a bar
on the grounds that there are likely to be too many Senegalese there,
Ray attacks him for despising his racial roots:

"In the modern race of life we're merely beginners. If this Renaissance
we're talking about is going to be more than a sporadic and scabby
thing, we'll have to get down to our racial roots to create it."
    "I believe in a racial renaissance," said the student, "but not in going
back to savagery."
    "Getting down to our native roots and building up from our own peo-
ple," said Ray, "is not savagery. It is culture."
    "I can't see that," said the student.

"You are like many Negro intellectuals who are belly-aching about
race," said Ray. "What's wrong with you all is your education. You get
a white man's education and learn to despise your own people. You read
biased history of the whites conquering the colored and primitive peoples, and it thrills you just as it does a white boy belonging to a great
white nation."

(Banjo, pp. 200–1)

There are another two hundred and eighty words in Ray's speech, in
which he advises the Martiniquan to read Russian novels, to learn
about Gandhi, and to be humble before the simple beauty of the
African dialects instead of despising them. This does not bring about
a change in the Martiniquan's life. But he does not appear in the
novel again.

There are easier examples to discredit, where Ray's views are more
controversial, and where there is not even the pretence of a living situation. This seems to be a fair selection, however, and I want to argue
from it that even when we agree with what McKay wishes to declare,
and when we share the author's passion, it is still difficult for us as
readers of fiction to accept such blatant manipulating of character and
event as occurs in the novel. It is a central weakness that McKay uses
Ray to state authoritatively points of view which do not strictly arise
out of the presented life of the novel.

Another weakness becomes apparent when we consider the passages
in which McKay takes us into the consciousness of the fictional character. A good example comes at the end of the novel when Ray's attitude to Banjo's method of raising funds becomes the occasion of a
two-thousand-word authorial reportage of Ray's thoughts, culminating in McKay's theory of cultural dualism or legitimate difference:

The more Ray mixed in the rude anarchy of the lives of the black boys
—loafing, singing, bumming, playing, dancing, loving, working—and
came to a realisation of how close-linked he was to them in spirit, the
more he felt that they represented more than he or the cultured minority the irrepressible exuberance and legendary vitality of the black race.
And the thought kept him wondering how that race would fare under
the ever tightening mechanical organisation of modern life. . . .

The grand mechanical march of civilisation had levelled the world
down to the point where it seemed treasonable for an advanced thinker
to doubt that what was good for one nation or people was also good
for another. But as he was never afraid of testing ideas, so he was not
afraid of doubting. All peoples must struggle to live, but just as what
was helpful for one man might be injurious to another, so it might be
with whole communities of peoples.

(Banjo, pp. 324–5)

The reverie is only slightly motivated, and is so prolonged that it
loses sight of the immediate situation (Banjo waiting for a reply to

a question), but what really matters here is that Ray's consciousness is entered into not for the sake of creating a sense of that consciousness but only as a variation on speech-making. McKay's view of himself as a misfit in White civilization had lent itself in *Home to Harlem* to the presentation of a tortured, uncertain mind. The key to the novel's dramatic interest lay in the sensed need for something more than what the life of the boys had to offer: "Life burned in Ray perhaps more intensely than in Jake. Ray felt more and more and his range was wider, and he could not be satisfied with the easy, simple things that sufficed for Jake" (p. 265). By the time that *Banjo* comes to be written, McKay's position has changed: the life of vagabondage is desperately held to be the only preservative value in a decadent White world.

The belief is successfully embodied in the presentation of Banjo, the protagonist. He dominates the all too brief first part of the novel in which McKay sets the scene and introduces the tramps of the seafront: "It was as if all the derelicts of all the seas had drifted up here to sprawl out the days in the sun" (p. 18). From the mimetically impressive opening sentence, however, McKay asserts life: "Heaving along from side to side, like a sailor on the unsteady deck of a ship, Lincoln Agrippa Daily, familiarly known as Banjo, patrolled the magnificent length of the great breakwater of Marseilles, a banjo in his hand" (p. 3). Through the spontaneity, improvisation, and unconventionality of Banjo and his beach boys, McKay suggests the rhythmic quality of unquenchable life. But Banjo the folk artist of the jazz world is presented circumstantially as a person, and it is this which allows us to accept him as standing for a way of life. The supremacy of the new faith is made evangelically clear when Jake is reintroduced to spell out his allegiance. He is married to Felice but has taken a seaman's job: " 'I soon finds out . . . that it was no joymaking business for a fellah like you' same old Jake, chappie, to go to work reg'lar ehvery day and come home ehvery night to the same old pillow. Not to say that Felice hadn't kep' it freshin' up and sweet-smelling all along. . . . But it was too much home stuff, chappie' " (pp. 292-3).

The new faith obviously turns Ray into a zealous preacher. But at one moment, the character affirms to himself that "civilisation would not take the love of colour, joy, beauty, vitality and nobility out of *his* life and make him like one of the poor mass of its pale creatures. . . . Rather than lose his soul, let intellect go to hell" (pp. 164-5). And at another point the same character is represented thus in authorial reportage: "From these boys he could learn how to live—how to exist as a black boy in a white world and rid his conscience of the used-up hussy of white morality. He could not scrap his intellectual life and be entirely like them. He did not want or feel any urge to 'go back' that way. . . . Ray wanted to hold on to his intellectual ac-

quirements without losing his instinctive gifts. The black gifts of
laughter and melody and simple sensuous feelings and responses" (pp.
322–3). These two statements suggest that McKay is still in doubt. But
none of this uncertainty informs the characterization. Ray comes over
as a learned interpreter of Negro values, and a critic of Babylon. The
author's unresolved tension, and his unhappiness with the authorita-
tive figure he has created are allowed to break in at the end of the
novel, however, when Ray and Banjo set off together on a life of
vagabondage. " 'Youse a book fellah . . . and you' mind might tell
you to do one thing and them books persweahs you to do another.' "
There is fulfilment in every sense in the new world of *Banana Bottom*.

Home to Harlem and *Banjo* had ended with the departures of ex-
iles. *Banana Bottom* begins with the return of a native. The characters
of the first two novels extracted a living on the edges of society, the
characters of the third are rooted in a landscape. The violent debates
of the earlier works, in which there is only a thin line between author
and character are now succeeded by the controlled idyllic tone of a
distanced narrator. The central character is not a figure of *malaise*
like Ray of the preceding novels, nor does McKay find it necessary to
externalize *malaise* in the form of a complementary but separated pair
such as Jake and Ray or Banjo and Ray. The polarized pair of heroes
of the first two novels are replaced by a single heroine. Bita Plant, the
daughter of a Jamaican peasant, is brought up by the Reverend Malcolm Craig and his wife Priscilla. After seven years abroad at an English University and on the Continent, Bita returns to her native land.
Banana Bottom tells the story of how she gradually strips away what
is irrelevant in her English upbringing, and how she marries
Jubban the strong silent drayman in her father's employ. To put it
in this way is to make it clear at once that McKay's theme is still cultural dualism. The differences between *Banana Bottom* and the other
novels are differences in art. Bita Plant is the first achieved West Indian heroine and *Banana Bottom* is the first classic of West Indian
prose.

The action of the novel alternates between the village of Banana
Bottom where Bita spends her early years, and the adjoining town of
Jubilee where she is groomed by the Craigs; and McKay makes unob-
trusive use of the nominal difference between the two in order to symbolize Bita's final liberation and embrace of the folk. But our first impression is of the community:

> *That* Sunday when Bita Plant played *the* old straight piano to the
> singing of *the* coloured Choristers in the beflowered schoolroom was the
> most exciting in the history of Jubilee.
> Bita's homecoming was an eventful week for the folk of the tiny coun-
> try town of Jubilee and the mountain village of Banana Bottom. For she

was the only native Negro girl they had ever known or heard of who
had been brought up abroad. Perhaps the only one in the island. Educated in England—the mother country as it was referred to by the Press
and official persons.

(Banana Bottom, p. 1)

The communal memory is of specific times and specific events: *"That
Sunday when Bita played"*; it has its landmarks, its familiar items and
its own institutions—*"the* . . . schoolroom . . . *the* . . . piano" and
"the coloured Choristers." The private experience "Bita's homecom-
ing" is also an event for the folk. In the second paragraph the authorial voice glides mimetically into the communal voice. From these
opening moments of the novel, McKay steadily builds up a sense of a
way of life. Its constitutive elements are tea-meeting, picnic, market,
harvest festival, pimento picking, house-parties and ballad-making. Its
people range themselves across an ordered spectrum of swiftly and
vividly drawn individuals: Squire Gensir, the Englishman in exile;
Reverend and Mrs. Craig, the missionaries with a civilizing purpose;
Belle Black, the village free-living maid, and her friend Yoni Legge;
Tack Tally and Hopping Dick, the village dandies; Kojo Jeems and
Nias Black, drummers; Phibby Patroll, the roving gossip; Herald Newton Day, the pompous theological student, local boy being groomed
by the Craigs for stardom with Bita; Crazy Bow, the wandering flute
boy; the Lambert brood on the weary road to whiteness; the mulatto
Glengleys, and Wumba the obeah man.

The main action takes place against a background buzzing with
life and implication. But it is more than this. Bita belongs to a
sustaining community just as a Naipaul character sticks incongru-
ously out of a crowded depressing canvas. It is because Bita belongs,
and because the community is realized as having spontaneous values
of its own that we can credit her fictional process. The incident with
Crazy Bow which leads to Bita's adoption by the Craigs illustrates
how McKay enriches the background life of the community by draw-
ing out one of the background characters to perform a specific significant function and then letting them slip back into his independent
life again. The incident also illustrates how McKay at last integrates
music (a recurrent vitalizing element in the other novels) into the
action and meaning of the novel without signs of straining.

In what looked at first only like a charming anecdote in the novel,
McKay establishes Crazy Bow as the village's wandering musician:
"Unheralded he would thrust his head into the doorway of a house
where any interesting new piece of music was being played" (p. 6).
Breaking into the village choir rehearsals, he would not be induced
"to participate in a regular manner . . . but no one wanted to stop
him, everybody listened with rapture" (p. 6). The account continues:

He was more tractable at the tea meetings, the unique social events of
the peasantry, when dancing and drinking and courting were kept up
from nightfall till daybreak. Then Crazy Bow would accept and guzzle
pint after pint of orange wine. And he would wheedle that fiddle till
it whined and whined out the wildest notes, with the dancers ecstatically
moving their bodies together to follow every twist of the sound. And
often when all was keyed high with the music and the liquor and the
singing and dancing Crazy Bow would suddenly drop the fiddle and go.

(Banana Bottom, p. 7)

To be noted here is that McKay has dispensed with the hyphenated
words, the impressionistic dots, and the ancestral transports of dancers
and players which characterized music passages in the earlier novels.
But it is difficult to resist the rhythmic re-creation in the passage. It
is difficult to resist not only because of the mimetic quality of the
language, but because McKay's description is firmly attached to the
scene and the participants. In another passage, McKay's tact is even
more impressive. Crazy Bow is a frequent visitor to the home of
Jordan Plant:

And whenever Crazy Bow was *in the mood* he would take the fiddle
down from the wall and play. And sometimes he did play in a way that
moved Jordan Plant inside and made tears come into his eyes—tears
of sweet memories when he was younger down at Jubilee and fiddled, too,
and was a gay guy at tea-meetings. Before the death of his father. Before
he became a sober member and leader of the church.

(Banana Bottom, p. 8)

Because the community has replaced a vague ancestral land, like that
evoked in *Banjo,* and because each character in it has a specific past
to which to refer, McKay's rendering of the moving power of the
music needs no authorial insistence. It is not in keeping with the spirit
of the passage to indicate too strongly that McKay has stealthily
infiltrated a polemic point about the deadening weight of civilization
represented by the church, for our responsive gaze is fixed on the dis-
solving character.

Relating Crazy Bow to the earlier novels we might note that he
combines vagabondage with music. A brilliant student at school, he
shoots "right off the straight line" after the first year "and nothing
could bring him back" (p. 5). The school piano turns him "right
crazy. . . . It knocked everything else out of his head. Composition
and mathematics and the ambition to enter the Civil Service. All the
efforts of the headmaster were of no avail" (p. 6). Crazy Bow represents
the same kind of protest against civilization as the guitar-playing
Banjo, but McKay's well-proportioned world does not admit of that
protest being over-insistent nor of the protesting character being central. The value that Crazy Bow represents is a real one which the

society must assimilate. But it does not set itself up as the only value. Where Matthew Arnold fails, McKay triumphs sweetly.

It is with all this insinuated, the ravishing power of Crazy Bow's music and the tenseness of the fiddler, that the crucial incident takes place. Crazy Bow, the harmless idiot, often frisks with Bita by the riverside. As they do one Saturday:

> As they romped, Bita got upon Crazy Bow's breast and began rubbing her head against his face. Crazy Bow suddenly drew himself up and rather roughly he pushed Bita away and she rolled off a little down the slope.
>
> Crazy Bow took up his fiddle, and sitting under a low and shady guava tree he began to play. He played a sweet tea-meeting love song. And as he played Bita went creeping upon her hands and feet up the slope to him and listened in the attitude of a bewitched being.
>
> And when he had finished she clambered upon him again and began kissing his face. Crazy Bow tried to push her off. But Bita hugged and clung to him passionately. Crazy Bow was blinded by temptation and lost control of himself and the deed was done.
>
> *(Banana Bottom,* p. 10)

The setting is idyllic. Bita is drawn like a natural creature "creeping upon her hands and feet up the slope to him" and Crazy Bow is involuntarily possessed. The incident does not call for a moralizing gloss. The ballad-makers put it into "a sugary ditty" (p. 14). The stabilizing community absorbs and transforms the deed "and soon the countryside was ringing" with songs:

> You may wrap her up in silk,
> You may trim her up with gold,
> And the prince may come after
> To ask for your daughter,
> But Crazy Bow was first.
>
> *(Banana Bottom,* p. 15)

This is one of the ways in which McKay suggests the distinctive value of the Banana Bottom society but there is an attempt to use the incident in a more explicit way. We are returning to the question of how presented life in fiction relates to authorial theory.

Burning to deliver herself of the news, Sister Phibby Patroll travels the fifteen miles from Banana Bottom to Jubilee by foot. Her overnight trek gives her a decisive lead:

> So Sister Phibby told the tale to Priscilla Craig. And although she thought it was a sad thing as a good Christian should, her wide brown face betrayed a kind of primitive satisfaction as in a good thing done early. Not so that of Priscilla Craig's. It was a *face full of high-class anxiety, a face that generations upon generations of Northern training in*

reserve, restraint, and Christian righteousness have gone to cultivate, a
face fascinating in its thin benevolent austerity.

(*Banana Bottom,* pp. 15–16)

For much of *Banana Bottom,* McKay expresses cultural dualism not
by setting up explicit contrasts but by celebrating the *Banana Bottom*
community. This is why it is possible to read the work as a serene
evocation of the loved place. In this passage, however, McKay does
not resist the temptation to make an easy hit. It is plausible enough
that Sister Phibby should show the kind of satisfaction McKay describes—and the satisfaction derives from Sister Phibby's understanding of what is likely to be Mrs. Craig's view on the subject. But in the
section I have italicized McKay seems to be stating his case according
to an authorial preconception or prejudice about a type, and not in
relation to the individual character in the interview. The whole is
re-done with much less self-consciousness and with great effect a few
lines later:

> "Poor child!" said Priscilla Craig.
> "Yes, poor child," said Sister Phibby. . . . "But she was ober-womanish
> ob a ways the folkses them say."
> "That's no reason she should have been abused," said Priscilla Craig.
> "Temptation, Missis," sighed Sister Phibby, "and the poor fool was
> mad! What kyan a poah bady do ag'inst a great big temptation?"
> "Pray to God, of course, Sister Phibby," said Mrs. Craig.

(*Banana Bottom,* p. 16)

The conversation comes close to the truth of the presented incident.
And the Banana Bottom ethic proves to be a more flexible one than
that represented by Mrs. Craig. It does so simply by being itself.

The Crazy Bow incident establishes Bita's natural connection with
the Banana Bottom world. Her transference to Jubilee and tutelage
under the Craigs is an artificial thing. When Bita returns after her
seven years abroad she is still herself. The character who is a returned
native presents McKay with a plausible medium for the nostalgia
expressed in his poems and in the earlier novels. Bita goes to the
market. McKay describes the wealth of the land collected in one place
and records the sounds and sights of the higgling scene. Then:

> Bita mingled in the crowd, responsive to the feeling, the colour, the
> smell, the swell and press of it. It gave her the sensation of a reservoir
> of familiar kindred humanity into which she had descended for bap-
> tism. She had never had that big moving feeling as a girl when she
> visited the native market: And she thought that if she had never gone
> abroad for a period so long, from which she had become accustomed
> to viewing her native life in perspective, she might never have had that
> experience. . . .
> The noises of the market were sweeter in her ears than a symphony.

Accents and rhythms, movements and colours, nuances that might have passed unnoticed if she had never gone away, were now revealed to her in all their striking detail. And of the foodstuff on view she felt an impulse to touch and fondle a thousand times more than she wanted to buy.

(Banana Bottom, p. 41)

But this is not simply plausible nostalgia, it is part of a dramatic process that is to end with the marriage of Bita to her father's drayman. I shall return to this process later. After her experience at the market, Bita meets the dandy Hopping Dick.

In *Banana Bottom,* McKay reveals a comic talent for the first time. " 'Such hands like yours, Miss Plant, were trained for finer work than to carry common things like pineapples.' " Thus gallantly begins the courtship of Bita by the village dandy, grogshop customer, horse-gambler and notorious feminine heart-breaker. " 'There's more big-foot country gals fit to carry pines than donkeys in Jamaica. Please give me the pleasure to relieve you, as I am walking your way' " (p. 42). With the swelling disapproval of big-foot Rosyanna, servant of the mission and sister in the church, the trio pursue their way:

Hopping Dick turned on his dandiest strut walking up the main street with Bita. Out of the corner of his eye he saw a group of his set in the door of the grogshop watching him open-mouthed; but apparently unseeing he strutted more ornamentally, ostentatiously absorbed in conversation with Bita. . . . After the first compliments Hopping Dick was stumped of what to say. He was very ready-tongued with the local girls in the market and at the tea-meetings, but he felt he could not use the same talk upon a person like Bita, and he wanted to shine. So the few minutes between the market and the mission were mostly spent in perfecting his strut.

(Banana Bottom, p. 43)

The ungodly set are treated to the spectacle of Hopping Dick attending church and helping at choir-practice, and the grogshop gossipers of Jubilee provide a running commentary. The latest ballad is about the fall of Gracie Hall and one of the boys sitting on top of a cracker barrel has just been whistling the tune:

"Well, dat was one to fall down," said a little-sized brown drinker. "Wonder who be the next?"

"De nex' is you," said the barkeeper. "You habent call fer a roun' yet."

"Set him up, set him up deah," said the little one. "Dis is one way a falling, but de way Gracie fall is anodder. . . ."

"To fin' out de nex' you mus' ask Hopping Dick," said a tall black. "Hoppin' Dick ain't nuttin'," said the little one contemptuously.

"Him get a look in on the miss in de mission, though. . . ."

(Banana Bottom, p. 106)

Matters reach a dramatic head when Mrs. Craig sends the following telegram to Jordan Plant:

> "Bita ruining her reputation with worthless man. Please come at once." (p. 219)

For McKay has more than a comic use for Hopping Dick. Bita's association with the strutting young man is the occasion for a conflict between Mrs. Craig and Bita:

> "He's not a fit person for you to be seen in the street with, Bita. And he had no right to take advantage of your ignorance and force his company upon you. He is a brazen bad young man."
>
> "He didn't force himself on me. He asked me if he could come and I said all right."
>
> ". . . You know there are certain things we just can't do, simply because they reflect on the mission."
>
> "But I don't think walking and talking a little with Mr. Delgado could have anything to do with the mission. Even if he's not a person of the best character."
>
> "Bita, my child! Don't try to be ridiculous. A mere child even could see the right thing to do. You have received an education to do the correct thing almost automatically. Even Rosyanna feels a certain responsibility because she is connected with the mission. . . ."
>
> *(Banana Bottom,* p. 45)

The clash between Bita and Mrs. Craig is successfully dramatized as a particular one between two incompatible people. From this sound beginning it develops into a confrontation between two ways of life. Instead of the rhetoric of an authorial voice, we move into the consciousness of a character seeking a *modus vivendi:*

> Bita retired to her bed. And the more she thought of the incident the more resentful she became. She wondered now that she had come home to it after all the years of training, if she would be able to adjust herself to the life of the mission.
>
> *(Banana Bottom,* p. 45)

With matters thus poised, the scene shifts from the town of Jubilee to the lush village of Banana Bottom for the week of festivities beginning with the celebration of Emancipation Day. It is thirty years before Great Gort and Jack O'Lantern and before the march to Independence square in *Season of Adventure,* so we have to make do with Nias Black, and Kojo Jeems:

> Kojo Jeems, the drummer, had a fine set of drums and he was loved for his wonderful rattling of the battle-drum. His son beat the big drum. They went playing down the hill followed by a few ragged kiddies, to the hub of the village. There they were joined by the fiddler and the flute-blower and played and played, with the sun mounting higher and

hotter, until there was gathered together a great crowd. And all marched
swaying to the music, over the hill, and picking up marchers marking
time along the wayside, up to the playground.

(Banana Bottom, p. 63)

At the picnic on Table Top Plateau, McKay's feel for the dialect and
his vivid sense of people swiftly contribute to our impression of a
known and bounded world. "First among the rum-shop fellows was
Tack Tally, proudly wearing his decorations from Panama: gold
watch and chain of three strands, and a foreign gold coin attached
to it as large as a florin, a gold stick-pin with a huge blue stone, and
five gold rings flashing from his fingers. He had on a fine bottle-green
tweed suit with the well-creased and deep-turned pantaloons called
peg-top, the coat of long points and lapels known as American style.
And wherever he went he was accompanied by an admiring gang"
(p. 66). Contained in the Banana Bottom world too are the "Misses
Felicia, Elvira and Lucinda Lambert . . . cashew-brown daughters of
the ebony parson. They were prim of manners, precise and halting
of speech as if they were always thinking, while talking, that they
were the minister's daughters" (p. 65). It is a world of gossip and
ballad and anecdote. But it is a world whose laws are framed from the
outside.

Bita explains to the exiled Englishman Squire Gensir that her function at the mission prevents her from dancing and from attending
tea-meetings. Gensir nevertheless persuades her to attend Kojo Jeems's
tea-meeting. Under this unofficial teacher's tutelage, Bita's rebellion
begins. At Kojo's tea-party, Bita looks at the dancers and declares "I'm
going to join them"; about possible disapproval "Oh, I don't care
anyhow." Wilfully she begins:

And Bita danced freely released, danced as she had never danced since
she was a girl at a picnic at Tabletop, wiggling and swaying and sliding
along, the memories of her tomboyish girlhood rushing sparkling over
her like water cascading over one bathing upon a hot summer's day.

The crowd rejoiced to see her dance and some girls stood clapping
and stamping to her measure and crying: "Dance, Miss Bita, dance you'
step! Dance, Miss Bita, dance away!" And she danced forgetting herself,
forgetting even Jubilee, dancing down the barrier between high breed-
ing and common pleasures under her light stamping foot until she was
one with the crowd.

(Banana Bottom, p. 84)

The roving reporter Phibby Patroll takes the news to Jubilee, and
Bita's second clash with Mrs. Craig occurs. The consequences are
softened by Bita's use of Gensir's chaperoning name but the Craigs
decide to speed up their plans for Bita's marriage with Herald Newton
Day.

McKay's presentation of Herald Newton Day is enhanced by the new sense of characterization and human relationships that we see in *Banana Bottom,* and by the newly discovered comic resources. Because Day poses a threat to the heroine we can enjoy his deflation—in the way it is not always possible to do when Naipaul deflates a peripheral character even in *A House for Mr. Biswas.* McKay lets Day's own pompous language do the work, and he allows Bita and Gensir to patronize him. Gensir tells Bita and Herald Newton that he had fruitlessly spent much of the previous day hunting for a rare flower about which Jubban had informed him:

> "I think I'll try again tomorrow," the Squire said.
> "By God's help you'll succeed in finding it, sir," said Herald Newton.
> Bita was shaking from suppressed laughter and Herald Newton, remarking a humorous expression on the squire's face wondered what he might have done. . . .
> "I wish I could be sure God will help me to find that flower," said the Squire, his eyes twinkling. "Do you think he could help me, really?"
> "I am sure He will if you ask him in faith," replied Herald Newton.
> "Let us play," said Bita, turning to the piano.
>
> (*Banana Bottom,* pp. 171–2)

Since Day is the willing protégé of the Craigs, McKay can satirize him plausibly as a Negro who gets a white man's education and learns to despise his own people. When Day proposes marriage " 'Everybody would be happy if we both get married' " and Bita feels bound to accept " 'I suppose we might as well do it and please everybody,' " Herald is gratified and insensitive:

> "You know at first when I began studying for the ministry and thinking of the great work before me, I thought that perhaps only a white woman could help me. One having a pure mind and lofty ideals like Mrs. Craig. For purity is my ideal of the married state. With clean hearts thinking and living purely and bearing children under the benediction of God.
> "I know you will understand," . . . Herald squeezed Bita's hand, but she felt that it was not she herself that inspired the impulse, but perhaps his thought . . . "just as Mrs. Craig would. For you have been trained like a pure-minded white lady."
> "I don't know about that," said Bita. "But whatever I was trained like or to be, I know one thing. And that is that I am myself."
>
> (*Banana Bottom,* p. 100)

Herald Newton Day is the same type as the Martiniquan attacked by Ray in the novel *Banjo,* but it is only within the regulating structure of *Banana Bottom* and with McKay's sense of Day as an individual in the fictional world that the satiric effect can be achieved without signs of authorial straining. But the art of *Banana Bottom* is not free from impurities; it seems to be an indication of a loss of control in the novelist as well that, by the most violent irony, "Herald Newton . . . suddenly turned crazy and defiled himself with a nanny goat. Consternation fell upon that sweet rustic scene like a lightning ball of destruction. And there was confusion among these hill folk, which no ray of understanding could penetrate" (p. 175). The plot demands that Herald Newton should be removed from the scene but one cannot help feeling that the author is indulging a spiteful impulse. The spite in this account may be compared with the humour and tolerance with which in a later section, McKay presents the scandal discovered by Sister Phibby Patroll, at the height of a religious revival, that Sister-in-Christ Yoni Legge is pregnant by a fellow convert Hopping Dick (see pp. 270–2).

Bita's conflicts with Mrs. Craig and her antagonism to Herald Newton Day are associated with her alienation from the town of Jubilee, and with her increasing preference for the village of *Banana Bottom* where she had spent her early childhood. She spends more and more time in the village. "It was so much pleasanter and freer at Banana Bottom" (p. 161). A number of images of immersion associated with constitutive elements of village life or with the landscape impress her belonging to Banana Bottom. An example of the first is her dance at Kojo Jeems's tea-meeting. The following example of the second illustrates incidentally the way in which McKay is able to make maximum dramatic use of the nostalgia felt by some West Indian writers who are abroad. On a visit to Banana Bottom, Bita wanders through her childhood haunts:

> All of her body was tingling sweet with affectionate feeling for the place. For here she had lived some of the happiest moments of her girlhood, with her schoolmates and alone. Here she had learned to swim, beginning in the shallow water of the lower end with a stout length of bamboo. She remembered how she screamed with delight with her schoolmates cheering and clapping their hands that day when she swam from one bank to the other.
>
> She slipped off her slight clothes and plunged into the water and swam round and round the hole. Then she turned on her back to enjoy the water cooling on her breasts. Now she could bear the sun above burning down.

> (*Banana Bottom,* p. 117)

The unpretentious manner in which this passage suggests Bita's belonging and her exultation is best brought out by a comparison with the poverty of declaration in the closing sentences of Neville Dawes's *The Last Enchantment* (1960): "I was a god again, drunk on the mead of the land, and massive with the sun chanting in my veins. And so, flooded with the bright clarity of my acceptance, I held this lovely wayward island, starkly, in my arms" (p. 288).

Bita's increasing sense of her rootedness in the Banana Bottom community is reflected in her deliberate flouting of Mrs. Craig's wishes. A climax of a kind is reached when with Herald Newton long banished, the two women clash over Hopping Dick's coming to the mission to escort Bita to a dance. Mrs. Craig wants to know if Bita loves Dick. Bita says she could love him:

> "A low peacock," said Mrs. Craig, "who murders his h's and altogether speaks in such a vile manner—and you an educated girl—highly educated."
> "My parents also speak broken English," said Bita.
> Anger again swept Mrs. Craig and a sharp rebuke came to her lips, but it was checked when her eyes noted Bita toying enigmatically and ostentatiously with Herald Newton's engagement ring on her finger.

> *(Banana Bottom,* p. 210)

Moving from this particular show of antagonism between the two characters, and with the weight of similar demonstrations in earlier episodes behind him, McKay enters the consciousness of Bita:

> Bita was certain now that the time had arrived for her to face the fact of leaving Jubilee. It would be impossible for her to stay when she felt not only resentment, but a natural opposition against Mrs. Craig. A latent hostility would make her always want to do anything of which Mrs. Craig disapproved. Bita could not quite explain this strong feeling to herself. It was just there, going much deeper than the Hopping Dick affair. Maybe it was an old unconscious thing now manifesting itself, because it was to Mrs. Craig, a woman whose attitude to life was alien to her, and not to her parents, she owed the entire shaping of her career.

> *(Banana Bottom,* p. 211)

The passage is a crucial one in the sense that the doctrine it contains plays a part in the conception of the novel, but it is also crucial in terms of Bita's growing self-awareness. The flat declaration of an attitude which we have just seen in action is followed by the tentative "could not quite explain," "maybe," groping for an explanation, and then a resolution repeated—"Bita knew that she was going to go"— which leads into a wave of disgust and an assertive action:

> She became contemptuous of everything—the plan of her education and the way of existence at the mission, and her eye wandering to the photography of her English college over her bed, she suddenly took and ripped it from its frame, tore the thing up and trampled the pieces under her feet. . . .

> *(Banana Bottom,* p. 212)

It is a much more convincing and suggestive process than Ray's generalization in *Home to Harlem* that "civilisation is rotten." The difference is one between understanding through art, and becoming constricted through polemics.

Bita's return to the folk is confirmed when she witnesses a religious ceremony held by a drumming cult during a period of drought: "Magnetized by the spell of it Bita was drawn nearer and nearer into the inner circle until with a shriek she fell down. A mighty shout went up and the leading woman shot out prancing around Bita with uplifted twirling supple-jack, but a man rushed in and snatched her away before she could strike" (p. 250). It is interesting to notice that George Lamming uses a religious ceremony in a similar scene in *Season of Adventure* (1960). But whereas Fola's season of adventure into her true self *begins* at the ceremony of the souls Bita's mesmerization occurs at the end of her particular process. Fola is involved by Lamming in a process of self-discovery. McKay's heroine, it is possible to see more clearly by comparison, is involved in a process of self-assertion. By the end of the novel, Bita has married Jubban, her rescuer at the ceremony, and the land has prospered under his hand. Bita herself is in full bloom: "Her music, her reading, her thinking were the flowers of her intelligence, and he the root in the earth upon which she was grafted, both nourished by the same soil" (p. 313). In the final scene, Aunty Nommy rejoices over the child of the marriage:

> "What a pickney, though! What a pickney!" Aunty Nommy was saying and playfully slapping little Jordan's bottom.
> "Showin' you' strength a'ready mi li't' man. Soon you'll be l'arnin' for square you' fist them off at me."

In the world of *Banana Bottom,* life is going on. The recurrent McKay experience of *malaise,* of being born "out of time," lies behind *Banana Bottom*. But the achievement of the artist in this work is the creation of a world that disperses *malaise*. The episode at Bita's childhood pool is only one example of the novel's characteristic imaging of the act of immersion:

> She slipped off her slight clothes and plunged into the water and swam round and round the hole. Then she turned on her back to enjoy the water cooling on her breasts. Now she could bear the sun above burning down. How delicious was the feeling of floating! To feel that one can suspend oneself upon a yawning depth and drift, drifting in perfect confidence without the slightest intruding thought of danger.

> *(Banana Bottom,* p. 117)

Art reveals possibilities. Mr. Naipaul's observed Tulsi world is a copy of a society from which it is necessary to escape. In *Banana Bottom,* Claude McKay imagined a community to which it is possible to belong.

Biographical Notes

THE EDITOR AND CONTRIBUTORS

M. G. COOKE is a professor of English at Yale University, specializing in English romanticism and West Indian literature. He is the author of *The Blind Man Traces the Circle: On the Patterns and Philosophy of Byron's Poetry* (Princeton: Princeton University Press, 1969) and of numerous articles and book reviews on romantic poetry, modern fiction, and autobiography.

JONATHAN BAUMBACH teaches English at Tufts University and is author of *The Landscape of Nightmare,* co-author of *Moderns and Contemporaries: Nine Masters of the Short Story,* and editor of *Writers as Teachers: Teachers as Writers.*

ROBERT BONE is a professor of English at Teacher's College, Columbia University, and the author of *The Negro Novel in America* and other studies of modern black fiction.

MICHEL FABRE teaches at the Institut d'Études Anglaises et Nord-Américaines at the Sorbonne and has a special interest in Richard Wright and James Baldwin.

JOHN HEARNE, a Jamaican, is staff tutor in the Department of Extra-Mural Studies at the University of the West Indies. He has worked as a broadcaster and journalist and is an accomplished novelist in his own right.

ABIOLA IRELE is a poet as well as a critic. A graduate of the University of Ibadan, he completed his doctoral work at the Sorbonne with a thesis on Aimé Césaire.

JANHEINZ JAHN is a theorist, critic, bibliographer, and anthologist of African literature.

ROBERT W. JULY has been Assistant Director for the Humanities at the Rockefeller Foundation of New York and has a professorial appointment at the University of Ibadan.

JEANNETTE KAMARA, née MACAULAY, born in Freetown, Sierra Leone, is a lecturer in French-African Literature at Fomah Bay College, University College of Sierra Leone.

GERALD MOORE is a lecturer at the School of African and Asian Studies at the University of Sussex and a member of the Committee of *Black Orpheus,* to which he contributes regularly.

EZEKIEL MPHAHLELE, born in South Africa, has been literary editor of *Drum* and co-editor of *Black Orpheus* and is at present a professor of English in Zambia. In addition to his criticism and fiction, he has published an autobiography, *Down Second Avenue*.

KENNETH RAMCHAND, a Trinidadian, is an editor as well as a teacher-scholar of West Indian Literature. He has taught at the University of the West Indies and the University of Edinburgh.

GORDON ROHLEHR is a graduate of the University of the West Indies. In addition to his work on West Indian Literature, he has a major interest in Conrad and modern British fiction.

ANNE TIBBLE, a versatile writer and editor, has, in addition to her work on African Literature, collaborated with her husband on editions and criticism of John Clare and on the books *Helen Keller* and *The Study of Education*.

KINGSLEY WIDMER, a teacher and scholar, has written books on *The Art of Perversity: D. H. Lawrence's Shorter Fiction, Henry Miller,* and *Ways of Nihilism: A Study of Herman Melville's Short Novels.*

THE NOVELISTS

CHINUA ACHEBE, born in Ogidi, Eastern Nigeria, in 1930, went to Government College in Umuahia, which he uses as a setting in his novels, and for his B.A. to the University of Ibadan. He has been Director of External Broadcasting for Nigeria and did official work for the Biafran authorities, including missions abroad, during the Nigerian civil war. His first novel, *Things Fall Apart,* won the Margaret Wrong prize and has been translated into three European languages. *No Longer at Ease* won the Nigerian National Trophy.

JAMES BALDWIN was born (1924) and educated in New York City. His first novel, *Go Tell It on the Mountain,* won the Eugene F. Saxton Memorial Trust Award; he also has held various literary fellowships. Besides his novels, he has published two plays, *The Amen Corner* and *Blues for Mr. Charlie,* and three volumes of essays, *Notes of a Native Son, Nobody Knows My Name,* and *The Fire Next Time.*

MONGO BETI, born in Mbalmayo, Cameroun Republic, in 1932, went to Paris at twenty-one to study in the Arts Faculties of Aix-en-Provence University and the Sorbonne. He has been a government official in the Cameroun Republic and is now a university lecturer. His third novel, *Mission to Kala,* won the Saint-Beuve prize. He writes in French.

RALPH ELLISON was born in Oklahoma City in 1914 and studied at Tuskegee Institute, majoring in music. He has lectured widely on American Negro culture, folklore, and creative writing. His first book, *Invisible Man,* garnered him the National Book award, the Russwurm award, and the National Newspaper Publishers award. Much of his recent work appeared in *Shadow and Act,* where the essays created a counterpoise to Ellison's fiction that is reminiscent of the relation of fiction and essays in James Baldwin.

WILSON HARRIS was born (1921) and educated in Guyana. Formerly a land surveyor in his home country, he now lives and writes in England.

CAMARA LAYE, born at Kouroussa, Guinea, in 1924, went to technical college at Conakry, studied engineering in France, and now works as a civil servant in his homeland. Besides his novels, which he writes in French, he has published a number of short stories in *Black Orpheus*.

CLAUDE McKAY (1890–1948) was born in Jamaica and educated there and in the United States. He was a journalist and polemical pamphleteer, as well as accomplished poet and novelist. His *Harlem Shadows* (1922) did a great deal to launch the Harlem Renaissance, in which McKay held a prominent, if also controversial place.

V. S. NAIPAUL was born (1932) and bred in Trinidad, went to Oxford at eighteen, and has made England his home. Of East Indian parentage, Naipaul has written on India (*An Area of Darkness*) and on the relation of the West Indies to Europe (*The Loss of El Dorado*) and to Africa (*The Middle Passage*). He is included here as a West Indian novelist.

RICHARD WRIGHT, born in Natchez, Mississippi, in 1908, movingly records his upbringing and sense of destiny in his autobiography, *Black Boy*, and his social interpretations (he was a contributing editor of *New Masses*) in *Twelve Million Black Voices* and *Black Power*. He began his literary career writing short stories; *Uncle Tom's Children*, his first publication, won the *Story* magazine prize in 1938.

Selected Bibliography

THE NOVELISTS

Abrahams, Peter (b. 1919)
Mine Boy. London: Faber & Faber, Ltd., 1954.
A Wreath for Udomo. London: Faber & Faber, Ltd., 1956.

Achebe, Chinua (b. 1930)
Things Fall Apart. London: William Heinemann, Ltd., 1958.
No Longer at Ease. London: William Heinemann, Ltd., 1960.
Arrow of God. London: William Heinemann, Ltd., 1964.
A Man of the People. New York: Doubleday & Co., Inc., Anchor Books, 1966.
Chike and the River. New York: Cambridge University Press, 1966.

Anthony, Michael (b. 1932)
The Games Were Coming. London: André Deutsch, 1963.
The Year in San Fernando. London: André Deutsch, 1965.
Green Days by the River. London: André Deutsch, 1967.

Baldwin, James (b. 1924)
Giovanni's Room. New York: The Dial Press, 1956.
Another Country. New York: The Dial Press, 1962.
Go Tell It on the Mountain. New York: The Dial Press, 1963.
Tell Me How Long the Train's Been Gone. New York: The Dial Press, 1968.

Bennett, Alvin (b. 1914)
God the Stonebreaker. London: William Heinemann, Ltd., 1964.

Beti, Mongo (b. 1932)
Mission to Kala. London: Muller, 1958.
King Lazarus. London: Muller, 1960.

Boles, Robert
The People One Knows. Boston: Houghton Mifflin Company, 1964.

Cain, George (1856–1919)
Blueschild Baby. New York: McGraw-Hill Book Company, 1970.

Carew, Jan (b. 1922)
Black Midas. London: Secker & Warburg, 1958.
The Wild Coast. London: Secker & Warburg, 1958.
The Last Barbarian. London: Secker & Warburg, 1961.

Clarke, Austin C. (b. 1896)
  The Survivors of the Crossing. London: William Heinemann, Ltd., 1964.
  Among Thistles and Thorns. London: William Heinemann, Ltd., 1965.
  The Meeting Point. London: William Heinemann, Ltd., 1967.

Drayton, Geoffrey (b. 1924)
  Christopher. London: William Collins Sons & Co., Ltd., 1959.
  Zohara. London: William Collins Sons & Co., Ltd., 1961.

Ekwensi, Cyprian (b. 1921)
  People of the City. London: Dakars, 1953.
  Jagua Nana. London: Hutchinson & Co. (Publishers) Limited, 1961.
  Burning Grass. London: William Heinemann, Ltd., 1962.
  Beautiful Feathers. London: Hutchinson & Co. (Publishers) Limited, 1963.

Ellison, Ralph (b. 1914)
  Invisible Man. New York: Random House, Inc., 1952.

Fair, Ronald (b. 1932)
  Many Thousand Gone. New York: Harcourt Brace Jovanovitch, Inc., 1965.

Harris, Wilson (b. 1921)
  Palace of the Peacock. London: Faber & Faber, Ltd., 1960.
  The Far Journey of Oudin. London: Faber & Faber, Ltd., 1961.
  The Whole Armour. London: Faber & Faber, Ltd., 1962.
  The Secret Ladder. London: Faber & Faber, Ltd., 1963.
  Heartland. London: Faber & Faber, Ltd., 1964.
  The Eye of the Scarecrow. London: Faber & Faber, Ltd., 1965.
  The Waiting Room. London: Faber & Faber, Ltd., 1967.
  Tumatumari. London: Faber & Faber, Ltd., 1968.
  The Sleepers of Roraima. London: Faber & Faber, Ltd., 1971.

Hearne, John (b. 1926)
  Voices under the Window. London: Faber & Faber, Ltd., 1955.
  Stranger at the Gate. London: Faber & Faber, Ltd., 1956.
  The Faces of Love. London: Faber & Faber, Ltd., 1957.
  The Autumn Equinox. London: Faber & Faber, Ltd., 1959.
  The Land of the Living. London: Faber & Faber, Ltd., 1961.

James, C. L. R. (b. 1901)
  Minty Alley. London: Secker & Warburg, 1936.

Khan, Ismith (b. 1925)
  The Jumbie Bird. London: MacGibbon & Kee, 1961.
  The Obeah Man. London: Hutchison & Co. (Publishers) Limited, 1964.

Killens, John (b. 1916)
  Youngblood. New York: The Dial Press, 1954.

La Guma, Alex (b. 1925)
  A Walk in the Night. Ibadan: Mbari, 1962.
  And a Threefold Cord. East Berlin: Seven Seas Books, 1965.

Lamming, George (b. 1927)
  In the Castle of My Skin. London: Michael Joseph, 1953.
  The Emigrants. London: Michael Joseph, 1954.
  Of Age and Innocence. London: Michael Joseph, 1958.
  Season of Adventure. London: Michael Joseph, 1960.

Laye, Camara (b. 1924)
   The Dark Child. London: William Collins & Sons Co., Ltd., 1955.
   The Radiance of the King. London: William Collins & Sons Co., Ltd., 1956.

McKay, Claude (1890–1948)
   Home to Harlem. New York: Harper & Bros., 1928.
   Banjo: a Story without a Plot. New York: Harper & Bros., 1929.
   Gingertown. New York: Harper & Bros., 1932.
   Banana Bottom. New York: Harper & Bros., 1933.

Mais, Roger (1905–1955)
   Three Novels. London: Johnathan Cape, 1966.

Marshall, Paule (b. 1929)
   The Chosen Place, the Timeless People. New York: Harcourt Brace Jovanovitch, Inc., 1959.

Mayfield, Julian (b. 1928)
   The Hit. New York: Vanguard Press, Inc., 1957.
   The Long Night. New York: Vanguard Press, Inc., 1958.
   The Grand Parade. New York: Vanguard Press, Inc., 1960.

Mittelholzer, Edgar (1909–1965)
   Corentyne Thunder. London: Secker & Warburg, 1941.
   A Morning at the Office. London: Hogarth Press, 1950.
   Shadows Move Among Them. London: Peter Nevill, 1952.
   Children of Kaywana. London: Secker & Warburg, 1952.
   The Life and Death of Sylvia. London: Secker & Warburg, 1953.
   The Harrowing of Hubertus. London: Secker & Warburg, 1954.
   The Adding Machine. Kingston, Jamaica: Pioneer Press, 1954.
   Kaywana Blood. London: Secker & Warburg, 1958.

Mphahlele, Ezekiel (b. 1919)
   In Corner B (stories). Nairobi: East Africa Publishing House, 1967.

Naipaul, Vidiadhar Surajprasad (b. 1932)
   The Mystic Masseur. London: André Deutsch, 1957.
   The Suffrage of Elvira. London: André Deutsch, 1958.
   Miguel Street. London: André Deutsch, 1959.
   A House for Mr. Biswas. London: André Deutsch, 1961.
   Mr. Stone and the Knight's Companion. London: André Deutsch, 1963.
   The Mimic Men. London: André Deutsch, 1967.
   A Flag on the Island (short stories). New York: The Macmillan Company, 1968.
   Loss of El Dorado. New York: Alfred A. Knopf, Inc., 1970.

Ngugi, James T. (b. 1938)
   Weep Not, Child. London: William Heinemann, Ltd., 1964.
   The River Between. London: William Heinemann, Ltd., 1965.

Ouologuem, Yambo (b. 1940)
   Bound to Violence. New York: Harcourt Brace Jovanovitch, Inc., 1971.

Patterson, H. Orlando (b. 1940)
   The Children of Sisyphus. London: New Authors, Ltd., 1964.
   An Absence of Ruins. London: Hutchinson & Co. (Publishers) Limited, 1966.

Reid, Victor Stafford (b. 1913)
  New Day. New York: Alfred A. Knopf, Inc., 1949.
  The Leopard. London: William Heinemann, Ltd., 1958.
Rhys, Jean
  Wide Sargasso Sea. London: André Deutsch, 1966.
Rive, Richard (b. 1931)
  Emergency. London: Faber & Faber, Ltd., 1964.
Selvon, Samuel (b. 1923)
  A Brighter Sun. London: Wingate, 1952.
  An Island is a World. London: Wingate, 1955.
  The Lonely Londoners. London: Wingate, 1956.
  Ways of Sunlight. London: MacGibbon & Kee, 1957.
  Turn Again Tiger. London: MacGibbon & Kee, 1958.
  I Hear Thunder. London: MacGibbon & Kee, 1963.
  The Housing Lark. London: MacGibbon & Kee, 1965.
Tutuola, Amos (b. 1920)
  The Palm-Wine Drunkard. London: Faber & Faber, Ltd., 1952.
  My Life in the Bush of Ghosts. London: Faber & Faber, Ltd., 1954.
  Simbi and the Satyr of the Dark Jungle. London: Faber & Faber, Ltd., 1955.
  The Brave African Huntress. London: Faber & Faber, Ltd., 1958.
  Feather Woman of the Jungle. London: Faber & Faber, Ltd., 1961.
Williams, Denis (b. 1923)
  Other Leopards. London: New Authors, Ltd., 1963.
Williams, John A. (b. 1925)
  Sissie. Garden City, N.Y.: Doubleday & Company, Inc., 1969.
  The Man Who Cried I Am. Boston: Little, Brown and Company, 1967.
  Sons of Darkness, Sons of Light. Boston: Little, Brown and Company, 1969.
Wright, Richard (b. 1908)
  Native Son. New York: Harper & Row, Publishers, 1940.
  The Outsider. New York: Harper & Row, Publishers, 1953.
  Lawd Today. New York: Walker & Company, 1965.
  Uncle Tom's Children. New York: Harper & Row, Publishers, 1969.
  The Long Dream. New York: Harper & Row, Publishers, 1959.
Wynter, Sylvia
  The Hills of Hebron. London: Jonathan Cape Limited, 1962.

CRITICAL WORKS

Abraham, Willie, *The Mind of Africa*. Chicago: University of Chicago Press, 1962.

Augier, Gordon, Hall, and Reckord, *The Making of the West Indies*. London: Longmans, Green & Co., Ltd., 1960.

Bigsby, C. W. E., ed., *The Black American Writer*, Vol. I ("Fiction"). Baltimore. Pelican Publishing Co., Inc., 1971.

Bone, Robert, *The Negro Novel in America*. New Haven: Yale University Press, 1956 (rev. ed., 1965).

Brignano, Russell C., *Richard Wright: An Introduction to the Man and His Works*. Pittsburgh: University of Pittsburgh, 1970.

Chapman, Abraham, ed., *Black Voices: An Anthology of Afro-American Literature*. New York: The Free Press, 1968.

Coulthard, G.R., *Race and Colour in Caribbean Literature*. London: Institute of Race Relations, 1962.

Cruse, Harold, *The Crisis of the Negro Intellectual: From Its Origins to the Present*. London: W. H. Allen, 1969.

Daly, P. H., *West Indian Freedom and West Indian Literature*. Georgetown: The Daily Chronicle Press Ltd., 1951.

Dathorne, O. R., "The Theme of Africa in West Indian Literature," *Phylon*, 26, pp. 255–76.

Davis, Arthur P., and Saunders Redding, eds., *Cavalcade*. Boston: Houghton Mifflin Company, 1971.

Eckman, Fern, *The Furious Passage of James Baldwin*. New York: Popular Library, Inc., 1966.

Edwards, Paul, ed., *Modern African Narrative: an anthology*. London: Nelson, 1966.

Ellison, Ralph, *Shadow and Act*. New York: Random House, Inc., 1964.

Emanuel, James A., and Theodore Gross, eds., *Dark Symphony: Negro Literature in America*. New York: The Free Press, 1968.

Feuser, W., "Negritude—the Third Phase," *New Africa*, 5 (1965), 63–64.

Ford, Nick Aaron, "The Ordeal of Richard Wright," *College English*, 15 (1953), 87–94.

Gibbon, Donald B., ed., *Five Black Writers*. New York: New York University Press, Gotham Library, 1970.

Goede, William, "On Lower Frequencies: The Buried Men in Wright and Ellison," *Modern Fiction Studies*, 15:4 (1969/70), 483–501.

Goveia, Elsa V., *Slave Society in the British Leeward Islands at the End of the Eighteenth Century*. New Haven: Yale University Press, 1965.

Harris, Wilson, *Tradition, the Writer and Society*. London: New Beacon Publications, 1967.

Hays, Peter L., "The Incest Theme in *Invisible Man*," *The Western Humanities Review*, 23:4 (Autumn 1969), 142–59.

Hill, Herbert, ed., *Soon, One Morning: New Writing by American Negroes, 1940–1962*. New York: Alfred A. Knopf, Inc., 1963.

Hughes, Carl M., *The Negro Novelist, 1940–1950*. New York: Citadel Press, Inc., 1970.

Hughes, Langston, ed., *An African Treasury*. New York: Crown Publishers, Inc., 1960.

Irele, Abiola, "The Tragic Conflict in Achebe's Novels," *Introduction to African Literature*. Ed. Ulli Beier. Evanston, Ill.: Northwestern University Press, 1967.

Jahn, Janheinz, *Approaches to African Literature*. Nigeria: Ibadan University Press, 1959.

————, *Muntu: An Outline of Neo-African Culture.* London: Faber & Faber, Ltd., 1961.

————, *A Bibliography of Neo-African Literature.* London: André Deutsch, 1965.

————, *History of Neo-African Literature.* London: Faber & Faber, Ltd., 1968.

James, Louis, ed., *The Islands in Between.* London & Ibadan, Nairobi: Oxford University Press, 1968.

Jones, LeRoi, and Larry Neal, eds., *Black Fire: An Anthology of Afro-American Writing.* New York: Apollo Editions, Inc., 1969.

July, Robert W., *Origins of Modern African Thought.* New York: Praeger Publishers, Inc., 1968.

————, *History of the African People.* New York: Charles Scribner's Sons, 1970.

Kesteloot, Lilyan, *Les écrivains noirs de langue Française: naissance d'une littérature.* Bruxelles: Université libre de Bruxelles, 1965.

Kostelanetz, Richard. "Ralph Ellison: Novelist as Brown Skinned Aristocrat," *Shenandoah, 20:*4 (Summer 1969), 56–77.

Ludington, Charles T., Jr., "Protest and Anti-protest: Ralph Ellison," *Southern Humanities Review,* 4:1 (Winter 1970), 31–39.

McCall, Dan, *The Example of Richard Wright.* New York: Harcourt Brace Jovanovitch, Inc., 1969.

Makward, E., "Négritude in the New African Novel," *Ibadan,* 22 (1965), 37–45.

Margolies, Edward, *Native Sons: A Critical Study of Twentieth-Century Negro American Authors.* Philadelphia: J. B. Lippincott Co., 1969.

————, *The Art of Richard Wright.* Carbondale, Ill.: Southern Illinois University Press, 1969.

Moore, Gerald, *Seven African Writers.* Cambridge: Oxford University Press, 1962.

————, and Ulli Beier, eds., *Modern Poetry from Africa.* Baltimore: Penguin Books, Inc., 1963.

————, ed., *African Literature and the Universities.* New York: Africana Publishing Corp., 1965.

Mphahlele, Ezekiel, *The African Image.* New York: Praeger Publishers, Inc., 1962.

————, *African Writing Today.* Harmondsworth, Middlesex: Penguin Books, Ltd., 1967.

Olderman, Raymond M., "Ralph Ellison's Blues and *Invisible Man,*" *Wisconsin Studies in Contemporary Literature,* 7:2 (Summer 1966), 142–59.

Pieterse, Cosmo, and Donald Murno, eds., *Protest and Conflict in African Literature.* London: William Heinemann, Ltd., 1969.

Ramchand, Kenneth, *West Indian Narrative: an introductory anthology.* London: Nelson, 1966.

————, *The West Indian Novel and Its Background.* London: Faber & Faber, Ltd., 1970.

Rive, Richard, *Modern African Prose.* London: William Heinemann, Ltd., 1965.

Salkey, Andrew, ed., *West Indian Stories.* London: Faber & Faber, Ltd., 1960.

————, ed., *Stories from the Caribbean.* London: Elek Books, Ltd., 1965.

————, ed., *Caribbean Prose.* London: Evans Bros., 1967.

Sartre, Jean-Paul, "Black Orpheus," *Massachusetts Review,* (Autumn 1964), 13–52.

Schmidt, Nancy, "Nigerian Fiction and the African Oral Tradition," *Journal of New African Literature and Art,* 5–6 (Spring & Fall 1968), 10–19.

Seary, E. R., ed., *South African Short Stories.* Cape Town: Oxford University Press, 1947.

Tibble, Anne, ed., *African/English Literature: a survey and anthology.* London: Peter Owen, Ltd., 1965.

Tucker, Martin, "Three West African Novelists," *Africa Today,* 12 (1965), 10–14.

Turner, Darwin, *Black American Literature: Fiction.* Columbus, Ohio: Charles E. Merrill, Publishers, 1968.

Webb, Constance, *Richard Wright.* New York: G. P. Putnam's Sons, 1968.

Whiteley, W. H., ed., *A Selection of African Prose,* Vol, 2 ("Written Prose"). London: Oxford Library of African Literature, 1964.

Wright, Richard, "Blue Print for Negro Writing," *New Challenge,* II, no. 2 (1937), 53–65.